Raymond Carver

Twayne's United States Authors Series

Frank Day, General Editor

Clemson University

TUSAS 633

RAYMOND CARVER
Reproduced by permission of Jerry Bauer. © Jerry Bauer

Raymond Carver

Adam Meyer

Fisk University

Twayne Publishers • New York
Maxwell Macmillan Canada • Toronto
Maxwell Macmillan International • New York Oxford Singapore Sydney

Twayne's United States Authors Series No. 633

Raymond Carver
Adam Meyer

Twayne Publishers   Maxwell Macmillan Canada, Inc.
Macmillan Publishing Company   1200 Eglinton Avenue East
866 Third Avenue   Suite 200
New York, New York 10022   Don Mills, Ontario M3C 3N1

Library of Congress Cataloging-in-Publication Data

Meyer, Adam.
    Raymond Carver / Adam Meyer.
        p.   cm. — (Twayne's United States authors series : TUSAS 633)
    Includes bibliographical references (p.   ) and index.
    ISBN 0-8057-3952-1
    1. Carver, Raymond—Criticism and interpretation.   2. Carver,
Raymond. I. Title. II. Series.
PS3553.A7894Z77   1994
813'.54—dc20   94-26516
                                                                    CIP

The paper used in this publication meets the minimum requirements of American
National Standard for Information Sciences—Permanence of Paper for Printed Library
Materials. ANSI Z3948–1984. ∞™

10 9 8 7 6 5 4 3 2 1 (hc)

Printed in the United States of America

For Nikki and Jillian

Contents

Preface

The film *Short Cuts*, directed by Robert Altman and released in the fall of 1993, brought the name of Raymond Carver to the movie-going public. To the reading public, however, Carver had been a well-known and important figure since the early 1980s, when his brand of short-story writing seemed, in both style and substance, to define a time and place, as well as spawn a host of imitators. At the time of his death in 1988, his life cut short (at 50) by lung cancer, Carver was seemingly at the height of his powers and popularity. Since his death, though, his popularity has continued to grow, along with critical estimation of his work. The number of tributes paid to him upon his death, the increasing amount of serious criticism that has been produced in an attempt to explain his world and works, and the appearance of Altman's film all testify to the lasting impact that Carver's career, however brief, has had on American life and letters. The fact that his writing has been translated into over twenty languages, including Hebrew and Japanese, shows that his influence has extended beyond the borders of the United States. Tess Gallagher, Carver's widow, has noted that "it was extremely unlikely that a writer growing up in a household where Zane Grey westerns and the newspaper were the only available reading materials would come to affect world literature to the extent that Raymond Carver has,"[1] yet Carver's influence is undeniable.

In this book I analyze Carver's life and career and account for his international following by examining most of his fictional output. I had hoped to discuss all of his stories, but space limitations precluded such an endeavor; even so, I provide full analyses of all but 15 of the tales in his major collections,[2] and I make brief comments on the ones that I have not been able to analyze in depth. While exploring the stories in their own right, I also define the shape of Carver's career, which moved through several different phases. Inevitably, Carver's name will be linked to the so-called minimalist movement, but I show that this appellation, if it applies at all, categorizes only one portion of Carver's work. Tracing the evolution of Carver's influential style, I liken the shape of his career to that of an hourglass—beginning wide, narrowing in the middle, and then widening again. In order to demonstrate the aptness of this metaphor, I examine a number of Carver's stories that have appeared in different versions in various collections.[3] Such an examination has the advantage of showing the meticulous care with which Carver approached the art and craft of fiction writing. Carver's poetry, which does not display the degree of mastery found in his short stories, has not received much attention from either readers or critics, and so I provide a brief introduction to it, explaining how it reflects and helps to clarify his fiction. On the whole, I hope the ensuing discussion will be enlightening to those who have read and loved Carver's works for years, as well as to those who have been introduced to him through Altman's motion picture.

Acknowledgments

Permission to quote from works cited in this book has been generously granted by the following parties:

Capra Press: excerpts from *Furious Seasons*. Copyright © 1977 by Raymond Carver. Reprinted by permission of Capra Press, Santa Barbara, California.

Tess Gallagher: excerpts from *Where I'm Calling From*, *Fires*, and *No Heroics, Please*. Reprinted by permission of Tess Gallagher. Copyright © 1983 by Tess Gallagher.

Alfred A. Knopf, Inc.: excerpts from *Cathedral*. Copyright © 1981, 1982, 1983 by Raymond Carver. Reprinted by permission of Alfred A. Knopf, Inc.

Alfred A. Knopf, Inc.: excerpts from *What We Talk About When We Talk About Love*. Copyright © 1981 by Raymond Carver. Reprinted by permission of Alfred A. Knopf, Inc.

The Helen Dwight Reid Educational Foundation: excerpts from "Now You See Him, Now You Don't, Now You Do Again: The Evolution of Raymond Carver's Minimalism" by Adam Meyer, in *Critique* 30, no. 4 (Summer 1989): 239–51. Reprinted with permission of the Helen Dwight Reid Educational Foundation. Published by Heldref Publications, 1319 18th Street, N.W., Washington, D.C. 20036–1802. Copyright © 1989.

Vintage Books, a Division of Random House, Inc.: excerpts from *Will You Please Be Quiet, Please* by Raymond Carver. Copyright © 1990 by Tess Gallagher. Reprinted by permission of Vintage Books, A Division of Random House, Inc.

In addition, I would like to thank many individuals for the roles they played in helping me to write this book. Among Carver scholars, I am indebted to Mark A. R. Facknitz and William L. Stull, who supported my endeavors and were instrumental in my taking on this project. At Twayne, I would like to thank Frank Day, Liz Fowler, Vida Petronis, and Mark Zadrozny; they made the agonizing process of getting the manuscript into shape less arduous than it otherwise would have been. To my colleagues at Vanderbilt—Fred Ashe, Ken Cooper, Julie Fesmire, David Guest, Christopher Metress, Lee Moore, Clay Railey, and, especially, Cecelia Tichi—I offer many thanks for your friendship, guidance, and encouragement. Finally, but most importantly, I owe an enormous debt of gratitude to my parents, Ralph and Selma Meyer, without whose constant love and support this book could not have been written, and to my wife, Nikki, and daughter, Jillian, without whose forbearance it would not have been completed.

Chronology

the University of California, Santa Cruz. "A Night Out" reprinted in *Best Little Magazine Fiction*.

1972   Teaches at the University of California at Berkeley; studies, under a Wallace Stegner Creative Writing Fellowship, at Stanford University.

1973   Teaches at the Iowa Writers' Workshop. "What Is It?" included in *Prize Stories, 1973: The O. Henry Awards*.

1974   Begins teaching at the University of California at Santa Barbara; forced to resign due to alcoholism. Files for second bankruptcy. "Put Yourself in My Shoes" published as a chapbook by Capra Press and reprinted in *Prize Stories, 1974: The O. Henry Awards*.

1975   "Are You a Doctor?" in *Prize Stories, 1975: The O. Henry Awards*.

1976   First collection of stories, *Will You Please Be Quiet, Please?*, published by McGraw-Hill. *At Night the Salmon Move* (poems) published by Capra Press. "So Much Water So Close to Home" in *Pushcart Prize* anthology. Hospitalized several times for acute alcoholism.

1977   Stops drinking 2 June. *Will You Please Be Quiet, Please?* nominated for National Book Award. *Furious Seasons and Other Stories* published by Capra Press. Separates from Maryann Carver; meets Tess Gallagher.

1978   Teaches at Goddard College in Vermont and at the University of Texas, El Paso.

1979   Begins living with Tess Gallagher. Awarded National Endowment for the Arts Fellowship.

1980   Appointed professor of English at the University of Syracuse.

1981   *What We Talk about When We Talk about Love* published by Alfred A. Knopf; title story included in *Pushcart Prize* anthology. "The Bath" wins *Columbia* magazine's Carlos Fuentes Fiction Award. "Chef's House" appears in the *New Yorker*.

1982   Divorces Maryann Carver. "Cathedral" included in *Best American Short Stories, 1982*.

1983   *Fires: Essays, Poems, Stories* published by Capra Press.

Cathedral published by Alfred A. Knopf; later nominated for National Book Critics Circle Award and Pulitzer Prize. "A Small, Good Thing" wins first place in *Prize Stories, 1983: The O. Henry Awards* and appears in the *Pushcart Prize* annual. "Where I'm Calling From" reprinted in *The Best American Short Stories, 1983*. Receives the Mildred and Harold Strauss Living Award from the American Academy and Institute of Arts and Letters.

1984   Resigns position at Syracuse and moves to Port Angeles, Washington. "Careful" included in *Pushcart Prize* volume.

1985   *Where Water Comes Together with Water*, poems, published by Random House; awarded *Poetry* magazine's Levinson Prize. Publication of *Dostoevsky: A Screenplay*.

1986   *Ultramarine*, poems, published by Random House.

1987   Cancer discovered; two-thirds of left lung removed. "Boxes" included in *The Best American Short Stories, 1987*.

1988   *Where I'm Calling From: New and Selected Stories* published by Atlantic Monthly Press. "Errand" awarded first place in *Prize Stories, 1988: The O. Henry Awards* and included in *Best American Short Stories, 1988*. Reappearance of cancer. Elected to American Academy and Institute of Arts and Letters; awarded honorary Doctor of Letters degree from the University of Hartford. Marries Tess Gallagher 17 June. Dies of lung cancer in Port Angeles 2 August.

1989   *A New Path to the Waterfall* (poems) published by Atlantic Monthly Press.

1992   *No Heroics, Please: Uncollected Writings* published by Vintage Contemporaries.

1993   Film *Short Cuts*, directed by Robert Altman and based on the writings of Raymond Carver, released. *Short Cuts*, selected stories, published by Vintage Contemporaries.

Chapter One

The Life of Raymond Carver

The mid to late 1970s was a hard time to be an American. A malaise seemed to have settled upon the country, "a general sense that things [had] not only gone wrong, but that they [would] never be right again."[1] This feeling grew out of such events as the assassinations of John and Robert Kennedy and Martin Luther King, Jr., the lingering effects of the debacle in Vietnam, and, as a kind of capstone, the Watergate scandal, which confirmed many of the public's worst fears about the possible misuses of power in the political system. Following the election of Jimmy Carter, moreover, the country moved into a pro- longed period of economic hardship—symbolized by the energy crisis— followed by the national embarrassment of the Iranian hostage crisis. The election of Ronald Reagan in 1980 seemed to indicate a new start, and it was for some; for many others, however, trickle-down economics failed to materialize, and as the gap between the rich and the poor widened, the life of the blue-collar worker became increasingly stressful and difficult. For the generation that came of age during this period, "the common denominators of . . . experience [were] death, loss, and futility, and it is inevitable that the fiction that reflects that experience reveals in its tone the natural reaction to such a history: fatigue, depres- sion, the loss of hope."[2] Of the writers who attempted to depict the his- tory of this "blue-collar despair,"[3] none did so as fully and accurately as Raymond Carver. His stories and poems brilliantly "reflected the down- beat mood, the sense of frustration and failure that worked its way into the fiber of individual lives."[4]

In many ways, Carver was perfectly suited to the task. As William L. Stull has pointed out, "Carver was a belated child of the Great Depression."[5] For him, the economic hardships his father endured in the 1930s were still weighing heavily in the 1970s, and his fiction naturally gave voice to those for whom the American Dream seemed more and more impossible. In many ways he lived the life of the down-and-out characters he wrote about. Like many of them, he drowned his problems in alcohol until alcohol became the only problem. What is fascinating about Carver's biography, however, refuting F. Scott Fitzgerald's dictum

1

that American literature has no second acts, is the abrupt and positive change that occurred in his life when he stopped drinking. By the time his writings struck a chord with the Reagan-era public, he had already moved beyond despair, "beyond Hopelessville."[6] Carver regarded his new life as a great gift, even when it took its final turn toward the cancer that would cause his death at the age of 50.

The Early Years

Raymond Clevie Carver, Jr., was born 25 May 1938 in Clatskanie, Oregon, although both of his parents had grown up in Arkansas. As Carver explains in his essay "My Father's Life," his father, Clevie Raymond Carver ("C.R."), had "walked, hitched rides, and rode in empty boxcars when he went from Arkansas to Washington State in 1934, looking for work."[7] After finding employment building the Grand Coulee Dam, C.R. returned to Arkansas to relocate his parents, and while there he met Ella Beatrice Casey, whom he promptly married and took with him to Omak, Washington. After the dam was completed the family relocated again, this time to Clatskanie, where C.R. had gotten a job at a sawmill. In 1941, the family—now including four-year-old Raymond—moved to Yakima, Washington, another mill town, and it was here that the young writer spent his formative years.

Although the 1940s were years of relative prosperity for the Carver family, the end of World War II brought renewed hardships. The family continued to move around, but that did not mean moving up. Raymond would later recall his embarrassment about living in the last house in the neighborhood without indoor plumbing. What made the situation even worse was C.R.'s increasing dependence on alcohol. In "My Father's Life," Carver recalls a horrific scene in which his mother knocked his father out with a colander when C.R., having been locked out of the house, drunkenly tried to climb in a window. Carver also recalls that "I tasted some of his whiskey once myself. It was terrible stuff, and I don't see how anybody could drink it" (F, 16), a consciously ironic statement in light of Carver's own severe alcoholism later in his life. When C.R. moved his family again, this time to Chester, California, he became so sick that he had to be taken back to Yakima, institutionalized, and given electroshock treatments. After he was released, finding work was almost impossible, and Ella had to support the family by waiting tables and performing other low-wage jobs. By the early 1960s, C.R. had recovered somewhat and the family relocated to Klamath, California, where C.R. died in 1967 at the age of 53.

In many ways, "My Father's Life" reads like one of Carver's own short stories (and a very good one at that). What the essay also shows us is that certain negative elements in Raymond Carver, Jr.'s, life—his difficulty finding economic success, his peripatetics, his alcoholism—can clearly be traced to his father's influence. On the other hand, Carver also acknowledged on several occasions that it was the father who made the son want to become a writer. In several interviews Carver related that, as a boy, he had loved to listen to his father tell stories, either about how C.R.'s grandfather had fought for both sides during the Civil War, or about how C.R. himself had ridden the rails during the 1930s. Carver also recalled his father reading to him from Zane Grey novels, although he soon preferred Edgar Rice Burroughs, Mickey Spillane, and fishing magazines. At a young age, Carver, inspired by his father, began to dream of becoming a storyteller himself. He decided that he wanted to be a writer, although, as he would later point out, he "didn't know beans"[8] about how to become one. There was no one to tell him what to read, for example, and so he read historical romances as well as *Argosy*, *Rogue*, and *True* magazines, and tried his hand at writing science fiction. He even enrolled in the Palmer Institute of Authorship, although he failed to complete the correspondence course.

On the whole, Carver's youth and adolescence were uneventful. He was deeply in love with the land, and became an avid hunter and fisherman, avocations that would continue to appear in his fiction. He later stated that "My childhood was given over to fishing and hunting and baseball" (*Con*, 135). What differentiated him from everyone else was his desire to be a writer: "I wanted to be right in there with all the rest of the guys," he once said. "But I also wanted to write. I was the nerd who always hung around the library, half ashamed to be seen carrying books home."[9] Despite his desire, the Carver family had not considered sending Raymond to college and had assumed that, after graduation from high school, he would join his father at the sawmill. Indeed, by the time Carver graduated from Yakima High School in 1956—the first person in his family to reach that educational benchmark—economic pressures were already beginning to assert themselves in his life. He immediately moved to Chester, California, and did indeed work with his ailing father for several months.

In 1955, when he was seventeen, Carver began dating Maryann Burk, who was three years his junior and attended a private girls' school. She encouraged his desire to obtain an education and become a writer, and she even introduced him to some writers he had not yet read but who would become important to his development: Tolstoy, Chekhov,

and Flaubert. Toward the end of 1956 he returned to Yakima to be closer to Maryann, and on 7 June 1957—four days after she graduated from
high school—Carver, 19, and Burk, 16, were wed. In December of that
year their first child, a daughter whom they named Christine LaRae, was
born. Maryann was to have gone to the University of Washington to
study law, but instead she took care of the baby. A son, Vance Lindsay,
was born in October of the following year. At this time the family was
living in an apartment attached to the office of their family doctor, and
having their rent paid in exchange for housekeeping; Raymond was also
attending Yakima Community College, as well as working as a part-time
delivery boy for a local pharmacist. Before his twentieth birthday, then,
Carver found himself responsible for supporting a family of four. The
need to earn money began to wage a fierce battle with, and eventually
would prevail over, his desire to be a writer. He would later note in his
autobiographical essay "Fires" that "I really don't remember much about
my life before I became a parent. I really don't feel that anything happened in my life until I was twenty and married and had the kids. Then
things started to happen" (*F*, 32). Most of the "things" that Carver is
referring to here are negative, as the rest of "Fires" goes on to show, and
they would continue to trouble him for the next 15 long and difficult
years.

The Years of Struggle

The impetus behind the writing of "Fires," Carver explains in the afterword to the volume later published under that name, was "an invitation
to contribute something to a book on 'influences.'"[10] He felt that his
children had been the biggest influence on his life as a writer, an influence he had found largely "oppressive and often malevolent" (*F*, 28). His
life had become a continual effort to keep the family afloat financially
while he and Maryann also pursued their educational and career goals;
for the next 13 years, one or both of them would be enrolled in a college
or university while also holding a series of what Carver would later call
"crap jobs" (*F*, 34). At various times he was employed pumping gas,
sweeping hospital corridors and fast-food restaurants, managing an
apartment complex, and even picking tulips. Inevitably, Carver's family
began to follow the pattern that C.R. had established of frequent relocations in search of work opportunities. Their first move, in 1958, was to
Paradise, California, where Maryann's mother and sister had moved, and
where they could rent a house for twenty-five dollars a month. This relo-

cation would prove to be one of the most significant in Carver's life, for he was able to enroll part-time at Chico State College. There he met the first person who would significantly influence his writing, the novelist John Gardner.

Gardner was teaching at Chico because, although he had written several of the novels that would later make him famous (*Nickel Mountain*; *October Light*), he had yet to publish any of them. Even so, he was the first real, practicing writer that the young and impressionable Carver got to know, and he was an impressive and inspiring figure. Carver's style may not owe much of a debt to Gardner's, but the apprentice did learn a number of important lessons from the older writer; he always credited Gardner as a mentor, most notably toward the end of "Fires" and in the essay "John Gardner: The Writer as Teacher," which he wrote following Gardner's death in 1982. One of the ways Gardner helped Carver was by sharpening his reading tastes, thereby introducing him to a number of important writers he had never heard of before. He also introduced Carver to the "'little' magazines," telling him (and the rest of the class) that "this was where most of the best fiction in the country and all of the poetry was appearing" (*F*, 44). Moreover, Gardner was willing to sit down with the aspiring writer and go through his stories line by line, urging him to use the language of common people and to eliminate unnecessary verbiage. Carver notes in "Fires" that Gardner "made me see that absolutely everything was important in a short story. It was of consequence where the commas and periods went" (*F*, 38). Gardner also taught Carver the importance of revision, a lesson that the student never forgot.

Perhaps Gardner's most helpful act, however, was extracurricular: He knew that Carver, in the midst of family and work responsibilities, was having a hard time finding a peaceful place to write, and so he lent him the key to his office to use on weekends. One result of this gift proved to be an embarrassment to the young writer: Carver snooped in Gardner's manuscript boxes, stole titles he liked, and affixed these to his own work, which he resubmitted to Gardner. The older writer promptly reprimanded him, and then explained the concept of authorial proprieties. A more positive aspect of Gardner's gift to Carver of a room of his own, though, and the reason he later called it "a turning point in my life" (*Con*, 77), is that that room was where Carver completed his first serious story, "The Furious Seasons." He would later include this story in *Selection*, the college literary magazine he had founded, and a revised version of it would eventually serve as the title story of his second collection.

Above all, Carver learned "a writer's values and craft" (*F*, 45) from Gardner, and these were fundamentally important lessons indeed. Throughout his writing career, even after Gardner's death, Carver "felt Gardner looking over his shoulder when he wrote, approving or disapproving of certain words, phrases and strategies."[11]

After Carver had spent two years at Chico State, however, economic reasons again forced him to relocate. Although he had been sweeping floors and working in the school library, and although Maryann was working for the telephone company, they couldn't manage to make ends meet in Chico, and so they moved to Eureka, California, where Carver had gotten a job through his father at a Georgia-Pacific sawmill. He began to work at the mill at night (Maryann still worked for the phone company) and take classes at nearby Humboldt State College during the day. There he fell under the sway of another important writing teacher, Richard C. Day, and his craft continued to advance. Day was very impressed with the first story Carver showed him, the vignette "The Father" (later included in *Will You Please Be Quiet, Please?*), and Day published it in *Toyon*, the college's literary magazine. In the spring of 1962, Carver received a boost when, on the same red-letter day, he received notification that his story "Pastoral" had been accepted by the *Western Humanities Review* and that his poem "The Brass Ring" had been accepted by a small journal called *Targets*. By this time he had been able to stop working at the mill, having gotten a job in the college's library, and Maryann had started to attend Humboldt as well. Carver graduated in February 1963, and that spring he edited an issue of *Toyon* in which he included three of his stories and one of his poems; two of the pieces appeared under the pseudonym John Vale, which Carver used so as not to seem immodest.

After graduation, Carver moved to Berkeley, where he had a job in the University of California's biology library. When Maryann finished her Humboldt semester in June, she and the children joined him. In the fall, however, they were on the move again, this time to far-off Iowa City. Day, who had studied at the famous Writers Workshop at the University of Iowa, encouraged Carver to attend the school and even managed to get him a small grant. Although the experience did help Carver as a writer—while there he wrote several of the stories that would appear in his first collection—financial problems again complicated his life. It was in an Iowa City laundromat that he realized the full impact his children were having on his life, causing him to feel, he writes in "Fires," "that my life was a small-change thing for the most part, chaotic, and without much light showing through" (*F*, 33). The five hundred dollars the workshop had given him didn't go far, and even with his working in the university library and Maryann's waiting tables at the University Athletic Club they had trouble getting through the first year of what was a two-year master's program. The workshop offered him a grant for the second year, but the situation was impossible, and so the family moved again, this time to Sacramento, where C.R. and Ella were living.

Life in Sacramento proved to be at least as hardscrabble as it had been in Iowa City. Carver couldn't find steady work, and was employed as, among other things, a hotel desk clerk and a stockboy. Moreover, he was becoming increasingly depressed over the family's financial situation; as he wrote in "Fires": "For years my wife and I had held to a belief that if we worked hard and tried to do the right things, the right things would happen. It's not such a bad thing to try and build a life on. Hard work, goals, good intentions, loyalty, we believed these were virtues and would someday be rewarded. But, eventually, we realized that hard work and dreams were not enough. Somewhere, in Iowa City maybe, or shortly afterwards, in Sacramento, the dreams began to go bust" (*F*, 34–35). When Carver got hired as a custodian at Mercy Hospital, he was glad for the job. He was even more pleased when he was able to transfer to the night shift, which would afford him more time to write. All in all, Carver worked at Mercy Hospital for three years, while Maryann worked in door-to-door sales, and later for *Parents* magazine. He continued to write during this period—several of the stories would later appear in his first collection—and he also enrolled in Dennis Schmitz's poetry-writing class at Sacramento State College.

After he had been working at the hospital for a while, however, his routine began to change, and instead of going home to write after he got off his shift he would go out for a drink. He would later explain that "I was just too young to be a father with much too much responsibility to keep the family going. Those needs kept me doing odd jobs which didn't fit my personality at all. When all I really wanted to do was write. So that's why drinking took hold at a certain point in my life" (*Con*, 74). Whatever the reasons, alcohol itself got to be a problem—Carver later said that he "took to full-time drinking as a serious pursuit" (*Con*, 37)— and, with debts mounting, the Carvers opted for declaring bankruptcy in 1967. It was also in 1967 that C.R. died.

If Carver's personal life was failing, his writing career was beginning to succeed. His story "Will You Please Be Quiet, Please?," which had originally been published in the small journal *December*, was selected to appear in the *Best American Short Stories* annual, edited by Martha Foley. This was his first national honor, and he reveled in it. Carver later recalled that he was so excited when he received his copy of the book that he took it to bed with him. Foley's selection of the story was at least as big a turning point in his life as Gardner's bestowal of the key had been. In 1968, moreover, Carver's first book, a collection of poems entitled *Near Klamath*, was published, albeit by the English Club of Sacramento State College.

Encouraging though these events were, the problem of earning a living remained foremost in Carver's mind, giving him very little time to write. Shortly after he left his job at Mercy Hospital—and after an abortive stay in Iowa City, studying library science at the university there—Carver was hired as an editor by Science Research Associates (SRA), a textbook publishing firm. It was his first white-collar job, and it was something of a step up when the family moved to Palo Alto. Since he was making decent money, and Maryann had left a good job in Sacramento, she returned to school at San Jose State, and in 1968 she applied for and received a scholarship from the California State College Study Abroad Program. Given their choice of destinations, the Carvers picked Tel Aviv over Uppsala and Florence because it offered an additional five hundred dollars. Carver, granted leave from SRA, eagerly anticipated the trip; the family had been promised a villa on the Mediterranean, and he had idyllic dreams of living the writer's life. The trip, however, proved to be a disaster, with the accommodations much less luxurious than promised and the children placed in a non-English-speaking school. Carver would later look at the trip "as a low point, a final straw" (*Con*, 91). Although the Carvers were supposed to be in Israel for a year, they ran out of money after four months and returned to California, this time to Hollywood, where Carver began selling theater programs. What the failed sojourn signaled to Carver was that his life was over, that he would never get the Mediterranean villa, that "the world wasn't my oyster" (*Con*, 91). On returning from Israel, he turned to drinking once again. He would later say that "I began to drink heavily once I realized that the things which I wanted most in my life, writing and having a wife and kids, were not lined up neatly waiting to be had" (*Con*, 75). He had received such knowledge in Iowa City, and again in Sacramento, but he seemed to take the insight gained in Tel Aviv as a third strike. In 1969 Carver returned to his job at SRA, where he would remain for almost two years. His promotion to advertising director—complete with expense account—only led to further alcohol abuse.

Throughout this bleak period, however, Carver continued to write, and to gain further recognition. Several more of the stories that would eventually make up *Will You Please Be Quiet, Please?* appeared in little magazines, and one of them ("Sixty Acres") was chosen for *The Best Little Magazine Fiction, 1970* anthology. *Winter Insomnia*, a second volume of poems, was published, this time by Kayak, a commercial press. Carver was also awarded a National Endowment for the Arts Discovery Award for poetry, which brought him a bit of money. He planned to quit his job at SRA, but instead, due to a corporate reorganization, he was fired, which proved to be a fortunate occurrence since it allowed him to draw both severance pay and unemployment. For the first time in his life, Carver had enough money so that he didn't have to work, and he would spend most of the next year writing while Maryann finally finished her undergraduate degree and began a high-school teaching career. Carver marked his being fired from SRA as another turning point in his life, for it was during the period of his NEA fellowship in 1970 and 1971 that he completed the bulk of the stories in *Will You Please Be Quiet, Please?*, many of which would be published in magazines and journals over the following six years until the collection as a whole was finally issued.

Another milestone was reached in 1970 when "Neighbors" became the first of Carver's stories to be accepted by a major magazine, *Esquire*. The fiction editor there, Gordon Lish, would soon rival John Gardner as an influence in Carver's writing career, as he acknowledges in "Fires," and their association would last for over a decade. Carver had in fact first met Lish while he was working for SRA in Palo Alto, and Lish was working for a different textbook publisher across the street. The two would frequently get together for lunch. When Lish became the fiction editor at *Esquire*, Carver sent him some stories; Lish rejected them, but he encouraged the young writer to submit more, and he finally accepted "Neighbors." Lish did more than just publish Carver's work—he began to have an effect on the work itself, moving Carver towards an even more pared down style; where Gardner had urged him to use 15 words instead of 25, Lish told him to use 5 instead of 15. When Lish left *Esquire* it was for a job at the McGraw-Hill publishing firm, and it was through this association that *Will You Please Be Quiet, Please?* was eventually accepted and published. More than anything else, Carver came to appreciate the fact that Lish "was a great advocate of my stories, at all times championing my work, even during the period when I was not writing, when I was out in California devoting myself to drinking, Gordon read my work on radio and at writers conferences and so forth" (*Con*, 234–35). Lish believed in Carver when no one else did, and it was largely through his efforts that the wider world began to become aware of Carver's skills. *Esquire* went on to publish several more of Carver's stories (and James Dickey, the poetry editor there, printed several of his poems) during the early 1970s, as did other mass media magazines such as *Harper's Bazaar*. Carver's stories continued to garner acclaim, as evidenced by the inclusion of "A Night Out" (later "Signals") in *The Best Little Magazine Fiction, 1971*.

In 1971, moreover, the year "Neighbors" appeared in *Esquire*, Carver—whose combined severance pay/unemployment/grant money had almost expired—took up a new form of employment: teaching. Although Carver would become a good teacher, and although there were certain appealing aspects to the job—it was a lot easier than working at the sawmill, for example, and gave him a lot more time to write—it was not something that came naturally to him. He would later tell an interviewer, in fact, that teaching was "a terrifying prospect" (*Con*, 6), since he had always been "the shyest kid in class" (*Con*, 219). Because he was uncomfortable in this new role, he began to drink even more heavily; Maryann Carver actually dates the severe change in his drinking pattern to his first teaching job. The jobs were also always temporary, and as such necessitated an additional series of relocations, although these moves took place largely within the San Francisco area. Carver's first one-year visiting lecturer position, for example, was at the University of California, Santa Cruz, and so the family moved from Sunnyvale (where they had been living for the past year) to Ben Lomond; his second position, for the 1972–73 academic year, was at the University of California, Berkeley, causing the family to move again, this time to Cupertino, where they bought a house. During that year he was also studying at Stanford University under a Wallace E. Stegner Fellowship. For the 1973–74 academic year, Carver was appointed to a visiting lecturer post at the Iowa Writers Workshop, where he had formerly been a student, and so he moved to Iowa City (although his family stayed behind). John Cheever, a writer whom Carver greatly admired, was also teaching at Iowa that year, and the two of them, as Carver later recalled, "did nothing *but* drink. . . . I don't think either of us ever took the covers off our typewriters," he noted, but "we made trips to the liquor store twice a week in my car" (*Con*, 40). On top of this, Carver was trying to maintain a teaching job in California (at UC Santa Cruz) and was commuting between the two schools without either one being aware of it. The craziness of this life-style led to further alcohol abuse. Carver's next job was at the University of California, Santa Barbara, for the 1974–75 school year, but by that point his alcoholism had gotten so bad that he rarely met his classes and was forced to resign in December, after which the Carvers filed for their second bankruptcy. For the next two years Carver lived in Cupertino and primarily drank.

Between 1971 and 1976, then, Carver did little writing, for he did not write when he was drunk and, according to Maryann, "for five years Ray didn't draw a sober breath."[12] Nevertheless, many of the stories that would later appear in *Will You Please Be Quiet, Please?* continued to be published and to gain recognition; Carver had works included in *Prize Stories*, the O. Henry Awards annual, in 1973 ("What Is It?"), 1974 ("Put Yourself in My Shoes," which had previously appeared in a limited edition chapbook from Capra Press), and 1975 ("Are You a Doctor?"). Despite this string of publications, Carver was unable to find a publisher for the collection as a whole, a situation that no doubt exacerbated his other problems. It was not until the spring of 1976, with the aforementioned urging of Gordon Lish, that McGraw-Hill finally issued *Will You Please Be Quiet, Please?*, which collected most of the fiction Carver had written during the previous fourteen years. The book received almost unanimously favorable reviews, and was even nominated for the National Book Award the following year, although the collection failed to sell many copies. A story not included in the collection, "So Much Water So Close to Home," was included in the first *Pushcart Prize* anthology. A third book of poetry, *At Night the Salmon Move*, was also brought out in 1976, again by Capra Press.

Such achievements and accolades failed to quiet Carver's personal demons of economic hardship and alcoholism, however, and the 1976–77 period was in many ways the low point of his life, a time when he felt that "the only light at the end of the tunnel was an oncoming train" (*Con*, 19). Between October and January he was hospitalized for acute alcoholism on four separate occasions, and one doctor even told him that his next drink would likely be his last. The house in Cupertino had to be sold to try to cover some of the debts and, more significantly, Carver and Maryann, whose marriage had managed to survive up to this point, began to live separately. Carver would later say of this period in his life that "I made a wasteland out of everything I touched," and that "toward the end of my drinking career I was completely out of control and in a very grave place. Blackouts, the whole business. . . . I have an image of myself sitting in my living room with a glass of whiskey in my hand and my head bandaged from a fall caused by an alcoholic seizure. Crazy! . . . I was dying from it, plain and simple, and I'm not exaggerating" (*Con*, 38).

It seemed as though Carver's promising career was already over, even as it was (to the wider public) just beginning. He would later explain at the end of "Fires" that following the 1970 publication of "Neighbors" in *Esquire* his life "took another veering, a sharp turn, and then it came to a dead stop off on a siding. I couldn't go anywhere, couldn't back up or go forward." Even after the long-awaited publication of *Will You Please Be Quiet, Please?*, Carver "was still off on the siding, unable to move in any direction. If there'd once been [an artistic] fire, it'd gone out" (*F*, 39).

The Years of Recovery

On 2 June 1977 Raymond Carver took his last drink. He would later state that he considered regaining his sobriety to be his "greatest achievement" (*Con*, 69), "the most profound thing that ever happened to [him]" (*Con*, 247). He looked at that day in 1977 as "the line of demarcation" (*Con*, 89) between his two very different lives. Earlier that spring, Carver—separated from his wife, estranged from his children, unemployed, broke, and drinking again following his fourth stay at a detox center—had moved to a small house in McKinleyville, California, near Humboldt. Richard Day, Carver's former teacher, had made the arrangements and looked after the troubled writer. Carver stayed sober for a few weeks in February and again in April, but when he went to a San Francisco publishers convention in May he began to drink again, and to experience blackouts. He returned drunk to McKinleyville, but after a few days he didn't drink again, and then those days became weeks, and then months; along with frequent trips to AA meetings, Carver was able to break the habit that had held him under its sway for 10 years and had very nearly killed him. Although he was never fully able to account for his strength to remain sober, Carver later explained that he realized first that he "was not going to be able to drink like a normal person," and second that he "wanted to live" (*Con*, 90). During the disastrous trip to San Francisco Carver had secured an advance to write a novel that he described as an epic set in "German East Africa during World War I, involving . . . patrician German military officers" (*Con*, 6), and which, it seems safe to assume, he never had any intention of writing. With this money he was able to continue living in McKinleyville. When Maryann rejoined him in the fall it was clear that his life was at last taking a positive turn.

In November 1977, Carver's second collection of short stories, entitled *Furious Seasons*, was published by Capra Press. This volume included all of Carver's writings that had not appeared in *Will You Please Be Quiet, Please?*, with the exception of the early *Toyon* pieces. At this time, however, there were no new stories forthcoming (although Carver did write a few poems during this period, most notably "Rogue River Jet-boat Trip, Gold Beach, Oregon, July 4, 1977"); he later explained that "it was so important for me to have my health back and not be brain-dead any longer that whether I wrote or not didn't matter any longer. I just felt like I had a second chance at my life again. But for about a year or so, I didn't write anything" (*Con*, 236). By early 1978 Carver was feeling well enough to return to teaching, though, and he moved to Plainfield, Vermont, where he taught a brief course at Goddard College. Among the other teachers there were Tobias Wolff and Richard Ford, two men of whom Carver would later fondly write in an essay entitled "Friendship" (*NHP*, 217–22). Around this time he was also awarded a John Simon Guggenheim Fellowship, and that spurred him to begin writing again. His first post-alcohol stories, "Why Don't You Dance?" and "Viewfinder," signaled that he had indeed returned from the brink. In the spring of 1978 Carver returned to Iowa City, where he and Maryann were again reunited, for what would prove to be the last time (although they would not officially divorce until 1982). In the summer he moved again, this time to El Paso, Texas, where he had been appointed visiting distinguished writer-in-residence for 1978–79 at the University of Texas, El Paso.

In El Paso, Carver became reacquainted with Tess Gallagher, a poet whom he had met briefly at a writers conference in Dallas the previous year, the first such gathering he attended after he stopped drinking. Gallagher was attending another writers conference, this one at UTEP, and the two writers discovered that they had much in common. She, too, had grown up in the Northwest (in Port Angeles, Washington) where her alcoholic father had relocated from Missouri to find work during the Great Depression. Having escaped that life to pursue her education and to fulfill her desire to become a writer, she had fallen on hard times as well, and was recovering from her second divorce while living alone in Port Angeles and writing. Gallagher and Carver struck up an instant rapport, and, following a series of visits and phone calls, she returned to El Paso where, on New Year's Day 1979, the two began living together, an arrangement that continued until Carver's death. Over the next decade Tess Gallagher became as prominent a figure in Carver's life and writing career, as important a "help and inspiration" (*Con*, 49), as Maryann Burk, John Gardner, and Gordon Lish had been earlier. She does, as she has written, "bear a special relationship to his writing" (*NHP*, 15). Her diligent example sparked a renewal of Carver's interest in producing creative work, and she became the first person to read and critique his new stories and poems as he wrote them. He would frequently tell interviewers that they "influence[d] each other's work" (Kellerman, C17); following his death she wrote that "we helped, nurtured and protected each other . . . He gave me encouragement to write stories and I gave him encouragement to write his stories and poems."[13] Their collaboration as writers and companions would prove to have a vital impact on Carver's greatest works.

After living in El Paso the pair followed teaching jobs to Tucson, Arizona, and Syracuse, New York, where Carver began his first permanent teaching job at the University of Syracuse in 1980. More importantly, he continued to write and publish at an ever-increasing pace. He began work on a novel, *The Augustine Notebooks*, although the project was scrapped following the appearance of one chapter in the *Iowa Review* in 1979. His short story "The Calm" also appeared in 1979, with "Gazebo," "A Serious Talk," "Want to See Something?" (later "I Could See the Smallest Things"), and "Where Is Everyone?" (also known as "Mr. Coffee and Mr. Fixit") following in 1980, and "One More Thing" in 1981. With Gallagher's encouragement Carver also began to write book reviews and essays, such as the aforementioned "Fires," and he received another National Endowment for the Arts Fellowship, this time for fiction. In 1981 *What We Talk about When We Talk about Love* appeared, his second collection of stories to be issued by a major publishing house. The text was once again edited by Gordon Lish, who moved Carver toward an extreme conciseness; several of the stories from *Furious Seasons* appeared in radically pared-down versions, for example. This style gave rise to Carver's work being labelled minimalist, a slippery and controversial critical term that will be examined more closely in the next chapter. The collection received a great deal of praise, including a glowing front-page assessment in the *New York Times Book Review* and the statement from Robert Towers in the *New York Review of Books* that the author was "one of the true contemporary masters of an exacting genre."[14] This was to be the volume that would firmly establish Carver as an important writer, "a major force in contemporary fiction."[15]

Although Carver previously had trouble getting *Will You Please Be Quiet, Please?* published because "editors found the stories too depressing, or not in tune with what the culture wanted to read" (Halpert, 53), it now seemed that the "culture [had] finally caught up [and] the disillusionment of the seventies and eighties now suddenly found itself reflected in his work" (Halpert, 70). Carver would later tell an interviewer that, "after the reception for *What We Talk about*, I felt a confidence that I've never felt before. Every good thing that's happened since has conjoined to make me want to do even more and better work" (*Con*, 49). By the end of 1981 "The Bath" had been awarded *Columbia* magazine's Carlos Fuentes Fiction Award and "What We Talk about When We Talk about Love" had been included in the *Pushcart Prize* anthology. "Chef's House," a story too new to be included in the collection, appeared in the *New Yorker*, Carver's first publication in the country's most prestigious magazine for short stories. Not only was Carver back, but he was now in a position of eminence that had seemed improbable if not impossible during the dark days of his drinking. His recovery was now complete, and his life and career continued to move steadily forward.

The Years of Triumph

Following the publication of *What We Talk about When We Talk about Love*, Carver again found himself in a period in which he did not write. After a few months, however, he began to work again, and the first story he produced, "Cathedral," marked a significant departure in his work. He would later explain to an interviewer that the story was "totally different in conception and execution from any stories that have come before. I suppose it reflects a change in my life as much as it does in my way of writing. . . . There was an opening up when I wrote the story" (*Con*, 44). His life had moved in a positive direction—he felt more hopeful and more optimistic since he was no longer drinking and had become involved with Tess Gallagher—and such a change was naturally reflected in his fiction, which became open, expansive, and generous, rather than rigorously pared down. During the next eighteen months he produced a dozen new stories, many of which continued the trend toward fullness and affirmation. John Gardner, editing the *Best American Short Stories, 1982* anthology, chose "Cathedral" to be the leadoff story. Another of the new stories, "A Small, Good Thing" (a revised and expanded version of "The Bath" from *What We Talk about When We Talk about Love*), was awarded first place in the O. Henry Awards' *Prize Stories, 1983* collection and was included in the eighth *Pushcart Prize* anthology; the story "Where I'm Calling From" was included in *The Best American Stories, 1983*, edited by Ann Tyler.

Nineteen eighty-three was in many ways a banner year for Carver. In the spring, Capra Press published *Fires: Essays, Poems, Stories*. This volume included the titular essay and a piece called "On Writing" that had originally appeared as "A Storyteller's Notebook" in the *New York Times Book Review*[16]; selected (and frequently revised) poems from Carver's first three small-press collections, as well as some newer verse; and a group of stories, several of which had appeared in *Furious Seasons* and, in minimalized versions, in *What We Talk about When We Talk about Love*, and which were now restored to their fuller forms in keeping with Carver's new direction. Later that spring, Carver was awarded, from the American Academy and Institute of Arts and Letters, one of the first Mildred and Harold Strauss Livings, a fellowship that guaranteed an annual stipend of $35,000, with the requirement that the recipient have no other job. Carver promptly resigned his position at the University of Syracuse and was able to devote himself entirely to writing without having to worry about economic survival. The stories that had been pouring out of him during the previous year and a half were collected and, in the fall, Carver's third major-press book, *Cathedral*, was published. *Cathedral* is undoubtedly Carver's masterpiece, and it was greeted with widespread and glowing critical acclaim, including Irving Howe's front page analysis in the *New York Times Book Review*. With the volume's nomination for both the National Book Critics Circle Award and the Pulitzer Prize, Carver's triumph was complete and he had clearly arrived at the forefront of American letters.

Not only was Carver acknowledged as a master within the literary world, but his awards made him something of a celebrity as well, evidenced by profiles in the *New York Times Magazine*, *Vanity Fair*, and even *People* magazine. Finding it increasingly difficult to work amid the hubbub in Syracuse, Carver removed to Gallagher's house in Port Angeles in early 1984. He intended to continue writing fiction—he was again at work on a never-to-be-completed novel—but instead he found himself writing poetry, something he hadn't done for several years. In the space of two months, he had produced enough material for a new collection, which would be titled *Where Water Comes Together with Other Water* when Random House published it in 1985, and which would be awarded *Poetry* magazine's Levinson Prize. In the summer of 1984 Carver and Gallagher traveled to South America, and when they returned he began writing poems again. Another collection, *Ultramarine*, was published in 1986. During this time Carver was also publishing book reviews and essays, as well as an unproduced screenplay about the life of Dostoevsky on which he and Gallagher had collaborated for director Michael Cimino[17]; Carver also wrote another screenplay for Cimino, "Purple Lake," about juvenile delinquents, but it was neither produced nor published. During this period Carver became an editor and anthologizer as well, compiling a special issue of the journal *Ploughshares*, guest editing *The Best American Short Stories, 1986*, judging *American Fiction, 88*, and collaborating with Tom Jenks on a volume entitled *Short Story Masterpieces*. He and Gallagher divided their time between Port Angeles and Syracuse, where she was still teaching; they also traveled to England and Europe to promote editions of his books that were being published there.

Two years after the publication of *Cathedral* Carver finally returned to writing fiction. In the space of a few months he produced seven new stories, beginning with "Boxes." Once again he told an interviewer that "these new stories are different from the earlier ones in kind and degree" (*Con*, 186). Between February 1986 and June 1987 these stories appeared in the *New Yorker*, *Esquire*, and *Granta*. "Boxes" was included in *The Best American Short Stories, 1987*, edited by Ann Beattie, while "Errand," which would prove to be Carver's last story, was awarded first place in the O. Henry *Prize Stories, 1988* and included in *Best American Short Stories, 1988*, edited by Mark Helprin. In 1988, more significantly, Atlantic Monthly Press published *Where I'm Calling From: New and Selected Stories*, a collection that represents the best of Carver's fiction. The volume once again received outstanding notices—the poet Hayden Carruth, for example, pronounced it "the only certifiable masterpiece produced in the United States during the past quarter-century" (Stull 1989, 212)—and it firmly cemented Carver's position as the most significant short story writer of the day. Later in the year, in conjunction with his fiftieth birthday, he received a Creative Arts Award Citation for Fiction from Brandeis University, an honorary Doctor of Letters degree from the University of Hartford, and induction into the American Academy and Institute of Arts and Letters. By this point in time Carver had unquestionably become "as successful as a short story writer in America can be,"[18] as well as the most influential writer of his generation; it was only fitting that, in *Esquire* magazine's depiction of the Literary Universe in 1987, Carver was placed at the red-hot center. Unfortunately, these awards and honors were to be his last triumphs.

The Final Years

In the fall of 1987, Carver, who had always been a heavy smoker (he had once called himself "a cigaret with a body attached to it" [*Con*, 4]), was diagnosed with lung cancer. On 1 October doctors in Syracuse removed two-thirds of his left lung. Carver remained optimistic about his prognosis, but in March 1988 a new tumor was detected, this time in his brain, and he began a series of radiation treatments in Seattle. By June, when the cancer reappeared in his lungs, it became clear that the disease was going to be fatal. Nevertheless, Carver pressed on, working on another volume of poems, *A New Path to the Waterfall*, which would be published posthumously. Later that month he and Tess Gallagher were married in Reno, Nevada. In July the couple made a brief fishing trip to Alaska. On the morning of 2 August 1988 Raymond Carver died in his home in Port Angeles.

During this period of illness Carver refused to pity himself. He steadfastly maintained, even in interviews conducted a few weeks before his death, that he was going to recover, since he had "fish to catch and stories and poems to write" (Kellerman, C17). In any event, he asserted (echoing Lou Gehrig) that "I feel—I think I'm one of the luckiest men around" (*Con*, 249). As he noted in one of his final poems, after he had stopped drinking the rest of his life—"these past ten years. / Alive, sober, working, loving and / being loved by a good woman"[19]—had been pure gravy, a gift that he hadn't counted on and that was better than he had any right to expect. Carver certainly enjoyed the recognition he received, but he wore his honors lightly and remained humble in the face of such accolades, surprised that, after his life's struggle, he had finally arrived at the place he had set out to reach. Following his death a number of friends and fellow writers paid tribute to him in the form of such touching memoirs as Tobias Wolff's "Raymond Carver Had His Cake and Ate It Too" in *Esquire* and Jay McInerney's "Raymond Carver: A Still, Small Voice" in the *New York Times Book Review*, but the greatest testament to his indomitable spirit will remain the writings that he left behind. Small though his oeuvre may be, it is sure to last, to be read and appreciated for generations to come.

Chapter Two

The Work of Raymond Carver: An Introduction

Bill Buford, the editor of the British journal *Granta*, began his introduction to a special 1983 issue with the following statement: "A new fiction seems to be emerging from America, and it is a fiction of a peculiar and haunting kind. It is not only unlike anything currently written in Britain, but it is also unlike what American fiction is usually understood to be."[1] Two years later, Kim A. Herzinger, the editor of the *Mississippi Review*, began her introduction to a special issue with a very similar statement: "The following group of essays came to be gathered here in the following way and for the following reasons: Along with others, I imagined that there was a new kind of fiction being produced out there—the evidence was in the tone and texture of books recently published by major American literary publishers and in the amount of attention these books were given in the national press."[2] For both Buford and Herzinger, the writer who defined this "new fiction," who gave it its prevailing "tone and texture," was Raymond Carver. His writings were featured prominently in both issues. He was not the only writer to whom Buford and Herzinger were referring, certainly, but he was undeniably at the forefront of the emerging literature with which they were concerned.

In this chapter, then, I will map out the shape of this "new fiction," particularly with regard to the role Carver's own writings played in the movement (if indeed that is an appropriate term to use about something which, like most literary movements, was neither well-organized nor well-defined, even by the aforementioned editors). In addressing these topics, I shall examine both the matter and the manner of Carver's fiction, that is the kinds of people, places, and situations he wrote about as well as the way in which he wrote about them. A short discussion of "minimalism," the term that became the most commonly used shortcut in talking about Buford and Herzinger's "new fiction," will follow. In this way I will lay the groundwork for the discussions of individual texts in the ensuing chapters.

The Confines of "Carver Country"

In his essay "On Writing," Carver asserts that "every great or even every very good writer makes the world over according to his own specifications" (*F*, 22). Thus there is one world according to John Irving, for example, and a different world according to Flannery O'Connor. Although he doesn't say so himself, there is certainly a world according to Raymond Carver. There is a particular milieu associated with his stories that sets them apart from those of any other writer. As such, a piece of critical shorthand like "Carver Country" makes perfect sense to anyone familiar with Carver's works. We should keep in mind, though, as Tess Gallagher has noted, that the term denotes "an amalgam of feelings and psychic realities which had existed in America, of course, even before Ray began to write about them. But because of his writing we began to give these feelings and patterns more credibility" (Gallagher, 8). We should also keep in mind, as we try to enumerate the characteristics of this world, that one thing Carver Country is not is a particular geographic location. While it is true that many of Carver's stories are set in small towns in the Northwest, and that at one time he was interested in local color writing, by and large his stories "could take place anywhere" (*Con*, 247), as Carver himself has noted. In his view, "men and women behave pretty much the same whether in Port Angeles, or Bellevue, or Houston, or Chicago or Omaha or New York City" (*Con*, 134–35).[3] The great majority of Carver's stories, moreover, take place in regionally anonymous indoor settings. One of the reasons for this lack of regionalism, Carver explained, is that he "moved around too much, lived in too many places, felt dislocated and displaced, to now have any firmly rooted sense of 'place'" (*Con*, 50–51). What unifies his world, then, is not so much a physical as an "emotional landscape" (*Con*, 247); Carver Country is anywhere certain kinds of people congregate, whether East or West, North or South.

   One of the distinguishing features of the characters who inhabit Carver Country is their very rootlessness. It is not uncommon for a Carver story to include a number of characters, all of whom are from somewhere else. What drives them is a search for something better, the hope that their lives will be different in a different environment. All too often, though, in this as in their other dreams and aspirations, their troubles follow them. And most of the characters in Carver Country are troubled; almost every story represents, in the words of a character from one of them, "another tragedy in a long line of low-rent tragedies."[4] In fact,

Carver's fictional people are nearly always "losers who are thoroughly thrashed by life in the first round" (Facknitz 1986, 287).

Although Carver does occasionally focus on a writer or a teacher or a doctor, his characters are primarily employed, when they are employed at all, as blue-collar workers—waitresses, mill or factory workers, mechanics, mail-carriers, sales clerks, motel managers, hairdressers. For relaxation they play bingo, watch television, or go fishing or hunting. Often they are transient, moving between jobs or between locations to try to find a new and better way of life. They are ordinary people and they have fairly ordinary desires. Nevertheless, the vast majority of them "don't get the little they want" (*Con*, 81) and they find themselves struggling to survive. Their marginal lives are filled with failure, deterioration, disenchantment, and despair, leading many critics to designate Carver Country as "Hopeless-ville." Anatole Broyard, for example, has stated that Carver's "stories are rather like the proletariat fiction of the 1930's, although these are proletariats of the psyche, not of economic forces"[5]; in fact, Carver's characters are both, and one of Carver's salient achievements is to demonstrate how psychological and economic factors are intricately bound up with each other in a vicious cycle of depression and bankruptcy from which there seems to be no escape. The characters' marriages and relationships are often a shambles, and too frequently those characters turn to alcohol as a temporary sop. Alcoholism only exacerbates the situation. Feelings of emptiness are prevalent, and violence never seems to be too far from the surface; its occasional eruption is almost expected in these "drab, bleak, and disappointing lives."[6]

In many ways, Carver Country is "a kind of modern wasteland."[7] Carver's characters find themselves isolated, lonely, and often lost or bewildered by what has happened to them. As the writer himself has said of his creations, "Most of my characters would like their actions to count for something. But at the same time they've reached the point— as so many people do—that they know it isn't so. It doesn't add up any longer. The things you once thought important or even worth dying for aren't worth a nickel now. It's their lives they've become uncomfortable with, lives they can see breaking down. They'd like to set things right, but they can't. And usually they do know it, I think, and after that they just do the best they can" (*Con*, 42). Their best, of course, is never quite good enough. As Tobias Wolff has very accurately stated, most of Carver's stories are "about the endless losing war our good intentions wage against our circumstances and our nature."[8]

Some critics, however, have taken Carver to task for being overly pessimistic, for "painting too dark a picture of American life" (*Con*, 183). Others have accused him of demonstrating an ironic or sarcastic intent, "as if [he] is winking at us behind his characters' backs."[9] Both attitudes represent a serious misrepresentation of his aims. Carver always depicts his characters, however down and out, with dignity and respect; he is never cynical. On the contrary, as one critic has written, "he approaches them with sympathy, and respect for their inherent mystery" (*Con*, 133). Carver himself said that "I'm not talking down to my characters, or holding them up to ridicule, or slyly doing an end run around them" (*Con*, 185). "I've known people like this all my life. Essentially, I *am* one of those confused, befuddled people" (*Con*, 112). Therefore he "could never write down to them" (Stull 1989, 199).

Ironically, it is such empathy with the downtrodden that may help to account for Carver's characteristically choosing to depict that moment in a person's life at which, as bad as things are, they are about to get worse. The mood he creates is one of suspension, where the characters always seem to exist in the position of Damocles, with a sword balancing precariously over their heads; "the threat of catastrophic failure seems always imminent" (Goodheart, 634), although it has not arrived quite yet. Carver, according to one critic, tells us "not only [of] what has already gone wrong, but of the accident around the next curve" (*Con*, 244). The word most often used to describe this sense of foreboding in Carver's works is "menace," a notion that reiterates remarks Carver made in the essay "On Writing." There he stated that "I like it when there is some feeling of threat or sense of menace in short stories. I think a little menace is fine to have in a story. For one thing, it's good for the circulation. There has to be tension, a sense that something is imminent, that certain things are in relentless motion, or else, most often, there simply won't be a story" (*F*, 26). This mood is established in so many of Carver's stories that it has become almost a critical commonplace to speak of the way he is able to establish a feeling "of strangeness and dread."[10] Carver, in reviewing a volume of tales by William Kittredge, noted that "there's God's plenty of 'dis-ease' in these stories, a phrase Camus used to describe a certain terrible kind of domesticity" (*NHP*, 179), and a phrase that applies equally well to Carver's own works.

Not only do the characters in these stories experience the menace, but so does the reader, since it is rare for Carver to actually produce the disaster. Thus, as Michael Wood explained in reviewing Carver's first collection, "the expected catastrophe, though absent as crisis or melodrama, is perpetually present as fear."[11] There is the threat of violence without the violence itself to provide any kind of catharsis. Such a situation results in a fearful suspension for both actor (character) and observer (reader). Carver achieves this effect partially through his very brief stories and poems, which often border on (and in the case of the poems, cross over into) the vignette. Carver has expressed approbation for V. S. Pritchett's definition of a short story as "'something glimpsed from the corner of the eye, in passing'" (*F*, 26), and he has attempted to put into practice his belief that "the short story writer's task is to invest the glimpse with all that is in his power" (*F*, 27). Because Carver's stories move "from A to B without delimiting A or B," as the critic Marc Chenetier has noted, characters and readers alike exist in the "suspended seconds between blinding thunderbolt and crashing thunderclap."[12]

To further add to this effect, Carver's stories "frequently end in a static tableau,"[13] or else they "end on an edge with their 'lives' left hanging in an air of uncertainty."[14] The result, as one of Carver's most astute critics, William L. Stull, has written, is that "Carver's stories work by implosion, with detonation delayed until just after the closing sentence. . . . For reader and character alike, the shock is subliminal, more felt than understood."[15] Carver's endings are therefore often referred to as being "open" or "ambivalent" or "indeterminate," and this condition does place something of a burden on the reader. The open ending invites collaboration between author and reader, but many readers have complained about being left "holding the bag."[16] They feel that Carver is abandoning his responsibility as a writer by not providing a resolution. Michael Gorra, for example, analyzing the last paragraph of Carver's story "Preservation," asks, "Why should it end there? It is in no way an ending in their lives. . . . What makes this extremely thin slice better than one further down the loaf, what makes Carver's choice of an ending anything more than arbitrary?"[17] In his own defense, Carver stated during one of his most significant interviews that

> it would be inappropriate, and to a degree impossible, to resolve things neatly for these people and situations I'm writing about. . . . The writer's job, if he or she has a job, is not to provide conclusions or answers. If the story answers *itself*, its problems and conflicts, and meets its *own* requirements, then that's enough. On the other hand, I want to make certain my readers aren't left feeling cheated in one way or another when they've finished my stories. It's important for writers to provide enough to satisfy readers, even if they don't provide "the" answers, or clear resolutions. (*Con*, 111)

Occasionally Carver fails in his aim and the reader does feel cheated, but this is not often the case if the reader is being attentive. The ending of "Preservation," for example, as we shall see when we come to examine the stories in *Cathedral*, follows logically from and resolves the conflicts in the story; we don't find out what happens to the characters in the rest of their lives, but we do have enough evidence to arrive at a reasonably certain projection of the future. Such an ending may be "preseismic" (Chenetier, 167), but the reader can sense the impending cataclysm. Carver doesn't have to push us into the abyss; he need only lead us to the edge of the precipice for us to see that it is there.

The difficulty these critics have with Carver's denouements is that such endings don't proclaim the grandiose statement that many readers have come to expect from literature. For the same reason, many critics assert that Carver's characters fail to achieve any sort of understanding or epiphany.[18] Alan Davis, for example, complains that "one thing happens, then another thing happens, then the story stops, sometimes with an arresting image but hardly ever with an earned epiphany"[19]; other critics have faulted Carver for being "content with taking literary snapshots of life's murk without offering insights."[20] Once again, though, these are misreadings. Carver's characters for the most part do indeed learn and grow, albeit in a muted, implicit way. And what they almost always learn is that they are limited beings and that their lives are going to present them with limited possibilities, much as Carver himself realized the unlikelihood of his dreams coming true during his moment of insight in the Iowa City laundromat, when understanding came to him "like a sharp breeze when the window is thrown open" (*F*, 33). According to Graham Clarke, "many of Carver's stories involve such a moment of recognition and insight in which the fictions by which we live are viciously wiped out. Characters find themselves looking into a void: desperate in their attempts to understand such sudden and disastrous knowledge" (Clarke, 111). Carver emphasizes the importance of the moment of epiphany in his essay "On Writing" when he explains that one of the statements he has hanging above his typewriter is the following fragment from one of Anton Chekhov's stories: ". . . and suddenly everything became clear to him" (*F*, 23). Carver's epiphanies don't usually take this traditional form, yet they are almost always there. In many cases, however, the characters do not know how to respond to them. Ironically, then, the revelatory moments in Carver Country only add to its menace, constraining its denizens even more securely within its borders.

The Survival of the Short Story
and the Return of Realism

Some critics have claimed that, far from lacking in epiphanies, Carver's stories are actually nothing but epiphanies. Gordon Weaver, for example, states that "Carver treats the story as epiphany, his brutally spare slices of life so thin as barely to establish viable contexts for their moments of ironic statement or awareness."[21] This emphasis on the revelatory moment may help to account for Carver's having concentrated his fictional efforts in the genre of the short story. At the time he was beginning to write, such a decision went against the prevailing publishing winds, which stressed the novel. Yet his choice has led, in many ways, to a renaissance of the form. We should not think, however, that aspirations to the literary vanguard influenced his decision. The reason Carver focused on writing stories, he explains in "Fires," was much more prosaic:

> During these ferocious years of parenting, I usually didn't have the time, or the heart, to think about working on anything very lengthy. The circumstances of my life, the "grip and slog" of it, in D. H. Lawrence's phrase, did not permit it. The circumstances of my life with these children dictated something else. They said if I wanted to write anything, and finish it, and if ever I wanted to take satisfaction out of finished work, I was going to have to stick to stories and poems. . . . I had to sit down and write something I could finish now, tonight, or at least tomorrow night, no later, after I got in from work and before I lost interest. (*F,* 34)

Furthermore, the writers whom the young Carver looked up to and tried to model himself upon were ones who had concentrated largely, if not exclusively, on the short story. A list of these authors would include John Cheever, Frank O'Connor, Flannery O'Connor, Sherwood Anderson, Ernest Hemingway, Isaac Babel, and, perhaps most importantly, Anton Chekhov.

Whatever the impetus that pushed Carver in the direction of the short story, it proved to be the perfect genre for exploring and presenting the kind of worldview that prevails in Carver Country. Even when his financial situation no longer compelled him to write in the shorter form, it was still the one he chose to use. As Carver notes in "Fires":

> To write a novel, it seemed to me, a writer should be living in a world that makes sense, a world that the writer can believe in, draw a bead on, and then write about accurately. A world that will, for a time anyway,

stay fixed in one place. Along with this there has to be a belief in the
essential *correctness* of that world. A belief that the known world has reasons for existing and is worth writing about, is not likely to go up in
smoke in the process. This wasn't the case with the world I knew and was
living in. My world was one that seemed to change gears and directions,
along with its rules, every day. (*F*, 35)

The short story, Carver indicates, rather than the novel, is the proper
genre in which to portray the feeling of 'dis-ease' that is so central to his
conception. Most critics have concurred with his assessment. Graham
Clarke, for example, notes that the form is "wholly appropriate to the
fragmented and disparate America of post-Vietnam and Watergate"
(Clarke, 104), while Reamy Jansen asserts that "the short story reflects
an essential condition of our modern age, our sense of marginality in the
world and our often tenuous sense of self."[22] In Carver, form and content
are perfectly matched.

However, Carver's turn to the short story was a risky proposition at
the time, a period in which the genre's very survival was in question.
When Carver notes in "Fires" that he began writing stories because he
"wanted to see tangible results" (*F*, 35), he certainly didn't have financial
considerations in mind. As he explains in an early interview, his career
had trouble getting off the ground because "publishers [were] not interested in collections of short stories," even ones by "established writers,"
since they would "not sell more than 1,500 to 2,000 copies" (*Con*, 11);
"beginning short story writers," such as himself, "could not give away
their collections" (*Con*, 176). Throughout the early part of Carver's
career, pressure was constantly brought to bear on him to write a novel,
which was viewed as a more significant undertaking. Carver did at one
point take an advance to write a novel, although his motivation was
mostly to get some money on which to live while he was trying to dry
out; he also once published a chapter from a novel-in-progress, *The
Augustine Notebooks*, but that was as far as he ever got on the book. By
the mid-1980s, though, the situation of the short story had changed. In
one of his last interviews, Carver spoke of the revival of the genre as "the
single most eventful literary phenomenon of our time" (*Con*, 224), pointing out that "some short story writers can [now] command advances
every bit equal to some of the advances being paid for novels. The bottom line is always how many copies are being are sold, and books of
short stories are being sold these days like never before" (*Con*, 225). His
own *Cathedral*, for instance, racked up quite impressive hardcover sales

of over 20,000. Although Carver was reluctant to claim too much personal credit for this resurgence of the form—demurring to Cheever and Ann Beattie, among others—there is no doubt that he played a significant part in that development. More than one critic has written to the effect that "since 1979, a period virtually coinciding with that of Raymond Carver's success, many publishers and critics have noted that the short story seems to be undergoing a renaissance" (*Con*, 86).

Simultaneously, Carver played a significant part in another revival, that of realistic writing. When Carver was first beginning to write, the dominant literary mode, according to the critics if not the general reading public, was a kind of experimental postmodernism that has been variously called metafiction, surfiction, self-reflexive fiction, or fabulism. The style is marked by such features as an exploration of the arbitrariness of language, an abundance of writing whose main concern is writing itself, and a fascination with complex and convoluted forms and structures. The leading practitioners of this difficult style included John Barth, William Gass, William Gaddis, Thomas Pynchon, Robert Coover, John Hawkes, Ronald Sukenick, and Kurt Vonnegut. By and large, however, such writing failed to appeal to Carver. In several interviews he expressed his view that these writers' works are "all texture and no flesh and blood" (*Con*, 110), that they are "full of gimmicks, and they're ultimately boring. . . . I get bored with writers writing about writing" (*Con*, 18). Carver similarly noted in one of his book reviews that "fiction is not, as some writers believe, the ascendance of technique over content" (*NHP*, 184). As far as Carver was concerned, the experiment of postmodernism had failed. He asserted that "when people look back on that period fifty years from now it's going to be looked on as an odd time in the literary history of the country" (*Con*, 183), a period remarkable for "such an excess of ambition crowned by so little success" (*Con*, 195).

In 1967 Carver published one story in the "self-consuming mode of 'superfiction' that swept through American literature in the late 1960s" (*NHP*, 17–18). However, "Bright Red Apples" remains an anomaly in his oeuvre, an experiment that was not repeated and that he subsequently seemed to disown. Carver concentrated instead on the kind of fiction that, he felt, matters, fiction that has "some bearing on how we live and how we conduct ourselves and how we work out the consequences of our actions" (*Con*, 229). Carver thus placed himself firmly "in the realist tradition" (*Con*, 184), no matter how unpopular or out of step with the times that move was; throughout his career he spoke in favor of "the traditional (some would call it old fashioned) methods of storytelling" (*NHP*, 136). Carver also championed realism in the anthologies he edited. For example, in the introduction to the 1987 volume *American Short Story Masterpieces*, which he coedited with Tom Jenks, he writes that "the bias of this collection . . . is toward the lifelike—that is to say, toward realistically fashioned stories that may even in some cases approximate the outlines of our own lives. Or, if not our own, at least the lives of fellow human beings—grown up men and woman engaged in the ordinary but sometimes remarkable business of living and, like ourselves, in full awareness of their mortality" (*NHP*, 148). A bit later in that same piece, he notes that, following the dominance of experimental writing in the 1970s, "the wheel has rolled forward again and fiction that approximates life . . . has reasserted itself" (*NHP*, 148). He reiterated this claim in several interviews at the time. He told David Applefield, for example, that "I think there's a very real and definite turning away from fabulism and metafiction. Literature is coming back to the things that count, the things that are close to the writer's heart, the things that move us" (*Con*, 207). Carver may have been unwilling to accept much personal credit for the revival of realism, just as he was unwilling to accept credit for ensuring the survival of the short story, but it is undeniable that he played a large part in helping the wheel to turn.

The Miasma of Minimalism

While Carver is quite accurate in stating that "my fiction is in the realistic tradition (as opposed to the really far-out side)" (*Con*, 113), David Applefield is just as accurate in stating that Carver is "not just telling stories in a conventional late 19th-century realist mode" (*Con*, 207). Indeed, no one would confuse a page of Carver with a page of Charles Dickens or George Eliot or William Dean Howells or Henry James, or even such contemporary realistic writers as John Updike or Anne Tyler. Carver's work may mark a return to mimesis, but it is a mimesis saturated with a postmodern worldview. The subject matter is different, certainly, and it is this aspect of Carver's oeuvre more than any other that has caused British observers to call his work, and that produced by some of his contemporaries, "Dirty Realism," a term popularized by Bill Buford in the 1983 special issue of his journal *Granta*. Carver's style is also different, however, and is in fact the more radical departure from the tradition. His is in many ways a highly mannered style, one that is new to American literature. The critical term that has come to be used for Carver's style—as well as that of several other writers who write in a similar manner—is minimalism. That term's use was formalized to an extent by Kim A. Herzinger in the 1985 special issue of the *Mississippi Review*. In her introduction, however, Herzinger pointed out several problems with the term, which is "at best misleading and at worst devaluative" (Herzinger, 9). For one thing, the word *minimalism* had been used before with regard to music (as applied to such composers as Philip Glass and Steve Reich) and the visual arts (with regard to such artists as Ad Reinhardt and Frank Stella). When applied to literature, the term's fit was awkward, taking in (according to various critics) everyone from Joan Didion and Renata Adler, on the one hand,[23] to William S. Burroughs, J. G. Ballard, and Thomas Pynchon on the other.[24] Even after the term was more precisely applied, no two critics ever quite agreed on who was or wasn't a minimalist; Carver's name was always mentioned, but the rest of the list, depending on the compiler, variously included such writers as Ann Beattie, Mary Robison, Bobbie Ann Mason, Richard Ford, Tobias Wolff, Frederick Barthelme, Jayne Anne Phillips, Amy Hempel, and such younger writers as Jay McInerney (who had been one of Carver's students at Syracuse), Bret Easton Ellis, and Tama Janowitz. Interestingly, almost all of these writers repudiated the term when it was applied to their own works. Carver, for example, expressed his dissatisfaction with the label in his important *Paris Review* interview, asserting that "there's something about 'minimalist' that smacks of smallness of vision and execution that I don't like" (*Con*, 44). Indeed, as time went on the term gained largely negative connotations.

Arriving at a consensus definition of minimalism is difficult, although there are certain features that do seem to be characteristic of the style. Herzinger, for example, says that minimalist fiction is "loosely characterized by equanimity of surface, 'ordinary' subjects, recalcitrant narrators and deadpan narratives, slightness of story, and characters who don't think out loud" (Herzinger, 7). John Barth—ironically, a practitioner of "metafiction"—offers a succinct discussion in his essay "A Few Words about Minimalism"; he states that "a cardinal principle [of the minimalist aesthetic] is that artistic effect may be enhanced by a radical economy of artistic means, even where such parsimony compromises other values: completeness, for example, or richness or precision of statement."[25] Barth also presents a minimalistic definition of minimalism by repeating the oft-made contention that "less is more" (Barth, 1), a notion followed up by Geoffrey Wolff's statement that a minimalist "is a taker-outer rather than a putter-inner" (Halpert, 112). Probably the salient feature of minimalism, then, is what is not there—it is a style that thrives on omission. Indeed, many of Carver's stories are marked by what is absent—in "characters, events, and setting"[26]—as much as, if not more than, by what is present. As John W. Aldridge explains, in the minimalist method "what is barely stated about a person or an experience is given a kind of subaqueous luminescence as well as a certain air of menacing fatality by the materials that are left out but the presence of which is nevertheless hauntingly *there*, lurking just behind the venetian blinds of the shuttered prose."[27] Once again, then, in regard to Carver's works, style and content work in perfect harmony.

Once minimalism caught on, it caught on like wildfire. By the mid-1980s, in fact, a number of editors, including Tom Jenks of *Esquire*, Nicholas O'Connell of the *Seattle Review*, William Abrahams of the *O. Henry Awards* annual, and, most eloquently, David Jauss of *Crazyhorse*, complained that the majority of submissions they were receiving were attempts by lesser talents to write like Carver. Minimalistic stories soon began to seem ubiquitous, and almost as quickly there appeared an anti-minimalist backlash the likes of which American literary trends had never seen before. This backlash was frequently aimed at Carver, although it was really calling into question the works of his putative sons and daughters, who generally wrote a "kind of narrow-gauge minimalism that Carver's style unwittingly encouraged but scarcely exemplified" (Dickstein, 512). From the beginning, critics "almost unanimously [found] 'minimalist' fiction somehow lacking" (Herzinger, 10). Even in the special "Minimalist Fiction" issue of the *Mississippi Review*, for instance, Linsey Abrams asserts that "we are witnessing a retreat, in this kind of fiction, from the generative abilities of consciousness, from both the language of thought and the language of emotion."[28] Joe David Bellamy, along the same lines, claims that "a case can be made that the latest fiction is nothing so much as a kind of literary Republicanism, a kind of mid-eighties undulation of the conservative groundswell."[29] Such criticisms were repeated in many other publications as well, and by critics who favor traditional realism as well as by those who champion fabulistic postmodernism.

By the late 1980s, minimalism's fashionable status was "clearly in transition or on the wane" (Sassone, S40). Like a comet, the style was fading away shortly after it had gained its ascendancy. Carver sensed this as early as 1987 when, in his contribution to *Michigan Quarterly Review*'s "A Symposium on Contemporary American Fiction," he wrote: "'Minimalism' vs. 'Maximalism.' Who cares finally what they want to call the stories we write? (And who isn't tired to death by now of that stale debate?)" (*NHP*, 153). Furthermore, the fact of Carver's member-ship in the minimalist fraternity has never been fully and firmly estab-lished. He certainly did not view himself as belonging to any such group (if, indeed, any such group actually existed); as he wrote of himself, Richard Ford, and Tobias Wolff in the touching essay "Friendship," "they don't see themselves as belonging to, or spearheading, a movement" (*NHP*, 217). Randolph Paul Runyon echoes such concerns when he notes that "Carver has been the most influential minimalist . . . while at the same time the least representative."[30] Mark A. R. Facknitz similarly states that Carver "may be a founder [of the school] though not, ulti-mately, a fellow."[31] Part of the problem with using a term such as *mini-malism*, of course, is that it lumps together a number of writers who share certain features but are in other ways quite different from one another. Another part of the problem, though, and one that is crucial in understanding Carver's work, is that the use of such labels doesn't allow for a writer's development. Carver's writing, however, went through a number of phases. As I have noted elsewhere,[32] and as I will show at greater length throughout the ensuing discussion, Carver's career actu-ally follows the pattern of an hourglass—beginning wide, moving through a narrow stage (during his "arch-minimalist" period), and then widening again. The following analyses of Carver's stories and poems will try to help clear the miasma that the use of the term *minimalism* has placed over Carver's writings. Such a dispelling of confusion will help us to better appreciate his true achievement.

Chapter Three

Early Fiction I:
Will You Please Be Quiet, Please?

One of the most striking aspects of *Will You Please Be Quiet, Please?*, Raymond Carver's first major collection of stories, is that it doesn't read like a first book. Carver is firmly in control of his material even at this early stage in his development. One reviewer of a 1992 reissue of the volume, which was originally published in 1976, noted that "Carver had found both his fictional people and, most importantly, a spare ironic style exactly right for chronicling the terror barely contained by everyday routine" (Davis, 654). In other words, the aforementioned elements of Carver Country—with regard both to matter and manner—have been constants almost from the beginning. As Ewing Campbell puts it, in these first stories Carver had "already found his voice and the motifs that [would] preoccupy him for the rest of his life" (Campbell, 3).

Carver had also already found this themes, or, as he preferred, "obsessions" (*Con*, 199), which, as he once told an interviewer, were "the relationship between men and women, why we oftentimes lose the things we put the most value on, [and] the mismanagement of our own inner resources. I'm also interested in survival, what people can do to raise themselves up when they've been laid low" (*Con*, 199). He produced another such list of obsessions in his introduction to *The Best American Short Stories, 1986*, which he edited; there he stated that the "things that count" are "love, death, dreams, ambition, growing up, coming to terms with your own and other people's limitations" (*NHP*, 140). Critics have offered alternative (and equally valid) lists, such as Campbell's "motifs of the grotesque, of otherness, the reconciling factor of characters imagining others' lives, and the opposite—characters failing to make the imaginative leap that will connect them with others," along with "characteristic topics of alcoholism, infidelity, insomnia, and despair" (Campbell, x–xi). Although neither Carver nor Campbell explicitly mentions it, I would agree with William Stull's assessment that "failure of communication is Carver's abiding theme" (Stull "RC" 1985, 242). All of these obsessions are present and active in the stories that make up *Will You Please Be Quiet, Please?*

"Fat"

The leadoff story in this first collection, "Fat" is one of Carver's early masterpieces, and serves as an introduction to a number of the motifs that will become constants in his work. In particular, the story is set very clearly in a blue-collar environment. The unnamed first-person narrator is a waitress in a second-rate restaurant, and the other characters include the other waitresses (Harriet and Margo), a busboy (Leander), a cook (Rudy), who also happens to be the narrator's lover, and her friend, Rita. The catalyst for the story's development is a new patron at the diner, an incredibly fat and rapacious man—one so large, in fact, that he refers to himself as "we." The scene seems ripe for irony, but Carver is instead interested in depicting the hard life of a waitress. He has the narrator note that, when the fat man sat down at her station, she also had "other tables, a party of four businessmen, very demanding, another party of four, three men and a woman, and this old couple."[1] Through his empathy, Carver demonstrates the value he places on the working class, people who would ordinarily not be deemed worthy of serious literary consideration. Carver explores the effect that the mysterious fat man has had on the waitress, and the story concludes with a particularly Joycean revelation. As a result of the incident, the narrator comes to reevaluate her relationship with Rudy, and at the end of the story she asserts that "My life is going to change. I feel it" (*WYP*, 8). She realizes that what she had earlier said to the fat man, "A person has to be comfortable" (*WYP*, 5), applies to herself as well.

Carver's concern with the fragility of interpersonal relationships, particularly as they are exacerbated by economic struggle, is readily apparent here. When we first meet Rudy he is depicted, like the rest of the story's characters, as being rather boorish in his response to the new patron. The narrator herself is initially somewhat repulsed by (and very curious about) the fat man—in trying to act nonchalant, she spills a glass of water in his lap—but she soon begins to reconsider her prejudices. As she waits on and converses with him, "there is a movement toward recognizing her own difference in the fat man" which "suggests a link between the two" (Campbell 13). Although she cannot clearly articulate her emotions to Rita when she tells her the story, the reader can sense that "the fat man is a being with whom, on a deeper, personal level, the narrator strongly identifies."[2] When Leander makes a comment about the man's weight, for instance, she tells him, "He can't help it, . . . so shut up" (*WYP*, 5). Harriet refers to the customer as "old tub-of-guts" (*WYP*, 6) and tells Rudy that he is a "fat man from the circus"

(*WYP*, 7). When the narrator defends the man, Rudy mocks her, saying that she is "sweet on fat-stuff" (*WYP*, 7). At this point in the narrative the reader has no indication that this conversation is anything but tasteless jocularity, so it comes as a surprise when we later learn that Rudy is also the narrator's boyfriend. She is clearly put out with Rudy as a result of his insensitivity to the man. Rudy thus becomes a kind of ogre, and the narrator attempts to avoid contact with him. What the reader comes to understand is "that the waitress is being suffocated by [Rudy] and that, curiously enough, the fat man represents to her everything Rudy lacks" (Nesset, 298). When Rudy initiates sex, she rather unwillingly submits, but then something strange happens; she reports to Rita that: "When he gets on me, I suddenly feel I am fat. I feel I am terrifically fat, so fat that Rudy is a tiny thing and hardly there at all" (*WYP*, 8). Here, then, Carver is already exploring a theme, an obsession, that will run throughout his works: "the principle of self-discovery in the other, with its implications of change" (Campbell, 12).

In "Fat" we also have the first of Carver's trademark endings, one which can lead to several interpretations. The sense of power in the image of being so much bigger than Rudy—an overcompensation created by her realization of how "dwarfed and submissive she has been"[3]— clearly indicates a positive change for the narrator, who has been empowered by the fat man to break off her relationship with the insensitive cook and look for something better. As the story ends, however, this break-up has not yet occurred, and we can only anticipate the problems the narrator is going to have in ending the relationship. The narrator's resolve at the end—"My life is going to change"—seems strong, but it is still in the future tense, and in the passive voice (Nesset, 300). There remains a degree of menace about the period between now and then, and thus a great deal of ambiguity about the conclusion of the story. Several critics take a dim view of the narrator's abilities to make true changes. Kirk Nesset, for example, asserts that "the sense of the story's close, ultimately, is that the waitress will not act but will continue to be acted upon" (Nesset, 301). Alan Wilde similarly claims that her assertion "deceives neither us nor, ultimately, herself" (Wilde, 118). Ewing Campbell, on the other hand, takes a more generous, if cautious view; he writes of "hints of a vaguely altered future" (Campbell, 12) and concludes that "her renewal, although recognizable and foreshadowed, must not be viewed as finished or in any way static, for she is in the fluid state of becoming" (Campbell, 13). I would agree with this position, emphasizing that in Carver Country change is a positive virtue, for the alternative to epiphany is paralysis. The ending is typical of Carver in its inconclusiveness, although I take the story to be more optimistic than many in the collection.

"Fat" can also be seen as an early expression of Carver's lifelong obsession with communication. In many ways, "Fat" is a study of storytelling. The opening line of the story is: "I am sitting over coffee and cigarets at my friend Rita's and I am telling her about it" (*WYP*, 3). Already, then, there is a double narrative framework to the story, for the narrator is now telling us what she has already told Rita about something that has happened even earlier. The first part of the narration is taken up largely with a recounting of conversations that were held at the diner concerning the fat man, although, in one of Carver's stylistic trademarks, these conversations are retold in the present tense. Phrases such as "I say" and "he says" appear in almost every line; at one point the narrator goes to the kitchen to get the man's dessert, and "Rudy says, Harriet says you got a fat man from the circus out there" (*WYP*, 7). The layering of stories provides almost a palimpsistic effect here. By the time she's done telling her story of the encounter with the fat man, the narrator realizes that Rita, who "sits there waiting, her dainty fingers poking her hair" (*WYP*, 8), has little understanding of the point she has been trying to make. She then tells the reader, "I feel depressed. But I won't go into it with her. I've already told her too much" (*WYP*, 8). As with the open ending, then, in a very real sense the monological nature of the story—its narrative form taken from the modern oral tradition—also makes the reader a very active participant: We are called upon, if we don't want to be dropped the way Rudy and Rita are being dropped, to be more sensitive listeners than they were.

Carver makes it clear that storytelling, communication, is a cathartic act, "a purgation" (Nesset, 300). The narrator is herself still coming to grips with her reaction to the fat man, for "she cannot pin down the reason for its having unsettled her so" (Saltzman, 23). Carver told an interviewer that the narrator of the story "can't quite make sense out of the story herself, all of the feelings that she experienced, but she goes ahead and tells it anyway" (*Con*, 211). In the very act of telling the story, moreover, she comes closer to understanding it herself. At one point, for example, she pauses to say "I know now I was after something. But I don't know what" (*WYP*, 6). As her narrative progresses, though, she makes connections and begins to see that the first concrete action to be taken involves severing her constrictive ties to Rudy. In the first sign of the narrator's disaffection from Rudy—following a story he has told about a boy he knew when he was growing up who was called simply "Fat"—she remarks to Rita that "I can't think of anything to say" (*WYP*, 8). This inability to communicate is an important component of many of Carver's stories of broken relationships, of which this is the first.

Some of Carver's stylistic trademarks are also apparent in this first story. David Kaufmann, for example, asserts not only that "the prose is disjunctive,"[4] but that "the paratactic sentence structure is not a stylistic quirk but is rather integral to the construction of the story" (Kaufmann, 99). Campbell similarly talks about "the hovering *it*" (Campbell 12), evident in both the opening and closing sentence; in the first sentence "it" refers to the encounter with the fat man, while in the last "it" refers to her change, and thus Carver again links the two occurrences. While several critics have made less than favorable comments about "Fat"— Kaufmann, for example, declares it "disturbingly inconsequential" (Kaufmann, 98)—I would argue that "Fat" is a strong story, and an almost textbook example of the Carveresque, in which "the crisis of the everyday that the fat man precipitates remains as enigmatic as it is inexpressible" (Kaufmann, 99). "Fat" can be read and appreciated on many different levels, and remains one of Carver's most appealing early works.

"Neighbors"

The next story, "Neighbors," the first of Carver's stories Gordon Lish accepted for publication in *Esquire*, is also one of Carver's strongest and most "quintessential" (Stull "RC" 1985, 237) early tales. Like "Fat," "Neighbors" reaches toward epiphany, but it ends on a very different, clearly pessimistic note. The story centers on Bill and Arlene Miller, a bookkeeper and a secretary, who come to feel that they have "been passed by somehow" in life (*WYP*, 9). They are envious of their across-the-hall neighbors, Jim and Harriet Stone, for "it seemed to the Millers that the Stones lived a fuller and brighter life" (*WYP*, 9). When the Stones go out of town they leave the key to their apartment with the Millers, who have agreed to look after the cat and water the plants. The first time Bill goes to the apartment he wanders around looking at the Stones' things, drinks some of their liquor, and becomes sexually aroused; he returns home and makes love to Arlene. The next day he leaves work early, makes love to Arlene again, and then goes to the Stones' apartment; the following day he once more visits the apartment, where he proceeds to masturbate in the Stones' bed and then try on some of Jim's clothes, and then some of Harriet's. As Carver explains, "with each subsequent trip to the Stones' apartment, Miller is drawn deeper and deeper into an abyss of his own making" (*NHP*, 103). That evening Arlene goes to feed the cat, and being in the neighbors' apartment also arouses her; she finds some pornographic pictures and, as Bill had done, she masturbates on the bed. Carver notes that she "has been doing pretty much the same kind of rummaging and prowling that he has been engaging in" (*NHP*, 104). When she admits her actions to Bill, the Millers decide to go to the apartment together. Living the Stones' lives will, they feel, be more exciting than living their own. In a sense, cat-sitting for the Stones becomes the Millers' own vacation, and Arlene even dares to hope that "'Maybe they won't come back'" (*WYP*, 15), that this excitement can become a new way of life. Bill, who had earlier wondered the same thing, notes that "'It could happen. . . . Anything could happen'" (*WYP*, 15).

Recounting the plot of a story like "Neighbors" is necessary because it is one of a number of Carver's stories that is driven by plot, just as "Fat" is driven by narrative. Action is particularly important in "Neighbors" because it is a story about the return of action, adventure, and excitement to the humdrum, run-of-the-mill lives of Bill and Arlene Miller. Although the opening paragraphs of the story do not indicate that their relationship was on the verge of breakup, they do show signs of a time-worn distance between the mates; as Nesset indicates, "the story deals less with love or passion than with its conspicuous absence and with the symptoms of love's withdrawal" (Nesset, 295). Bill's sexual advance in the afternoon, for example, is obviously quite out of the ordinary. It would thus seem that the experiences in the Stones' apartment have been beneficial to the Millers, and they certainly are looking forward to the time they can spend in the apartment before the Stones return. At the story's climax, however, Carver adds a final plot twist: not only did Arlene forget to feed the cat on her last trip to the Stones, but when they go over jointly to rectify the situation (and, we are sure, make love) they discover that she has locked the key inside. Bill and Arlene can no longer pretend to be the Stones—they are now locked out of that life—and they realize instantly that they must find some way to return to their real existence. As the story ends, Bill is comforting Arlene, telling her not to worry, and Carver writes that, "They stayed there. They held each other. They leaned into the door as if against a wind, and braced themselves" (*WYP*, 16). The story thus ends, not with Bill's statement that "'Anything could happen'"—which would align "Neighbors" with the protagonist's vocalized optimism in "Fat"—but on a more somber note.

The Millers' relationship had indeed been strengthened by their voyeurism and playacting, but whether this new excitement can be maintained remains very much in doubt; as the final image suggests, permanently reinvigorating their lives will be quite a struggle.

Thematically, "Neighbors" does bear certain parallels to "Fat," as several critics have shown.[5] The protagonists in both stories make use of a vicarious experience—imagining themselves as someone else—in order to reevaluate and redirect their own lives. In the case of the waitress from the first story, the breakthrough comes metaphorically, and so the hope that it can be actualized in some form remains alive; in the case of the Millers, however, their more literal breakthrough takes on a physical as well as emotional dimension, and the destruction of the one necessarily leads to the destruction of the other. "The Millers' psychosexual games are not without their negative implications" (Nesset, 196), and these become dominant as the husband and wife are unable to transfer their vicarious charge to the everyday reality of their marriage. The end result of their playacting and voyeurism[6] is to make them more fully realize the emptiness of their real lives. Ultimately they must face the fact that, for them, unlike the waitress in "Fat," who could feel the change even if she couldn't explain or fully express it, "no escape is possible."[7] The conclusion of "Neighbors," which shows the earlier "glimmer of something better" to be merely "the predictable prelude to inevitable letdown" (Wilde, 118), is thus more typical of Carver's work.

"Neighbors" also shows many of the typical stylistic signs of Carver's minimalism. The flatness of the third-person narration (compared to the first person of "Fat") is characteristic of the minimal voice. The sentences are short and clipped, unemotional even when describing the most surprising events. Of Bill's cross-dressing, for example, Carver writes that "He rummaged through the top drawers until he found a pair of panties and a brassiere. He stepped into the panties and fastened the brassiere, then looked through the closet for an outfit. He put on a black and white checkered skirt and tried to zip it up. He put on a burgundy blouse that buttoned up the front. He considered her shoes, but understood they would not fit" (*WYP*, 14). Such narration has the effect of making the bizarre seem quite normal, and so Carver draws us into empathizing with the Millers rather than pitying or laughing at them. The brilliant image at the end of the story—reminiscent as it is of the final image in John Milton's *Paradise Lost* (Saltzman, 26)—thus hits the reader as a slap in the face, just as it hits the Millers. They are left "in limbo, dissociated from both lives," and "they have only each other," however "tenuous that link is" (Boxer, 77). The menace that Carver has spoken of as being characteristic of his minimalist style is thus clearly apparent at the end of "Neighbors," where the protagonists are left forlorn, clinging together out of desperation. Carver himself said of the story that it "captured an essential sense of mystery or strangeness" (Stull "RC" 1985, 238), one of the hallmarks of the Carveresque.

"The Idea"

"The Idea" consolidates some of the motifs and obsessions explored in the first two stories, themes that will recur throughout the collection. In this text an unnamed first-person narrator tells us the story of her neighbor, who peeps "into his own bedroom window" (*WYP*, 18) while his wife undresses. In telling us this story, however, she also tells of that she and her husband, Vern, have spent the last three months watching their neighbor watching his wife. The frame of the story, then, is of a double-voyeurism. The neighbor's activity clearly leads to sexual arousal, and the narrator's voyeurism has much the same effect on her. The narrator's description of the way she and Vern watch the man—hiding in the dark so as not to be detected—contrasts with the neighbor's wife, who leaves the light on and the curtain open, and contains more than a hint of sexual tension. She knows that, although "Vern's a little embarrassed about watching," he does "enjoy it. He's said so" (*WYP*, 17). In the dark, she, too, enjoys it; she notes that it makes her "jumpy" (*WYP*, 19). When the light in the neighbor's house goes off and the one in the narrator's comes on, however, she presents a very different attitude. Feigning outrage, she threatens to tell the woman off the next time she sees her. When Vern suggests that "'maybe he *has* something there'" (*WYP*, 20), the narrator says, "anybody comes looking in my window . . . they'll have the cops on them" (*WYP*, 20). Although it seems that the narrator is looking forward to having sex with Vern, enhanced by thoughts of the neighbors, the act does not happen. Vern falls asleep and the story ends with the narrator again looking out the window and exclaiming "'That trash . . . The idea!'" (*WYP*, 21).

Carver makes it clear to the reader—even if it is not quite clear to the narrator herself—that she doesn't want to admit to her own sexual response to voyeurism, something that she was raised to think of as perverted. Watching their neighbors provides an opportunity for the narrator and Vern to reignite their own lives, similar to the opportunity Bill and Arlene Miller took advantage of in "Neighbors," but that renewal does not even occur momentarily, as it did for the Millers. After Vern goes to bed, the narrator's fears begin to coalesce around a group of ants that she finds crawling in and out of her garbage can; although she sprays—which is what keeps her in the kitchen longer than expected, so that when she gets to bed Vern is already asleep—she still feels as though the ants can come back at any time to watch her. This is the threat that prevents her from taking advantage of her own and Vern's renewed sexual feelings: Someone (or something) might be watching. Her attack on the neighbor's wife can thus be seen as arising from envy, for the narrator, too, has had "the idea," although she cannot bring herself to act on it. Like Bill and Arlene, she sees the neighbors' lives as being fuller than her own, but does not dare to enter those lives as the Millers entered the Stones'. In the final scene, then, the narrator is torn between her two impulses: repulsion and attraction, "Puritanism and prurience" (Boxer, 78). Because she is unable to become a part of the neighbors' sexual revolution, she comes to feel great rancor toward them, and is pushed "toward vicarious and symbolic gestures of retribution" (Campbell, 21), in this case the annihilation of the ants.

"They're Not Your Husband"

Although this story also hinges on the kind of sexual voyeurism that is at the center of "Neighbors" and "The Idea," "They're Not Your Husband" is more closely related to "Fat." In fact, it can be seen as a kind of radical revisioning of that story. The setting is once again at an all-night diner, and the story once again concerns a waitress and her personal relationships. But there the similarities end. The most significant change is that "They're Not Your Husband" focuses on the husband, Earl Ober, rather than the wife, Doreen. Earl is a salesman, although he is currently unemployed, and Doreen has taken a night job at a coffee shop. One evening Earl stops by the restaurant, hoping for a free meal, and overhears two businessmen commenting on Doreen's overly large backside. Already feeling "vulnerable to catastrophe" (Saltzman, 28), uneasy and unmanned by having to have his wife support him, Earl sees both a threat and an opportunity in the rude remarks. He decides that, if he can convince Doreen to lose weight, then her customers might make admiring lewd remarks, which would necessarily validate the manliness of her husband. One obvious sign of Earl's weakness is his allowing other people's opinions to have great sway over his own actions. In fact "all of his values come to him second-hand" (Campbell, 18), and he expects the same to be true of Doreen, except that he feels her values should come only from him, not from other people. Later on in the story, when Doreen tells Earl that some of the waitresses have been saying she looks pale and is losing too much weight, he tells her, "'Don't you pay any attention to them. Tell them to mind their own business. They're not your husband. You don't have to live with them'" (*WYP*, 27).

The emphasis here is clearly on Earl's point of view. Doreen remains entirely subservient the whole time, again in contradistinction to the narrator's raised consciousness at the end of "Fat." Doreen believes Earl's statements that she needs to lose weight, not understanding his ulterior motive, and he convinces her to, in effect, starve herself. Although he claims that he is so persuasive with her because he is "'a closer'" (*WYP*, 25), she is in fact the only sale he can make, for he is continually unable to land a job. Earl literally comes to treat her as an investment; Carver notes that "at night he counted up her tips. He smoothed out the dollar bills on the table and stacked the nickels, dimes, and quarters in piles of one dollar. Each morning he put her on the scale" (*WYP*, 26). After Doreen has lost almost twenty pounds, Earl returns to the diner and, when no comments about her figure are forthcoming, he attempts to elicit some, first from another waitress and then from a newspaper-reading patron. Earl says to the man, "'What do you think of that? . . . Don't you think that's something special?'" (*WYP*, 29). He even orders a sundae, knowing that Doreen's skirt will ride up when she bends over to scoop the ice cream, and nudges the other man to watch. In all of these ways, Earl—referring to her as "that"—is objectifying and dehumanizing Doreen.

When the other waitress sees what he's up to and asks Doreen "'Who is this joker, anyway?'" (*WYP*, 30), Doreen is forced to confess that "'He's a salesman. He's my husband'" (*WYP*, 30). The impact of the admission has not yet begun to hit Doreen as the story ends—she merely "began to shake her head slowly" (*WYP*, 30)—but Earl is already feeling its full force. Much like the Millers at the end of "Neighbors," he "put on his best smile. He held it. He held it until he felt his face pulling out of shape" (*WYP*, 30). He realizes that his plan has backfired, that what he hoped to use as a sop to his wounded vanity has in fact wounded him more deeply; his wounds are out in the open and everyone is staring. Wanting to avoid being seen as a joker—the initial customer's statement about Doreen was that "'some jokers like their quim fat'" (*WYP*, 22)—Earl obviously has become the biggest joker of them all. Earl knows what will happen to his reputation; "publicly identified as the sort of person he least wants to be" (Campbell, 19), Earl, like the Millers, must brace for a difficult period ahead.

Another way in which "They're Not Your Husband" revisions "Fat" is in its use of the metaphor of weight. While a fat patron causes a reassessment by a thin waitress in the earlier story, here a fat waitress causes a reassessment by a thin patron, who happens to be her husband.[8] Just as the waitress in "Fat" is bothered by the comments of her fellow workers with regard to the obese customer, so Earl is bothered by the comments of his fellow patrons with regard to the fat waitress. Unlike the waitress in "Fat," however, who comes to see that the fat man must be allowed to be fat, Earl agrees with the crowd, "he accepts the superimposition of the derisive perspective of her customers" (Saltzman, 28), and he prevails upon Doreen to lose weight. When his fantasy disintegrates at the end of the story, Earl realizes that his life has now permanently changed for the worse; his life is not beginning again, as it might have done had he been able to secure a job, but it is now effectively over. Doreen may eventually become enlightened to the abusive and punishing situation in which her husband is placing her, as the narrator of "Fat" gradually did, but the story ends before this change is indicated. Because the story focuses on Earl, it ends, as did "Neighbors," with a feeling of menace and impending doom.

"Are You a Doctor?"

A sense of menace is also apparent in "Are You a Doctor?" Here Carver tells the story of 24 hours in the life of Arnold Breit, 24 hours after which he will never be the same. The catalyst for such transformation is something as seemingly innocuous as a wrong number. As in several of Carver's stories, however, the telephone, a medium of communication, can become "an intrusive instrument, almost menacing in its power to disrupt and unsettle the lives of others" (Clarke, 115). In this case, the call certainly upsets the life of Arnold Breit, a rather mild, quiet, and lonely man. Expecting a phone call from his wife who is out of town on business, Breit answers the phone "'Hello, dear'" (*WYP*, 31). It is not his wife on the other end of the line, however, but Clara Holt, a total stranger who has called him because she found his number on a piece of paper left by her baby-sitter. The caller responds to the way Arnold answers the phone and attempts to extend the conversation. He would also like to talk but knows he shouldn't. After she tells him that "'You sound like a nice man'" (*WYP*, 32), Arnold reflects that "he should hang up now, but it was good to hear a voice, even his own, in the quiet room" (*WYP*, 32), so he continues talking.

The call seems to promise a positive change in his life. He fights it at first, but Arnold eventually succumbs to the temptation of meeting Clara. The whole time he is in her apartment, however, he continues to struggle with himself. Even as he climbs the stairs he feels sweaty and nervous. He knows that he should return home—he is expecting another call from his wife—but he is attracted to the idea of an affair with Clara, moreso than he is actually attracted to Clara. When he kisses her she intimates that she hopes he will visit again, but Arnold shakes his head negatively. He is too committed to his life with his wife, lonely as it often is, to break out so forcefully. As with the main characters in "Neighbors" and "The Idea," he cannot capitalize on the opportunity, and so a glimpse of the unattainable only makes his real life that much worse. He denies himself pleasure to return to the comfortable. Encounters with people like Clara will remain, as Arnold says, "'very much of a mystery to me[,] quite out of the ordinary I assure you'" (*WYP*, 38).

Later that night the phone rings again and this time, expecting Clara, he answers very formally, in contrast to the very familiar way he greeted Clara when he thought it would be his wife: "'Arnold. Arnold Breit speaking'" (*WYP*, 40). His wife, slightly intoxicated, kids him that he is being awfully formal, but Arnold is so taken aback to hear her voice on the line—almost as if hers were a voice from the distant past—that he cannot respond. As the story ends, "he remained silent and considered her voice. 'Are you there, Arnold?' she said. 'You don't sound like yourself'" (*WYP*, 40). In a very real sense he is no longer himself, or at least no longer the self that his wife knew him to be before she went away on business, "for he has played the role of another and thus feels alienated from his everyday reality" (May, 77). He is committed to his life with his wife, but he already knows that from now on it will be a series of disappointments. As the story ends, "Carver leaves [the Breits] on the verge of inevitable distance from one another" (Saltzman, 32), since Arnold can't think of anything to say. His epiphany, like so many in Carver's work, is his understanding of his own limitations, and so the end of the story has a decided tone of resignation.

"Nobody Said Anything"

Following "Are You a Doctor?" comes "The Father," the oldest and shortest of Carver's stories to be included in the collection, and one of the least effective. In contrast, "Nobody Said Anything" is one of the longer stories in the volume, and one of the best. The story is narrated in the first-person voice of an adolescent boy who senses the impending break-up of his parents and is made uneasy by it. He wakes up one morning to the routine sounds of his parents arguing and decides to play hooky. After his mother goes to work he watches TV, masturbates, smokes, and decides to go fishing. Much of the narration from this point on sounds like an adolescent version—or perversion—of Hemingway's "Big Two-Hearted River," with the narrator alternately catching fish and mastur-bating. Toward the end of the story, however, with the help of another kid, the narrator lands a huge fish.[9] After he and the other boy argue about who owns the giant animal, the narrator ends up cutting the fish in half and taking home only its huge head. The narrator has turned to the pastoral in an attempt to find solace, but he discovers, as will several other Carver protagonists, that "the realities [he] has sought to leave behind still enclose [him]" (Saltzman, 34). His fishing expedition proves to be something of a letdown, and the reader senses that the boy feels himself to be standing on a precipice.

At the end of the story he returns home, visibly proud of his achieve-ment and wanting to offer his parents the fish head as a kind of talisman around which to rebuild the family structure; he invests the fish with the "belief that somehow his victory will not only establish his manhood but also rescue his family from their malaise" (Saltzman, 37). He discovers his parents fighting, however, and their only response to the fish is to vent their anger at him. His mother tells him to "'take it out before I throw up'" and his father asks him, "'What in the hell is the matter with you? Take it the hell out of the kitchen and throw it in the goddamn garbage!'" (WYP, 61). The broken fish too closely resembles the broken home[10] to function as a unifying force, and the narrator's hopes are dashed. His attempt at mediation has proven entirely unsuccessful, and he is left with only a fish head for comfort, as indicated in the somber final lines: "I lifted him out. I held him. I held that half of him" (61). The boy is no longer merely standing on a precipice, but is beginning to fall into the chasm. The insight he has gained—reminiscent of the real-ization reached by the similarly adolescent protagonist of James Joyce's "Araby" (Campbell, 8)—is, once again, of his own limitations. His fami-ly is falling apart, and he learns that he can do nothing to stop its destruction (Campbell, 9). With the fish reduced to garbage, his hopes of reconciliation have also been trashed.

As the title "Nobody Said Anything" plainly indicates, Carver is here exploring one of his central motifs: the belief that communication prob-lems are endemic to failing relationships. As Ewing Campbell notes,

"Just as no one in the family listens, no one speaks up about unhealthy situations" (Campbell, 10). In the opening paragraph, for example, the narrator nudges his brother George hoping that he will "wake up and say something" to the fighting parents, but George verbally attacks him instead, says "'I don't care,'" and goes back to sleep (*WYP*, 43). The narrator reflects that, when his mother tried to tell him that his father "wanted to tear up the family," he "didn't want to listen" (*WYP*, 43). To cite another example of avoidance, the boy's mother, Edna, has given him permission to stay home from school, but before she leaves for work she sees that, against her orders, he has turned the TV set on. The volume is off, though, and her son is reading a book, so she "glanced at the TV but didn't say anything" (*WYP*, 45). On her way out of the house, "she stood in the doorway and turned the knob. She looked as if she wanted to say something else" (*WYP*, 45). But she does not. The narrator also wants to say something, but he finds it very difficult to do so. "On several occasions, he seeks to communicate with someone only to find himself without words" (Campbell, 9). When a woman gives the narrator a lift in her car, for example, he begins to think of the standard pornographic visions he has had of such a scene, but he is nervous and cannot "think of something to say" (*WYP*, 48). Finally, at the end of the story, the narrator does try to communicate as part of his attempt at mediation between his parents. In telling the reader how he hysterically attempted to divert his parents' attention to his heroic fishing feat, he explains that "my voice was crazy. But I could not stop" (*WYP*, 61). Since this attempt at communication is "crazy," the only result is that both parents displace their verbal attacks at each other onto him. They do talk to him, but the words prove to be even more damaging than the silence has been. He discovers that it is too late for there to be anything to be said. Thus, as Arthur Saltzman has pointed out, the title both "names the common response to hardship and serves as its principal symptom" (Saltzman, 34). Sad as it may be, such a situation is the predominant one in Carver Country.

"Nobody Said Anything" is rather unusual in Carver's canon, though, in that the theme is presented from the child's point of view rather than from the perspective of a parent. In many ways, the narrator shows himself to be more responsible than his elders are. Before Edna goes to work, for instance, she stresses to him that "'you don't need to turn the burners on for a thing'" (*WYP*, 45), yet when he returns to the house after having caught his fish he notes that "smoke was all over the kitchen. I saw it was coming from a pan on the burner. But neither of them paid any attention" (*WYP*, 60). The narrator also exhibits positive behavior in his encounter with the other young fisherman. He initially describes this boy as "look[ing] like a rat or something" (*WYP*, 53), and he feels confident that "I could have taken him if it came to that" (*WYP*, 58). Yet after the narrator has halved the fish, and they begin to haggle over who is going to get which end, he "didn't want to fight" (*WYP*, 58). He offers the boy an entire fish he had caught earlier in addition to the tail of the big fish, and that turns out to be an equitable solution; the two boys were on the verge of blows, but the narrator's mediation allows them to part as friends. Carver also points out that both fish seem diseased, as though the river is polluted. The giant one, for example, "was so skinny, too skinny for how long he was, and you could hardly see the pink stripe down his sides, and his belly was gray and slack instead of white and solid like it should have been" (*WYP*, 57). Even the natural world cannot entirely sustain itself amidst humankind's destruction, and so it is no wonder that the fish head is considered garbage by the narrator's father. The narrator has tried to salvage something from the chaos he perceives around him, but everything remains broken and seemingly irreparable, as in so many of Carver's stories. The narrative voice in "Nobody Said Anything" does make it distinctive, however, and the story is surely one of the most realized in this first collection.

"What's in Alaska?"

The next tale, "Sixty Acres," is in some ways the most atypical one in the volume, focusing as it does on a Native American narrator who is torn between his loyalty to his heritage and his desire to live a peaceful life. Although the story is effectively presented—and although it does refute some critics' charges that Carver is a one-trick pony—I have chosen to skip over it in the interest of space and because it is such a unique item in Carver's oeuvre.

Carver returns to more standard territory in the subsequent story, "What's in Alaska?," which centers on Carl, an auto mechanic living in a fairly limited but stable world. He gets off work early one day and buys a pair of shoes. He gets home and his wife, Mary, greets him warmly and says that a neighboring couple, Jack and Helen, have invited them over to smoke some marijuana in Jack's new water pipe. She also informs him that she has had a job interview and thinks that she is going to be offered a job in Fairbanks. Although this news is a shock to Carl's settled life, he seems to be intrigued at the prospect, stating that he's "'always wanted to go to Alaska'" (*WYP*, 78). When they arrive at the neighbors' house, however, Mary tells Jack and Helen that "'Carl's on a little bummer tonight'" (*WYP*, 80), thinking, perhaps, that her news has upset him. He resents the remark, mostly because he knows that her assumption about his bad mood is "'a good way to put me on one'" (*WYP*, 80). That is indeed what happens. When Jack and Helen begin to inquire about Carl and Mary's potential move, asking them "'What's in Alaska?'" (*WYP*, 84), Carl can only reply, "'I don't know'" (*WYP*, 84). Already his stable world is falling apart; his "sense of well-being has been shaken" (Boxer, 80) and he feels increasingly insecure.

His equilibrium is upset even further as the story progresses. First he discovers that Mary and Jack may be having an affair. They go into the kitchen together and Carl watches them: "He saw Jack reach up to a shelf in the cupboard. He saw Mary move against Jack from behind and put her arm around his waist" (*WYP*, 85–86). Subsequently, both Mary and Jack make verbal slips that confirm Carl's suspicions. As soon as Mary and Jack return from the kitchen, moreover, Carl spills some cream soda on his new leather shoes and ruins them, symbolizing the dissolution of his private life. By this time Carl is indeed on a bummer, and his attitude toward Alaska has become entirely negative. "'There's nothing in Alaska'" (*WYP*, 87) is his final opinion. He decides that it is time for him and his wife to leave the neighbors' house. Although there is some hesitation and awkwardness in their departure—"Carl stared at Mary, who was staring at Jack. Jack stared at something on the rug near his foot" (*WYP*, 90)—Mary does go along. On the way home she even says to her husband, "'When we get home, Carl, I want to be fucked, talked to, diverted. Divert me, Carl. I need to be diverted tonight'" (*WYP*, 91). As Arthur Saltzman points out, this desire to be diverted indicates that she does not want to confront "significant subjects" (Saltzman, 41), such as the unspeakable affair, but would rather be "numbed" (Saltzman, 42) by whatever is available—sex, drugs, food, or sleep. After sending Carl on several errands, Mary does indeed fall asleep before any sexual relations can take place. As with many other stories in this collection, communication has clearly broken down here, and the relationship is in jeopardy.

As the story ends, Carl sees something, presumably a mouse, running down the hall. The final note is typically Carveresque in its evocation of menace: "He kept staring and thought he saw it again, a pair of small eyes. His heart turned. He blinked and kept staring. He leaned over to look for something to throw. He picked up one of his shoes. He sat up straight and held the shoe with both hands. He heard her snoring and set his teeth. He waited. He waited for it to move once more, to make the slightest noise" (*WYP*, 93). Here we are left, once again, poised on a precipice. Carl is not even sure what he is fighting against, but he senses a malevolent force that has turned his life upside down in one day and is now "stalk[ing] him" (Nesset, 301). His only weapon of defense is a brand-new, but already hopelessly ruined, shoe. Whatever is out there, the "reader suspects that Carl is no match for it" (Saltzman, 43). In this abrupt ending, Carver is once again showing the reader "the emptiness of [a character's] life—something the protagonist feels as a growing 'disease'" (Stull "RC" 1985, 239). Like the Millers at the end of "Neighbors," Carl is bracing for what might come next.

Stylistically, "What's in Alaska?" is one of the most important stories in this volume, for it indicates the direction in which Carver's minimalism will increasingly move. There is very little action in the story, for example. The descriptions of emotions are held to a minimum, and the paragraphs and sentences are clipped. More significantly, "What's in Alaska?" is almost entirely conversational. Many of the conversations that make up the story, furthermore, are circular or incomplete. In addition to the usual problems of communication, the participants here are quite stoned—an effect Carver captures brilliantly. As in "Nobody Said Anything," Carver again portrays a couple whose "slow-motion collapse . . . is at once characterized and confirmed by the exasperated aimlessness of their interchanges" (Saltzman, 40). The following is a fairly typical example:

> Mary and Helen laughed.
> "What's funny?" Jack said. He looked at Helen and then at Mary. He shook his head. "I don't know about you guys," he said.
> "We might go to Alaska," Carl said.
> "Alaska?" Jack said. "What's in Alaska? What would you do up there?"
> "I wish we could go someplace," Helen said.
> "What's wrong with here?" Jack said. "What would you guys do in Alaska? I'm serious. I'd like to know."
> Carl put a potato chip in his mouth and sipped his cream soda. "I don't know. What did you say?"
> After a while Jack said, "What's in Alaska?"
> "I don't know," Carl said. (*WYP*, 84)

Passages such as this halting and almost incoherent conversation make up the bulk of the story. As David Boxer and Cassandra Phillips note,

"Little seems to be said, yet much is conveyed" (Boxer, 81), a phrase that captures the minimalist aesthetic. In many ways, as a matter of fact, "What's in Alaska?" directly presages "What We Talk about When We Talk about Love," the title story of Carver's most minimalist collection. Even as an early example of Carver's minimalism, this story remains one of the best; the writing contains all of the tautness and power, and all of the humor and terror, that the style is capable of creating.

"Collectors"

The next story in the collection, "Night School," shows some of the potential problems with the style, however. In describing a protagonist whose life is marked by aimlessness, the tale also seems to drift with no particular purpose and fails to reach any kind of satisfying climax. It may be a typical Carver tale, but it is not a particularly effective one. "Collectors," the piece that follows "Night School," contains many of the same elements, but they are delivered with a somewhat greater impact.

The first-person narrator of this story begins by telling us that "I was out of work. But any day I expected to hear from up north. I lay on the sofa and listened to the rain" (*WYP*, 102). Until he finds work his life is aimless, and it appears that he has already been unemployed for some period of time. Much of his energy seems to be devoted to avoiding the mailman, who might be delivering notices of overdue bills, but who might also be bringing news of the hoped-for job. In his hiding out, then, the narrator becomes actively resistant to any kind of positive change in his depressed condition. The opportunity is unexpectedly presented to him, but he turns it down. This potential catalyst for change is Aubrey Bell, a salesman who demonstrates and promotes vacuum cleaners. He arrives at the narrator's apartment because a Mrs. Slater has won a contest for a free vacuuming demonstration. The narrator's response, "Mrs. Slater doesn't live here" (*WYP*, 102), is rather ambiguous. Did his wife leave him? Is he even Mr. Slater? At first the salesman assumes that he must be Mr. Slater, but in the middle of the story he begins to wonder and refers to him several times as "Mr. . . ." (*WYP*, 103, 105), hoping that the narrator will fill in the blank. He refuses to do so, however, not willing "to surrender this last vestige of self" (Boxer, 87). At the climax of the story, a letter comes in the mail slot, but Bell uses his vacuum to prevent the narrator from getting it. He announces that the letter is "for a Mr. Slater," and puts it in his pocket, saying, "I'll see to it" (*WYP*, 109). The narrator can barely work up a challenge; he wants the letter, but he meekly allows Bell to walk off with it. He notes that "I kept watching him. That's all I did" (*WYP*, 109). If the narrator is indeed Mr. Slater, then it is possible that this letter is the news that he has been waiting for from "up north," but he'll never know, and as the story ends that situation seems agreeable to him.

The narrator of this story is one of the most enervated in all of Carver's fiction, a point that is stressed by the tale's seemingly obscure title. One of the special features of the vacuum cleaner Bell is trying to sell, he tells the narrator, is that it can clean mattresses and pillows, which are natural collectors of dead skin. He explains that, "Every day, every night of our lives, we're leaving little bits of ourselves, flakes of this and that, behind. Where do they go, these bits and pieces of ourselves? Right through the sheets and into the mattress, that's where" (*WYP*, 105). This image seems to encapsulate the narrator's zombielike existence, in which he loses bits and pieces of himself and slowly turns to dust. Bell can be seen as collecting "from the narrator his remaining dregs of self" (Boxer, 86), in addition to "his future" (Saltzman, 47), both of which are symbolized by the letter. As the story ends, the narrator, who has already told Bell that he doesn't have so much as a dollar, indicates that he does not want to buy the vacuum cleaner. He explains that "I'm going to be leaving here soon" (*WYP*, 110), although the reader has no reason to believe this optimistic statement. In the final line of the story, Bell leaves, carting off the narrator's "transient and precarious self. . . with the rest of the debris" (Nesset, 303). He "shut[s] the door" (*WYP*, 110), and it seems likely that a good deal of time will pass before the narrator willingly opens it again. Slater, if that is indeed his name, thus finds himself in much the same situation at the end of the story as he was in its beginning: depressed, disinterested, and nearly dead. The only change is an almost imperceptible one for the worse; the narrator begins at the bottom, and then he sinks a bit lower (Boxer, 86).

"What Do You Do in San Francisco?"

Just as "They're Not Your Husband" can be seen as a retelling of "Fat" from the cook's point of view, so can "What Do You Do in San Francisco?" be seen as a retelling of "Collectors" from the postman's point of view. Once again, letters and the question of identity are central to this story. Henry Robinson, the narrator, is indeed a postman, although the story, he tells us in the opening line, "has nothing to do with me. It's about a young couple with three children who moved into a house on my route the first of last summer" (*WYP*, 111). While the narrative does concentrate on the story of the mysterious Marston family—"Beatniks, I guess you'd have called them if you'd seen them" (*WYP*, 111)—it also reveals much about Henry Robinson. He inadvertently shows himself to be living a purely vicarious life, like so many of the characters we have seen in the stories in this collection. He complains, for example, that the rumors that have been circulating about the Marstons—that he is on the lam, or that she was a drug addict—were begun by Sallie Wilson, "who has been snooping and prying for years under cover of the Welcome Wagon" (*WYP*, 116), yet he has been snooping and prying under the cover of the U.S. Postal Service for quite a while himself. Robinson is fascinated by the Marstons and goes out of his way to try to discover their secret, something to do with their mysterious past in San Francisco.[11]

As the story progresses, however, Marston's wife leaves him for another man, and it is clear to the postman that Marston is "suffering" (*WYP*, 119) because of her departure. Robinson wants to offer solace, moreover, but he finds it difficult because "I didn't know what to say exactly" (*WYP*, 119). The only advice he can offer is for Marston to follow his own example of abnegating life in favor of work. He presents his gospel near the beginning of the story when he informs us that "I believe, too, in the value of work—the harder the better. A man who isn't working has got too much time on his hands, too much time to dwell on himself and his problems" (*WYP*, 111). Later in the story, Robinson, who has just delivered the letter from Marston's decamped wife that he has been so anxiously awaiting, lashes out at the woman. He tells Marston that "'She's no good, boy. I could tell that the minute I saw her. Why don't you forget her? Why don't you go to work and forget her? What have you got against work? It was work, day and night, work that gave me oblivion when I was in your shoes and there was a war on where I was. . . .'" (*WYP*, 120). Here Robinson unwittingly indicates that his desire to commiserate with Marston stems from his having been wronged in a similar way. While preaching his work ethic, Robinson displays his own vulnerability through the telling of his own divorce; perhaps his wife left him for another man as well. In any case, he, too, appears to have suffered at the hands of a woman, and he feels that the most Marston can hope for is to achieve oblivion, as he has done.

Marston does seem to be moving on at the end of the story however. Following the delivery of the letter he becomes at first suspicious of and then unconcerned with the postman, staring past him to the horizon that he is about to set out for. Robinson himself, on the other hand, remains in his comfortable rut. He appears to be afraid of getting involved here, of being forced out of his oblivion. He no longer wants to participate in life, for he has become perfectly content to watch from the sidelines. The story ends with his telling us of Marston: "The next day he was gone. He didn't leave any forwarding. Sometimes mail of some kind or other shows up for him or his wife or for the both of them. If it's first-class, we hold it a day, then send it back to where it came from. There isn't much. And I don't mind. It's all work, one way or the other, and I'm always glad to have it" (*WYP*, 121). Like the Millers at the end of "Neighbors," Henry Robinson has been forced to abandon his vicarious attachment; unlike them, however, he is glad to be heading back to his stable existence. He "reaffirm[s] the blessing of having work to engage his thoughts," Saltzman points out, and "manipulate[s] the few details about the Marstons at his disposal into supporting evidence for his personal philosophies regarding the treacheries of love and the compensations of oblivion" (Saltzman, 49).

Carver is dealing here with the same obsessions we have seen throughout the volume, but, as the quoted passages might indicate, the tone of "What Do You Do in San Francisco?" is unique among Carver stories. Henry Robinson is quite different from the sullen, almost incoherent narrators who are so common in Carver's work, and the narrative voice shows that difference distinctly. Robinson is garrulous, for one thing, and he talks directly to the reader, as opposed to other Carver texts, in which readers may feel that they are eavesdropping on the narrator's telling of the story to someone else. Robinson is also much more forthcoming about the details of his background. Near the opening of the story, for instance, he offers the following description of himself: "Henry Robinson is the name. I'm a postman, a federal civil servant, and have been since 1947. I've lived in the West all my life, except for a three-year stint in the Army during the war. I've been divorced twenty years, have two children I haven't seen in almost that long. I'm not a frivolous man, nor am I, in my opinion, a serious man. It's my belief a man has to be a little of both these days. I believe, too, in the value of work" (*WYP*, 111). Robinson also provides us with a much more detailed account of the story's setting than we usually receive. He notes that "Arcata is not a small town and it's not a big town, though I guess you'd have to say it's more on the small side. It's not the end of the world, Arcata, by any means, but most of the people who live here work either in the lumber mills or have something to do with the fishing industry, or else work in one of the downtown stores. People here aren't used to seeing men wear beards—or men who don't work, for that matter" (*WYP*, 113). Although the voice here is quite different from earlier Carver narrators, it is masterfully done. Critics who say that all of Carver's stories sound alike, that Carver was capable of only one style, should read "What Do You Do in San Francisco?," a unique item in his oeuvre.

"Put Yourself in My Shoes"

Carver is on more familiar ground again in the next story, "The Student's Wife," which depicts a relationship at the moment of breaking up and ends with a sense of menace and impending doom. This is a standard Carver situation, and his treatment of it here is nothing out of the ordinary. On the other hand, the following text, "Put Yourself in My Shoes," is one of the longest and most complex stories in the collection, and one of its finest. In addition, it brings together a number of the themes and images that have recurred throughout the volume. For example, it depicts the kind of interaction between two couples that we have seen in "Neighbors" and "What's in Alaska?"; in this case, the Myerses go to visit the Morgans, whose house they had lived in for a year while Professor Morgan and his wife were in Germany, but whom they have not seen since. Furthermore, the issue of empathy that surfaced in "Fat," "Neighbors," and "The Idea," the ability to visualize oneself in another's perspective, is so central here that it becomes the title of the story. What is different about this story, however, is its self-consciousness, its concentration on the role of the writer. In many ways, "Put Yourself in My Shoes" can be seen as Carver's metafictional comment on his own vocation, on storytelling itself.

　　Myers is a writer, although he hasn't sold anything yet and is currently not writing. He has quit his job to pursue his muse, but with little success. As the story opens he is depressed, "between stories and [feeling] despicable" (*WYP*, 134), when his wife calls to invite him to the office Christmas party. But he doesn't want to go, mainly because the textbook publishing company where she works is also his former place of employment. Like Marston in "What Do You Do in San Francisco?," Myers is feeling the guilt of the unemployed, which is exacerbated by the fact that he moves in a much more upscale milieu than is typical of Carver's protagonists. Myers is also reluctant to pay a holiday call on the Morgans, although his wife, Paula, finally convinces him to go. The meeting does turn out to be quite an uncomfortable occasion, however. As they approach the house, Myers narrowly avoids being attacked by the Morgans' dog. Shortly thereafter, following a seemingly innocuous discussion of writing, he is more directly attacked by the Morgans themselves. Edgar Morgan, from the beginning of their encounter, seems to be acting "odd" (*WYP*, 137) and on edge for some unknown reason. When Paula asserts that her husband "'writes something almost every day'" (*WYP*, 139), Edgar confronts him on the point. "'Is that a fact?' Morgan said. 'That's impressive. What did you write today, may I ask?'" Myers can only respond "'Nothing'" (*WYP*, 139), an answer that places him on an existential precipice. The response inevitably leads to questions about his identity, for what is a writer who doesn't write?

Edgar Morgan then proceeds to tell a story to test what Myers's imagination can do with some facts. The premise is that a university professor has had an affair with one of his students. He asks his wife for a divorce, and she throws him out of the house. While leaving, he is hit with a can of tomato soup thrown by the son, and he is now in the hospital in serious condition. Myers finds the story quite amusing, while Paula and Hilda Morgan are disgusted. Edgar tells Myers that a writer could look at this from the husband's point of view and get quite a story; Hilda says that the same is true of looking at the story from the wife's point of view, and Paula speaks up for the son's point of view. Edgar then tops them all by asserting: "But here's something I don't think any of you has thought about. Think about this for a moment. Mr. Myers, are you listening? Tell me what you think of this. Put yourself in the shoes of that eighteen-year-old coed who fell in love with a married man. Think about *her* for a moment, and then you see the possibilities for your story" (*WYP*, 141). Hilda responds that she has no sympathy for the girl at all, nor for the professor, but only for the wife and child. Myers apparently has no sympathy for any of the people involved. He can only see the black humor of the entire situation. This lack of empathy again calls into question the appropriateness of his vocation as a writer.

Hilda Morgan later narrates another story, that of a Mrs. Attenborough, an Australian woman who had collapsed and died while visiting them in their home in Germany. Hilda had left her purse (containing ID cards, a check, and some cash) in a museum, where Mrs. Attenborough had found it, minus the cash; she had taken a taxi to the Morgans' house to return it, but fell ill there. While the woman was lying unconscious, Hilda went through her purse in search of identification, only to find the missing money. When Hilda opines that "'Fate sent her to die on the couch in our living room in Germany'" (*WYP*, 148), Myers cannot restrain his laughter. As Myers continues to giggle, Morgan pounces on him: "'If you were a real writer, as you say you are, Mr. Myers, you would not laugh. . . . You would not dare laugh! You would try to understand. You would plumb the depths of that poor soul's heart and try to understand. But you are no writer, sir!'" (*WYP*, 149). Once again, though, the motivation of Morgan's attack is unclear, to Myers and to the reader.

At this point the Morgans move in for the kill, however, and the reader soon discovers the true reason for many of their strange actions. From the outset they have appeared to harbor malice toward the Myerses, as indicated by the way in which Edgar plays the gracious host but curses and throws things in the kitchen, and he now begins to explain the root of their resentment by telling another story. Saying "'Consider *this* for a possibility, Mr. Myers!'" (*WYP*, 149), Morgan tells of a couple, Mr. and Mrs. Y, who go to Germany for a year and lease their apartment to Mr. and Mrs. Z, a couple whom they do not know. Mr. and Mrs. Z violate the terms of the lease in several ways, such as bringing in a cat and using stored materials.[12] The reader quickly realizes that this is the story of the Morgans and the Myerses, and that the Morgans' anger over these violations accounts for the tension that Myers has been feeling throughout the evening. Myers is now forced to put himself into the other person's shoes, and he does not see much to admire when he looks at himself from that perspective. Edgar Morgan, ranting and raving about the invasion of Mr. and Mrs. Y's privacy by the tenants, explains that "'that's the *real* story, Mr. Myers'" (*WYP*, 150). Once again, however, Myers's only outward response to the story is to laugh. Paula seems to shrug off the meaning of the story entirely—as they drive away she remarks that "'Those people are crazy'" (*WYP*, 152)—but Myers shows himself to have been more deeply affected. The story's final lines show us a man who looks like a deer caught in headlights: "He did not answer. Her voice seemed to come to him from a great distance. He kept driving. Snow rushed at the windshield. He was silent and watched the road. He was at the very end of a story" (*WYP*, 152).

In addition to indicating how Myers's encounter with the Morgans will mark a change in his life, these final lines also remind us of the metafictional nature of the text. As Carver says, "by the end of the story [Myers is] ready to write, because he *has* a story, he's heard all kinds of stories" (*Con*, 61). The story that we are reading is, in fact, the result of Myers's rediscovered empathy and creativity. Since we know that Carver has really written all of these stories, however, it is easy to see "Put Yourself in My Shoes" as his way of commenting on his own writing. Carver seems quite concerned, for example, about the voyeuristic nature of the writer's craft, which, after all, involves putting oneself in another's shoes to report on life from that angle. One critic has even asserted that "the self-reflexive focus on writing-as-appropriation in 'Put Yourself in My Shoes' may indict the profession itself for this offense" (Saltzman, 53); another has gone so far as to state that the story demonstrates a kind of "warped self-scrutiny" (Skenazy, 79). Furthermore, if Myers is a stand-in for Carver, then Carver seems to be indicting himself for having a lack of sympathy for his characters, a charge that is often leveled against him by critics of minimalism.[13] Carver also acknowledges his propensity to see the black humor in a story, his tendency to laugh at tragedy, another reason some criticize him.[14] Or it could be, as Arthur Brown writes, that "Carver uses the stuffy, professorial Morgan to remind us of literature and its great tradition in order to make the point that those traditions are of the past—they will no longer work for today's stories or storytelling" (Brown, 130). In any event, the change that Myers experiences at the end of the story may be indicative of a change in Carver's writing as well, an increased attempt to see the story from all sides and evaluate the complexity of interrelationships.

"Jerry and Molly and Sam"

Despite its title, "Jerry and Molly and Sam" is actually the story of Al, one of Carver's most depressed and despairing figures. He seems to suffer from the malaise of many of the characters we have seen so far in *Will You Please Be Quiet, Please?* First of all, Al is worried about job security at the Aerojet plant where he works. In addition, he has recently moved into a new and rather expensive home at the urging of his wife, Betty. He is tense and nervous and can't relax. Despite being 31, he starts contemplating his old age. To top it all off, his sister-in-law, Sandy, has recently given his children a nonhousebroken mutt, Suzy. Feeling that his back is against the wall, Al knows that he must take some action and begin to put his life back in order. He decides that "there was only one solution. He had to get rid of the dog without Betty or the kids finding out about it. At night. It would have to be done at night. He would simply drive Suzy—well, someplace, later he'd decide where—open the door, push her out, drive away. The sooner the better. He felt relieved making the decision" (*WYP*, 153). Nevertheless, he has a great deal of trouble carrying out this plan. He can't find the proper place to leave Suzy because he is afraid of being discovered. He knows that, "held up to public view, without all the facts being in, it'd be a shameful thing to be caught abandoning a dog" (*WYP*, 158). He wants the mongrel to be adopted, not reported to the local pound, so he decides to leave her in his old neighborhood. When Al arrives at his old house he recalls his youth, and, thinking about his present state, he feels "even more insubstantial" (*WYP*, 160). Remembering Sam, the dog he had when he was a boy, Al pushes Suzy from the car and guiltily speeds away.

His attempt to reestablish control over his life, however, only leads to further difficulties. The next day he returns from work to find his daughter, Mary, distraught over Suzy's disappearance. His first reaction is to ask himself, "*My God*, heart lurching, *what have I done?*" (*WYP*, 164). Earlier he had been able to "justif[y] his treachery as the first step out of chaos" (Saltzman, 56), but now he realizes that he has made a grave mistake. He even contemplates suicide, a thought that occurs less often than we might expect among characters in Carver's bleak stories of blue-collar despair. Abandoning those "immoral" thoughts (*WYP*, 165), Al decides on a new course of action: finding the dog and bringing her home as a way of heroically reuniting the family. He now views himself almost as a medieval knight on a quest, attempting to salvage his own virtue by restoring peace to the lady, be it Betty or Mary or Suzy. Here Al reminds us of the protagonist of "Nobody Said Anything," who attempted to reunite his family through the office of an enormous fish head. Like that earlier character, moreover, Al's quest is doomed from the start. Even as he sets out, Al feels himself to be slipping; by the time he gets to the old neighborhood again he is crying. He does manage to find Suzy, but she refuses to go with him. The final lines of the story state that "He sat there. He thought he didn't feel so bad, all things considered. The world was full of dogs. There were dogs and there were dogs. Some dogs you just couldn't do anything with" (*WYP*, 169). This is one of Carver's more oblique and open-ended conclusions, but it indicates that, rather than carrying through on his attempt to put his life back in order, Al will most likely do nothing at all. His real problem is his lack of resolve; he can make decisions but he can't act on them, so he will continue to drift. As the story concludes, then, Al seems to be in much the same predicament as he was at its outset, only now even fewer of his limited options remain. Toward the end of the story he curses "what a weathervane he [is], changing this way and that, one moment this, the next moment that" (*WYP*, 169), but the metaphor does apply to him, and probably always will. Al seems to sound a note of humorous resignation in the final lines of the story, where he understands that, rather than saving the day as he has tried to do, he "will have to bear the brunt of this failure too" (Saltzman, 58). Even so, there is little evidence that his malaise has been altered in a significant way; if anything, he ends up a bit more depressed and despairing than he began.

"Why, Honey?"

"Why, Honey?" is one of the most technically dazzling stories in the collection. It is written as a letter in which a woman responds to a letter she has previously received, from someone whom she does not know. Her letter begins:

> Dear Sir:
>   I was so surprised to receive your letter asking about my son, how did you know I was here? I moved here years ago right after it started to happen. No one knows who I am here but I'm afraid all the same. Who I am afraid of is him. When I look in the paper I shake my head and wonder. I read what they write about him and I ask myself is that man really my son, is he really doing these things? (WYP, 170)

Since we have not seen the initial letter that prompted this reply, we are in the dark, having no idea to what "it" in "it started to happen" refers. Carver deliberately leaves the pronoun's antecedent unclear, although he imparts the sense even from this opening passage that the woman's son has become notorious through some diabolical behavior. We naturally assume that "these things" are awful. Why else would his mother be afraid of him? She goes on to confirm our suspicions when she notes two salient facts about her son's childhood: that he was once caught torturing the family cat, and that he was never able to tell his mother the truth. When she relates that he bought a gun and a knife, the reader becomes quite wary; when she tells of discovering a bloodstained shirt, we envision a stabbed body. She goes on to state that, when she finally confronted her son about these issues, he physically threatened her and then left the house, after which she never saw him again. She even moved away from the city and changed her name to avoid him, hoping that he would think she was dead.

The twist in the tale, however, is that her son is not an ax murderer; on the contrary, he is a powerful government official. Only as the story is rapidly concluding does Carver clarify the opening paragraph's hanging "it," when the mother writes that "he married that girl and got himself in politics. I began to see his name in the paper. I found out his address and wrote to him, I wrote a letter every few months, there was never an answer. He ran for governor and was elected, and was famous now. That's when I began to worry" (*WYP*, 175). The son obviously wants nothing to do with his mother, who is deathly afraid that, since she has become a potentially damning political liability, he is going to track her down and harm her. Her lament that "I should be the proudest mother in all the land but I am only afraid" (*WYP*, 176) seems perfectly valid. Once we realize the truth of her situation, the opening portions of the letter take on a new level of irony.

Even this O. Henry trick ending does not disclose the final layer of the story, however, for Carver also leads us to wonder about the identity of the initial letter writer. All we know is that the correspondent is someone the governor's mother doesn't know, and receiving the letter therefore raises her level of anxiety. She wonders how she has been found out and why she is being asked these questions about her son. Toward the end of the letter she expresses her fear of having been discovered, noting that "last week I saw a car on the street with a man inside I know was watching me, I came straight back and locked the door. A few days ago the phone rang and rang" (*WYP*, 176). The probability seems high that the person she has seen watching her, the person who has been calling, is also the person who has written the letter. She doesn't seem to consider this option, but Carver makes its likelihood implicit in the story's final lines: "I also wanted to ask how you got my name and knew where to write, I have been praying no one knew. But you did? Why did you? Please tell me why?" (176). Even if we assert that the watcher, caller, and writer are one and the same, however, the identity of that "you" remains unclear. Carver thus leaves the story rather open-ended. It is possible, as some critics have suggested, that the person is clandestinely employed by the governor. I get a very different sense. It seems logical to me that he or she is a reporter, one trying to expose the shady side of the powerful governor. The revelation that he has abandoned his mother, who lives in fear that he will find her and hurt her, would indeed destroy any of his future political activities. If this is so, then the letter that makes up the story is all the evidence the reporter needs. In fact, it contains more incendiary material than could have been hoped for. Published verbatim in a newspaper, this letter would effectually topple the governor's empire. The mother does not intend that end, nor does she understand the consequences of her response, but the irony is apparent. If she didn't have legitimate reason to fear her son before, she certainly does now. She feels relieved to have gotten the story off her chest, but the reader senses that this is only going to be temporary relief and that even worse times are ahead for her. Ironies such as this mark "Why, Honey?" as one of the more unusual stories of the collection, and indeed of all of Carver's works. The narrative voice here is not the one normally associated with Carver, but it is brilliantly done. He is also more successful here than elsewhere in his writings at creating a sustained air of mystery and suspense. Like "What Do You Do in San Francisco?," "Why, Honey?" should quiet the critics who deride Carver for only writing different versions of the same basic story.

"Bicycles, Muscles, Cigarets"

The same cannot be said, however for "The Ducks" and "How About This?," the two stories that come after "Why, Honey?" in the collection. They are indeed lesser variations on the typical Carver tale. "Bicycles, Muscles, Cigarets," on the other hand, is a masterful story. In telling a tale of a father-son relationship, Carver does an excellent job of establishing a tender mood that is not often seen in his work. What is ironic about this facet of the story is that an act of violence serves as the catalyst for the release of these tender and sincere emotions, some of the most honest and heartfelt communications of the entire collection. As the story opens, Evan Hamilton is called to a neighbor's house because of a situation in which his son Roger has become involved. The neighbor, Mrs. Miller, claims that her family had been out of town when Roger, his friend Kip, and a new kid in town, Gary Berman, used her son Gilbert's bicycle, deliberately broke it, and then failed to return it. When Hamilton arrives at Mrs. Miller's house, he immediately senses the animosity between his son and Gary, one of the other alleged conspirators. The tension becomes even more pronounced when Gary's father arrives at the scene and attempts to take over. As the story progresses, a fistfight appears imminent. The imagery, as one critic has pointed out, recalls a boxing match, as "the boys pair off with their respective fathers like fighters consulting with their corners between rounds" (Saltzman, 60). Roger had earlier admitted partial guilt, but Gary, after private consultation with his father, pleads total innocence. In fact, Mr. Berman, after telling Roger to shut up, complains that he has been "'dragged out at night because of a couple of roughnecks!'" (*WYP*, 202), referring to Roger and Kip. When Hamilton defends his son, Berman tells him to mind his own business. The two fathers bump each other, and physical violence does indeed erupt.

Despite the pugnacity of the elder Berman, Evan is surprisingly strong and is quickly able to pin him. Taking Berman by the collar, furthermore, he begins "to pound his head against the lawn" (*WYP*, 203). Mrs. Miller is outraged by the actions of these two parents. The boys, at least Roger and Kip, also seem quite shaken by the violence. Later, as they reach home, Hamilton apologizes to his son, saying "'I'm sorry you had to see something like that'" (*WYP*, 204). His apology stems from his recollection of how "he had once seen his father—a pale, slow-talking man with slumped shoulders—in something like this. It was a bad one, and both men had been hurt. It had happened in a cafe. The other man was a farmhand. Hamilton had loved his father and could recall many things about him. But now he recalled his father's one fistfight as if it were all there was to the man" (*WYP*, 205). Evan clearly sees the parallels between his thoughts of his father and his son's potential thoughts of him. He knows that, while his son might love him at the moment, the boy will eventually remember very little about his father. For his part, moreover, Evan is sorry to have continued the legacy of making a fistfight one of the most vivid of those memories. He had previously told his son the story of witnessing his father's brawl, and the boy naturally thinks of it after watching his own father engage in a similar fight. The realization of these parallels, in fact, leads to the most touching and revealing conversation in the story:

> "Dad, was Grandfather strong like you? When he was your age, I mean, you know, and you—"
>
> "And I was nine years old? Is that what you mean? Yes, I guess he was," Hamilton said.
>
> "Sometimes I can hardly remember him," the boy said. "I don't want to forget him or anything, you know? You know what I mean, Dad?" (*WYP*, 206)

Hamilton does indeed know what the boy means, for he has already largely forgotten the grandfather—his own father—and he knows that the same thing will eventually happen in his case. As Arthur Saltzman has pointed out, then, "Hamilton is chagrined, for he fears that the lesson he had wished to impart to his son—some paternal axiom about owning up to your wrongdoings or handling difficulties maturely—had been obliterated by the demonstration of the macho ethic of 'might makes right'" (Saltzman, 63).

Saltzman is right, but there's more to it than that, for the father is the one who really learns a lesson here, as he comes to better understand the passage of generations within a family. Hamilton is led to think about his attitudes toward his father by considering how his son might now be perceiving him. He is simultaneously looking at the past (his own father), the present (his current fatherhood), and the future (his son's potential view of him). Roger makes the significance of these cross-generational connections clear to Evan at the end of the story when he says, "'Dad? You'll think I'm pretty crazy, but I wish I'd known you when you were little, I mean, about as old as I am right now. I don't know how to say it, but I'm lonesome about it. It's like—it's like I miss you already if I think about it now'" (*WYP*, 207). Evan is touched by this sentiment, as is the reader, but he realizes that the boy, in his later years, will most likely lose this idealized view of his father. Someday, moreover, Roger will have to come to the same understanding of the passing of generations by dealing with his own son.

"What Is It?"

"What Is It?"—though brilliantly written—is one of the darkest and most despairing stories in the collection. In the words of one critic, it "is far scarier than anything by Stephen King" (Davis, 654). As the tale opens, the narrator tells us that Leo, the main character, is at the lowest point in his life; as the story progresses, however, he moves steadily downhill. The particularly appropriate image that Carver uses to structure this story of dissolution is bankruptcy. Leo and his wife Toni, who are about to go to court to declare bankruptcy, are trying to dodge the bill collectors and sell off some of their few remaining assets while they can. In particular, they want to sell their convertible. We are told that Leo sends Toni to used car lots to dispose of the vehicle, knowing that she will be able to get more money for it than he can. She understands the business as well, and she spends a long time getting ready, knowing that the salesmen will likely ask for something besides the car in return for a very good price. After Toni leaves, Leo reflects that not only is he monetarily bankrupt, but his whole life seems to have fallen apart. He even comes to question his very existence, and considers suicide, believing that "he would rather 'be dead' than have to wholly confront the psychic contours of his bankruptcy" (Nesset, 305). He also questions his manhood, particularly following his wife's phone call—six hours later—in which she tells him that she has sold the car and is now having dinner with the salesman. She also tells him that the salesman "'said personally he'd rather be classified a robber or a rapist than a bankrupt'" (*WYP*, 215). To top off his profound feelings of insignificance, Leo is offered insults by the very man to whom he has sent his wife, and with whom she will cuckold him.[15] When Toni finally returns at dawn, Leo is ready to strike her. Before he can, though, Toni attacks him, ripping his shirt and screaming "'Bankrupt!'" (*WYP*, 216). Earlier, while getting dressed, she had teased him by saying "'you don't have money, . . . your credit's lousy. You're nothing'" (*WYP*, 209), but now she seems to mean it. And he is willing to accept that definition.

The truth of the matter, though, is that Toni and Leo are equally responsible for the financial situation that they find themselves in. When they first began to make money, they splurged on the convertible, and from that point on their money was constantly being drained. The narrator tells us, for example, that "they gorged on food. He figures thousands on luxury items alone. Toni would go to the grocery and put in everything she saw. 'I had to do without when I was a kid,' she says. 'These kids are not going to do without'" (*WYP*, 212). In reality, however, her concern for not letting them do without puts them in precisely that position: Leo and Toni have had to send the children to stay with their grandmother. Leo also explains that they joined book and record clubs, purchased a pedigreed dog, and essentially fell victim to American consumerism: "They buy what they want. If they can't pay, they charge. They sign up" (*WYP*, 212). Naturally they find themselves in financial straits, and the only thing they have left of value is that initial extravagance, the convertible. By the end of the story, Leo comes to associate the selling of the convertible with the total bankruptcy of his whole life, as well as with his own mortality; he "undergoes a gradual death of self [and] considers himself, in the end, as 'nothing'" (Nesset, 306).

The story concludes with another Carveresque epiphany of limitations. Leo is considering making love to Toni: "He turns on his side and puts his hand on her hip. He runs his fingers over her hip and feels the stretch marks there. They are like roads, and he traces them in her flesh. He runs his fingers back and forth, first one, then another. They run everywhere in her flesh, dozens, perhaps hundreds of them. He remembers waking up the morning after they bought the car, seeing it, there in the drive, in the sun, gleaming" (*WYP*, 218). Leo's life no longer has that gleam; his moment of glory is far in the past, and receding quickly. The same is true for Toni, of course. Part of the anger she displays toward her husband when she returns from the night with the salesman is certainly displaced self-aggression, mixed, perhaps, with a sense of her own aging.

Despite her best efforts, she has only managed to get $625 for a car for which she and her husband had hoped to get $900. The marks on her body are the physical representations of the roads that they have not taken, and of the dead end that they now find themselves in, one that seems to be too narrow for them to turn around in or back out of. At the beginning of the story Leo had asserted that, come Monday, "'things are going to be different! . . . We start over'" (*WYP*, 211)—and at the end he briefly confronts the salesman and intones "'Monday'" (*WYP*, 218)— yet the reader has every reason not to believe that Monday will be a new beginning. "'Monday'—the key that Leo thinks may turn back the odometer of their misfortunes—if it ever comes, carries few promises," Kirk Nesset aptly points out, since the events of the story have led Leo to realize "the hopelessness of his hopes" (Nesset, 307).

In many ways, "What Is It?" is typical of the stories in *Will You Please Be Quiet, Please?* It recalls several of the earlier texts, for example, in its chronicling of "isolation and breakdown, as well as the ache, often acted out in voyeuristic terms, to connect with another life, however perverse or futile that connection might be" (Davis, 655). The lack of communication that is apparent between Leo and Toni, and the infidelity that is one of its results, also resounds throughout the collection. Stylistically, however, "What Is It?" anticipates many of the qualities of the stories in Carver's breakthrough collection, *What We Talk about When We Talk about Love*. It is told in the present tense, for example. The narrative voice, moreover, is very flat and controlled, as in the description of Leo's thoughts about suicide: "He listens to the traffic on the highway and considers whether he should go to the basement, stand on the utility sink, and hang himself with his belt. He understands he is willing to be dead" (*WYP*, 213). This kind of deadpan narrative will become a dominant feature of Carver's later writings. So will alcoholism, and Leo, significantly, is the first character we encounter who becomes an alcoholic in response to his problems. Leo drinks heavily throughout the story, even though this habit only serves to increase his anxiety and dread. The sense of menace that we see here, and that we have seen in so many of the other stories in this collection, also continues to pervade the stories in that later volume.

"Will You Please Be Quiet, Please?"

The theme of miscommunication as both a reason for and a symptom of a failing relationship is also central to the next story in the collection, "Signals," as the title might indicate. This theme is present yet again, although it is more expertly handled, in the final story in this collection, "Will You Please Be Quiet, Please?" Here, in fact, Carver examines another marital relationship at the point of dissolution and reprises many of the themes that have dominated the entire book. In several other ways, however, the story is unique. It is the only one in the collection to feature crowd scenes, for example.[16] Stylistically, it is "more writerly than most of Carver's [stories] and richer in background information and authorial guidance" (Boxer 88), traits at variance with minimalism. In addition, "Will You Please Be Quiet, Please?" contains an unusually overt nod to some of Carver's literary forebears. The title is clearly an echo of Hemingway's famous line from "Hills Like White Elephants": "'Will you please please please please please please please be quiet?'" More significant here, though, is the use to which Carver puts the Joycean epiphany. The life of Ralph Wyman, the story's central character, is a history of epiphanies. On his honeymoon in Mexico, for example, he saw his wife Marian looking over the hotel balcony—an image that put him "in mind of something from a film, an intensely dramatic moment" (*WYP*, 229) that is eerily reminiscent of Joyce's picture of Mangan's sister in the sunlight in "Araby." Looking at his wife as a voyeur would, Ralph Wyman already understands, as the boy in "Araby" eventually comes to, that he is an outsider, that he is not the type destined for romance. Not only does he realize his own lowly state, but he also perceives "the threatening mysterious sensuality of his own sensible-seeming wife" (Boxer, 89). This realization is a significant turning point in his life and marriage, but it is not the central epiphany. Toward the end of the story, when Ralph asks whether there are other men "who could look at one event in their lives and perceive in it the tiny makings of the catastrophe that thereafter set their lives on a different course" (*WYP*, 243), he is referring to the revelation that his wife has had sexual intercourse with another man. This is the knowledge that Ralph arrives at in the story's present, and it sends him reeling.

In the first part of the story, the narrator relates the history of Ralph Wyman and Marian Ross's love and almost fairy-tale success. It seems a life so good that the reader has trouble believing there isn't some distant threat lurking. A line like "he felt enormously happy" (*WYP*, 230) seems, in Carver Country, to summon forth a falling ax. The expected menace comes to materialize in the form of a sexual indiscretion, although the act is at first presented rather nonchalantly: "They considered themselves a happy couple, with only a single injury to their marriage, and that was well in the past, two years ago this winter. It was something they had never talked about since" (*WYP*, 230). Nevertheless, in recent days Ralph has begun to think of it more and more, "for he had taken it into his head that his wife had once betrayed him with a man named Mitchell Anderson" (*WYP*, 230). Marian, it seems, has also been thinking about it, and one day she lets her thoughts be known to Ralph. He immediately pounces on her and badgers her into admitting what actually happened that night. He feels sure that it was more than a few kisses, as she had earlier admitted to, and as the reader was also led to believe. When Marian confesses that she did indeed have sexual intercourse with Mitchell Anderson, however, Ralph is stunned. It is not really the answer he expected, or, if it is the one he expected, it is the one he hoped never to hear.[17] Immediately, everything becomes clear to him. He is struck by the knowledge, as emphasized by Carver's rhetoric: "Then suddenly he knew! His mind buckled. For a minute he could only stare dumbly at his hands. He knew! His mind roared with the knowing" (*WYP*, 238). This is clearly a description of an epiphany, and it is one that upsets everything the protagonist had previously believed about his own life and identity.

Ralph's response to this turmoil, this awful knowledge, is to rush madly from the house, but he finds the outside world overwhelming. He has to lean against a car when two couples in evening clothes walk past. When he witnesses a woman tossing her hair as she gets into a car, he notes that "he had never seen anything so frightening" (*WYP*, 240). Ralph takes refuge, first in a bar, then in a card game. In its depiction of a "carnival" world (Clark, 244), quite unusual in Carver's works, this part of the story brings to mind the Joyce of the "Nighttown" chapters of *Ulysses* (Nesset, 308). Ralph, who can no longer be the staid person he was when the story began, resurrects an alter ego, Jackson, he had adopted during his dissolute college years. During his carousals, Ralph "eavesdrops on vulgar conversations, drinks too much, urinates on his hands, [and] studies obscene graffiti" (Saltzman, 71), among other things. His "nightmarish odyssey" (May 77) thus confirms his statement that, "yes, there was a great evil pushing at the world, . . . and it only needed a little slipway, a little opening" (*WYP*, 241). Marian's adultery represents that slipway for him, and his life has now been turned upside down. He cannot hope to escape the stigma of being a cuckold, as Carver overemphasizes by having Ralph stand under "a rack of antlers" (*WYP*, 243). Later, quite drunk, Ralph goes to the pier, where he is mugged by two black men and left to lie barely conscious.

In the morning Ralph returns home, quite undecided as to what course of action he should take as a result of the previous evening's revelations. "What, after all, should he do? Take his things and leave? Go to a hotel? Make certain arrangements? How should a man act, given these circumstances? He understood things had been done. He did not understand what things now were to be done" (*WYP*, 249). Ralph makes his way past the children, who inquire about his bruised head and generally shabby appearance, and locks himself in the bathroom. After his bath, during which Marian has gotten the kids out of the house, he goes to bed, and she soon joins him there. The story ends on a note of sexual excitement, one that has been strategically hinted at throughout the text. Early in the story, for example, at a point when Marian has only admitted to a few kisses, there is an odd italicized section: "*'What did you do that for?' she was saying dreamily. 'Where were you all night?' he was screaming, standing over her, legs watery, fist drawn back to hit again. Then she said, 'I didn't do anything. Why did you hit me?' she said*" (*WYP*, 232). This seems to be a fantasy on Marian's part, one tinged with sexual overtones of a dominating man making her pay for her sins. Ralph has a similar fantasy that combines punishment and heightened sexuality: "he thought of Marian as he had seen her a little while ago, face crumpled. Then Marian on the floor, blood on her teeth: 'Why did you hit me?' Then Marian reaching under her dress to unfasten her garter belt! Then Marian lifting her dress as she arched back! Then Marian ablaze, Marian crying out, *Go! Go! Go!*" (*WYP*, 240). In thinking about this possible scenario, Ralph is obviously highly aroused. It is also true that Ralph was sexually aroused even while Marian was describing her encounter with Mitchell; the narrator notes that Ralph "felt a peculiar desire for her flicker through his groin" (*WYP*, 237). Thus it should not be entirely surprising—although it is unusual, given the characters in the rest of the collection—that the story ends with intercourse between Ralph and Marian. This is a different kind of bedroom scene, and here Carver "suggests, ironically, that the remedy for . . . dis-ease lies in its cause; for Ralph and Marian, sex will now—at least in part—restore what sex has earlier undertaken to destroy" (Nesset, 310).

For Ralph, sex brings on yet another revelatory moment, one that ends the story on a very powerful note: "He held himself, he later considered, as long as he could. And then he turned to her. He turned and turned in what might have been a stupendous sleep, and he was still turning, marveling at the impossible changes he felt moving over him" (*WYP*, 251). This final image, with its "expansive, lyrical cadences" (Stull "BH" 1985, 2), is one of the most striking in the entire collection, as well as one of the most optimistic. As William Stull claims, it "points toward a place beyond Hopelessville, a place where love can soothe us after the talking stops" (Stull "BH" 1985, 2).[18] Marian and Ralph had earlier been unable to talk about the problem, first because she wouldn't say anything, and then because, once she confessed, he didn't want to hear her excuses, and told her to "'please be quiet, please'" (*WYP*, 250). But now, in the silence of their embrace, they seem to have communicated all that is necessary for them to go on and face the rest of their lives. Ralph doesn't know what the "impossible changes" will be, but he is now ready to accept them. Having already faced and survived the worst, Ralph knows that he can abide and endure (Nesset, 312). This is the most anyone in Carver Country can hope for, and it is more than most of its inhabitants achieve.

Conclusion

The ending of "Will You Please Be Quiet, Please?," the last story in the collection, may call to mind the ending of "Fat," the first story. In both works a character is awakened to a new understanding of his or her life through a sexual encounter, a form of interpersonal communication. Both the unnamed waitress and Ralph Wyman, although they have gone through hard times, come to feel their lives moving and changing in positive directions. They are looking forward to new experiences. They don't know exactly what is coming, but they feel they can find a way to triumph over whatever it might be. Carver stated that one of his primary obsessions is "survival, what people can do to raise themselves up when they've been laid low" (*Con*, 199), and these two stories fully embody that idea. I would agree with Kirk Nesset that "we have to admire [these characters] for trying, and we also have to admire Carver for giving them the incentive to persist, often against great odds, in their trials" (Nesset, 314). Even so, "Will You Please Be Quiet, Please?" and "Fat" are clearly the exceptions in the volume. In most of the stories the characters succumb to their anomie rather than discovering a method of overcoming it. They remain isolated and noncommunicative, and their lives are filled with anxiety, dread, and menace. The majority of the stories in Carver's first collection "provide stark black-and-white images of lives of quiet desperation" (May, 77), and we must admire Carver for his ability to depict these lives, to bring them to us in a way that truly makes us feel the characters' despair.

As a whole, *Will You Please Be Quiet, Please?* is a remarkable book, fully deserving of the National Book Award nomination that it received. It sets out the contours of Carver Country and establishes the obsessions that will reappear throughout Carver's fiction and poetry, yet "as a collection it is hardly uniform in subject or voice" (Nesset, 292). This characterization should be a positive factor in the reception of a first book of stories, but the volume's disparateness may, in part, have accounted for its relative lack of success. The collection doesn't achieve the same kind of cumulative impact as *What We Talk about When We Talk about Love* or *Cathedral*. Nevertheless, there are a number of stories here that are worthy of much more consideration than they have received. Ewing Campbell has pointed out that "the quality of [Carver's] early writing has withstood the passage of time, careful scrutiny, and sober judgment remarkably well. Indeed, as so often happens with the work of our best writers, that early fiction has grown in stature" (Campbell, 30). I would agree. *Will You Please Be Quiet, Please?* is a generally underrated text, but one that will reward both first and repeated readings. Not every story in the collection is a masterpiece to be sure, but the volume does indicate that Carver's craft was already at a very high level even as his career was just taking off. As we turn our attention to his next collection of short fiction, the small-press book *Furious Seasons*, that opinion will only be reinforced.

Chapter Four
Early Fiction II: *Furious Seasons*

Will You Please Be Quiet, Please? was published in 1976, when Carver was at a very low point in his life. He was gratified that the book had finally appeared, and pleased that it had received a positive, if limited, response, but it didn't sell very well and it failed to arrest his economic and alcoholic slide. Furthermore, Carver had essentially stopped writing by that point. The chances for a speedy follow-up to capitalize on the initial success seemed slim. Nevertheless, Noel Young, whose Capra Press had earlier issued "Put Yourself in My Shoes" as a chapbook, was interested in bringing out more of Carver's works. The result was the 1977 publication of *Furious Seasons*, a collection of eight stories going all the way back to Carver's first publication, the title story from 1961, and including almost all of his fiction that had not appeared in *Will You Please Be Quiet, Please?* Although perhaps not quite up to the level of the first volume, this second one is a fine collection of stories, displaying Carver's talents in a variety of ways. *Furious Seasons* is also an important text for understanding Carver's later development, since seven of these stories would subsequently appear in his major publications, albeit in markedly different versions. Like most of the stories in *Will You Please Be Quiet, Please?*, the stories in *Furious Seasons* are fuller and richer than those of Carver's minimalist period; they thus provide a valuable contrast through which we can better appreciate the shape of Carver's career. This does not mean, however, that the stories are of interest only as drafts of later works, for they are certainly worthy of attention in their own right. Some of them, in fact, rank with the finest stories in Carver's entire canon.

"Dummy"

"Dummy" is a masterful story, and provides a strong start to the collection. It recalls two of the more fully developed stories from the first volume: "Nobody Said Anything," in its pastoral setting and emphasis on fishing, and "Will You Please Be Quiet, Please?," in its depiction of multiple epiphanies. Dummy, the partially deaf and entirely mute character whose nickname gives the story its title, undergoes at least two dramatic changes in his life. The first occurs when, having been prompted by the narrator's father, Dummy stocks his lake with bass; the narrator tells us that, "from that night, Father maintained, Dummy was a different person. The change didn't come about all at once, of course, but after that night, gradually, ever gradually, Dummy moved closer to the abyss."[1] Dummy becomes overly protective of his new bass, and even puts up an electrified fence and refuses to allow any fishing in the pond. The second turning point in Dummy's life occurs several years later when, despite these precautions, a flood carries all of his fish away. Dummy is despondent, since the bass have become his only friends, and he takes his anger out on his unfaithful wife. His desire for extreme control over the bass can be seen to have initially developed out his lack of control over his wife's affections (Saltzman, 78; Aldridge, 55), so when the fish swim away it is understandable that he should vent his frustration through an act of violence against his wife: he kills her, and then drowns himself in the pond. These two events—the stocking and unstocking of Dummy's pond—certainly represent cataclysmic changes in his life, but it is hard to say whether they are epiphanies, whether Dummy himself is aware of the momentous nature of these changes.

For the narrator's father, though, the events do take on such gravity. In the opening paragraph of the story, for example, the narrator informs us that "My father was nervous and disagreeable for a long time after Dummy's death, and I believe it somehow marked the end of a halcyon period in his life, too, for it wasn't much later that his own health began to fail" (*FS*, 9). The narrator's father had worked with Dummy and had felt himself to be Dummy's friend. He had refused to join the other workmen in laughing at Dummy's physical disabilities and his embarrassment about sexual matters. In urging Dummy to purchase the bass for his lake, he felt he was doing Dummy a favor. It is also true, however, that he was simultaneously looking out for himself, for naturally he "assumed that when the bass were large enough, he'd be able to fish there as often as he wished, Dummy being a friend" (*FS*, 13). Dummy, however, has a very different idea about the fish; they become pets to him, not game. After much wrangling, he does finally allow the narrator and his father to come fishing, but when the boy catches a huge bass, Dummy makes it clear that he wants the fish returned to the pond. While the men are arguing, the fish slips back into the water on its own. From that point on, the narrator's father shuns Dummy. He does express pity for Dummy's post-flood condition, but he feels that the deaf-mute has brought it on himself. Upon hearing of Dummy's suicide, though, he is quite shaken. The narrator tells us that "I looked at Father, who'd turned away, lips trembling. His face was lined, set. He looked older, suddenly, and terrified" (FS, 26). The real source of his terror, at least in part, is his feeling that he is in some way responsible for Dummy's demise. Perhaps he hadn't really treated him as a friend, but merely as a means to some good fishing. The narrator reports that "it seemed to me life became more difficult for [Father] after that, that he was never able to act happy and carefree any more. Not like he used to act, anyway" (FS, 26). The father's "entrance into the world of guilt and sorrow," to borrow a phrase from Flannery O'Connor, is clearly a revelatory moment for him.[2]

Nor are Dummy and Father the only characters to gain such insights. Although the narrative attempts to direct our attention away from the narrator, his epiphany is really at the heart of the story. As he notes in the second paragraph, "For me, Dummy's death signalled the end of my extraordinarily long childhood, sending me forth, ready or not, into the world of men—where defeat and death are more in the natural order of things" (FS, 9). The story clearly depicts an initiation for the young boy, who is 12 at the time the lake is stocked and 14 when he goes fishing there with his father. A fishing expedition is a traditional scene of initiation, as in Hemingway's "Big Two Hearted River" or Faulkner's "The Old People," and indeed the catching of the fish is a significant event in the boy's maturation process. The more significant fishing expedition for the boy, however, takes place at the end of the story, when he watches the police divers drag the pond for, and then hook onto, Dummy's body. "For myself," he says, "I knew I wouldn't forget the sight of that arm emerging out of the water. Like some kind of mysterious and terrible signal, it seemed to herald the misfortune that dogged our family in coming years" (FS, 26). The boy's realization of mortality, like the father's realization of personal guilt, ages him several years in a single moment. He, too, is no longer as carefree as he used to be; his childhood is over and he now must face the concerns of the adult world. In the story's penultimate paragraph, the narrator discloses himself to be an older person, "as old as my father was then" (FS, 26), who has been narrating an event from his youth. Since that time he has seen many other drowned bodies, but they no longer have the same effect on him. He has become jaded, "almost ruthlessly stoic about life" (Saltzman, 79). Even so, the fact that he is telling us this story indicates that such occurrences do remind him of the very profound effect this first initiation had on him.

"Distance"

Structurally, "Dummy" is a frame tale, and so is "Distance." The story opens in the present, with a father talking to his 20-year-old daughter. From the beginning it is clear that the family has been broken apart for some time; the opening paragraph tells us that "she's in Milan for Christmas and wants to know what it was like when she was a kid. Always that on the rare occasions when he sees her" (*FS*, 27). The daughter, Catherine, seems to be intent on learning about her childhood and about her parents' relationship so that she can understand what went wrong, why her father left her and moved to Italy. Her father obliges by telling the story of the "first real argument" (*FS*, 37) he and his wife had, which occurred when Catherine was about three weeks old. He begins his story by remarking that the new parents "were kids them-selves, but they were crazy in love, this 18-year-old boy and his 17-year-old girlfriend when they married, and not all that long afterwards they had a daughter" (*FS*, 28). Several weeks later, the boy (as the father con-stantly refers to himself in narrating the story) calls an old friend to go hunting, and his wife encourages him to go, saying that he deserves a break from the routines of being a new father. The morning of the out-ing, however, the baby is cranky and, at least from the mother's point of view, seems to be getting sick. An argument develops when the boy decides to carry out his hunting plans regardless of his daughter's condi-tion. His wife threatens him, saying, "You're going to have to choose" and "If you go out that door you're not coming back, I'm serious" (*FS*, 33), but he goes on to his friend's house. Once he arrives there, however, he changes his mind, telling Carl that he has to cancel so that he can help his wife take care of the baby. He returns home to find mother and child sleeping peacefully. Several hours later, after she awakens, the wife apologizes for her earlier outburst and cooks her husband a waffle. When he accidentally spills the contents of his plate into his lap, they laugh about it and begin to dance in the kitchen, kissing and assuring each other that "we won't fight any more" (*FS*, 36).

The frame tells us, however, that, while this might have been their first argument, it would be far from their last. In telling the story, the father is clearly looking back to that day with nostalgia and sentiment; he recalls it with a certain glow, as a kind of golden moment in their relationship. But Catherine presses him about what happened later, how they moved from this scene of joy to their eventual break-up. He explains that "things change. . . . Kids grow up. I don't know what happened. But things do change and without your realizing it or wanting them to" (*FS*, 36). As the story ends, furthermore, Carver indicates that the father, if he could, would return to that morning and try to preserve the emotional attachment of that scene: "He continues to stand at the window, remembering that gone life. After that morning there would be those hard times ahead, other women for him and another man for her, but that morning, that particular morning, they had danced. They danced, and then they held to each other as if there would always be that morning, and later, they laughed about the waffle. They leaned on each other and laughed about it until tears came, while everything froze, for a while anyway" (*FS*, 36). The moment is frozen in time. It continues to live with the father, but it exists only in memory; the reality of the situation was fleeting and transitory. He remembers the closeness that he and his wife felt on that morning, yet what is pervasive in the present of the story, as its title indicates, is distance, the realization of how far removed from that point in time he now is. He is distanced from his wife, from his daughter, even from the physical setting, as well as from his own past (a fact of which the story's framing structure makes us fully aware). He can look back on it, but he cannot return to or re-create that moment. For him, "the 'good old days' are a treacherous legacy whose primary effect is to highlight the failure to sustain the optimistic vision of their future" (Saltzman, 80). The focus here, in contrast to other Carver stories that focus on relationships in the midst of falling apart, is not so much on the dissolution itself as on the memories of the good times that existed in the earlier part of the relationship. At the end of the story both father and daughter "regret the loss of the galled, warm, commonplace life they have conjured."[3] "Distance" thus achieves a degree of pathos tinged with nostalgia that is unusual in Carver's fiction.

"The Lie"

Although one of the shortest stories in the collection, "The Lie" is quite complex. On the surface, it is another story of marital strife and discord. On a deeper level, though, it is an examination of the nature of truth. The plot of the story, not coincidentally, turns on a series of lies. As the tale opens, the protagonist, who has been told something unsavory about his wife by a mutual female acquaintance of theirs, confronts his wife with the charge. The wife denies it, claiming that the other woman is telling a lie and urging her husband to believe her rather than that "'bitch'" (*FS*, 37). He wants to believe her, but he is not entirely able to do so. What causes him the most concern, if the story is a lie, is that he can't decipher the informant's motive. Remembering an old friend who was "a chronic, unmitigated liar," he is overjoyed, for this person "could indeed bear out my wife's theory that there were such people in the world. I was happy again" (*FS*, 38). He turns to tell his wife that he no longer believes the informant, but she completely surprises him by confessing. "'It's true, God forgive me,'" she says, "'everything she told you is true. It was a lie when I said I didn't know anything about it'" (*FS*, 38). His stunned response is "'Is that true?'" (*FS*, 38). By this point, though, any reassurances she offers cannot be fully trusted. The distinction between truth and lies is becoming increasingly blurry.

Nevertheless, the husband seems convinced that his wife has indeed committed some indiscretion, and he feels assured that she is now telling him the truth—or at least the truth that he wanted to hear all along. He is willing to forgive her, and he becomes quite excited as she casually does a striptease for him and then begins to caress him. Yet he cannot put the problem of the lie behind him completely. He again demands the truth and, as the story ends, the wife returns to her initial story that the informant is lying because "'lying is just a sport for some people'" (*FS*, 40). It certainly seems to be a sport for the wife, as the story amply demonstrates. The conclusion Carver reaches is that we can never completely know what is true and what is not. This sounds fine in theory, but for the husband in the story it is small comfort. As the story ends, his position in his marriage is quite unclear, both to him and to the reader. There no longer seems to be any objectifiable reality. Truth is the one thing that "the overall structure of the text makes sure the reader cannot attain" (Chenetier, 176). The wife's final protestations of innocence, couched in baby talk, do seem to be winning him over. These claims seem obviously fraudulent, yet the husband appears to be succumbing to her wiles as the story abruptly concludes. He seems willing to accept an obviously fictionalized version of the truth. Perhaps Carver's point is that, since the husband can never be entirely sure what *the* truth is, he might as well accept the one that causes the fewest problems. He will continue to feel "uncomfortable" (*FS*, 37) about his life, but that cannot possibly be avoided. The reader, moreover, is put in the exact same position as the husband: We feel uncomfortable about "The Lie" because we don't know which is the lie and which is the truth, or whether that distinction even matters.

"So Much Water So Close to Home"

"So Much Water So Close to Home," which had already been included in the 1976 *Pushcart Prize* anthology, is this collection's masterpiece. Indeed, it is one of the finest of all of Carver's stories, bringing together many of the themes and techniques that have become constants in his work, but expressing them in a new and very compelling way. The story once again focuses on a relationship undergoing a moment of great vulnerability. Claire and Stuart Kane have been a happily married couple—and they have one son, Dean—but following one of Stuart's fishing expeditions their relationship changes dramatically. In the story's opening paragraph, Claire, our first-person narrator, remarks that "something has come between us though he would like to believe otherwise" (*FS*, 41). Stuart "wishes everything could have been as before" (*FS*, 37), but he knows this is not possible. Claire also shares in this desire to be deluded, to be "deinitiated" (Saltzman, 86); she wishes that Stuart had not gone "*miles away to fish*," especially since there is "*so much water so close to home*" (*FS*, 47). Nevertheless, Claire knows that she must find a way to come to terms with what has happened on that excursion.

Reminding us of "Nobody Said Anything," and thus of Hemingway (Clarke, 112),[4] "So Much Water So Close to Home" again presents the encroachment of terror in a formerly escapist, pastoral setting. Stuart goes on the weekend fishing trip with his friends, looking forward to the relaxation. Shortly after they arrive at the campsite, however, one of the men discovers the nude body of a dead girl floating in the river. Following a short debate, the men decide, rather than give up their fishing (and drinking and card-playing), to tie the girl's wrist to a tree so that she won't float away and to go on with their vacation. Four days later they return to town and call the sheriff, feeling that they have nothing to be ashamed of. When Claire hears the story, however, her reaction is one of outrage and horror that the men could have acted as they did. She pictures them as "they took their dishes down to the river and washed them a few yards from where the girl lay in the water" (*FS*, 44). Stuart becomes monstrous to her. She recalls that, when he first came home, "he put his heavy arms around me and rubbed his hands up and down my back, the same hands he'd left with two days before, I thought" (*FS*, 44). They had even made love that evening. He did not tell her the news until the morning. Now that she knows what has happened, however, she is repulsed by the thought of his hands. As the story progresses she moves further and further away from Stuart, finally moving into the guest bedroom. Her anger at Stuart is exacerbated by the fact that he doesn't see any real problem at all. He doesn't understand her reaction to the events of the fishing trip. As Ann Beattie notes, "what she perceives to be her husband's cold imperviousness to the girl's death epitomizes for her what is wrong with their own relationship" (Beattie, 181).

As far as Claire is concerned, Stuart has changed radically. So, necessarily, has their relationship. He might wish for life to go on "exactly as if nothing had happened" (*FS*, 46), but for her it cannot. His continuing denial of any wrongdoing clashes with her resolve not to allow these events to be passed over so lightly. Her real fear is that Stuart's wishes will come true, that they will in fact go on as before. She laments that "nothing will ever really be any different. I believe that. We have made our decisions, our lives have been set in motion, and they will go on and on until they stop. But if that is true, what then? I mean, what if you believe that, but you keep it covered up, until one day something happens that should change something, but then you see nothing is going to change. What then?" (*FS*, 49). Here we see her ambivalence, as "she both wishes for a return to routine and fears that this is precisely what is in store for her" (Saltzman, 87). "What then?" is the question that she strives to answer in assessing her future relationship with Stuart.

Much of the rift between Claire and Stuart is obviously gender-related. Claire naturally empathizes with the girl, and visualizes herself as being in the girl's position: "I look at the creek. I float toward the pond, eyes open, face down, staring at the rocks and moss on the creek bottom until I am carried into the lake where I am pushed by the breeze" (*FS*, 48). Thinking of the girl as a rape victim, she comes to reevaluate the way she herself has been sexually harassed. The dead girl has been identified as Susan Miller, a high school student from a community about 120 miles away, and Claire decides to attend her funeral. On the way out of town she stops at the gas station, where she is ogled by the boy at the pump. While driving, she is pestered by a male motorist; she pulls off the road to try to get away from him, but he only comes back to see if she needs help. The reader realizes that he is probably just being a good Samaritan, but Claire notices the way he looks at her breasts and legs. She sees in him only a threat. She locks herself in her car, much the way Susan Miller is now locked in her coffin. Thinking of these emotions, Claire becomes aware of the ways Stuart has taken sexual advantage of her. She is made irate when she considers how Stuart came home and made love to her as though nothing out of the ordinary had happened on the fishing trip. In fact, he continues trying to have sexual relations with her, although she rebuffs him every time.

The story ends following her return from the funeral. Stuart again attempts to initiate sexual contact, but she stamps on his foot. Throwing her down, he insults her and storms out of the house. The next morning he sends flowers and a sweet note, but the delivery boy's glances again make Claire feel sexually vulnerable. Stuart obviously cannot be blamed for the delivery boy's actions, but Claire moves her things into the extra bedroom anyway, signaling a formal change in their relationship. For her, "there can be no reconciliation" (Campbell, 39); life simply cannot go on as it had before, since that would mean succumbing to death as Susan did. The separation will be painful, she knows, and she does express pity for Stuart, but she feels she must fight to remain vibrant and alive. She must break out of the oppressiveness of men, represented by the rapist/killer on the one hand and, not so very differently, Stuart on the other. As she retells the story, she seems to become angry all over again and the story ends with a very strong conviction that her relationship with Stuart has been permanently altered. As Ewing Campbell explains, her act of identification with Susan Miller "has made life with Stuart, life as it was, impossible. Their responses to the event have revealed how little they have in common, and she does in fact make certain, by refusing to yield to him, that something will change" (Campbell, 40). Like the waitress in "Fat," Claire is on her way to resolving the situation by leaving the relationship. She has decided that, in this case, jumping off into the unknown is preferable to clinging to an outmoded status quo.

"The Fling"

As its title indicates, "The Fling" is another story of infidelity. This extramarital affair is a particularly sordid one, however. The participants here are the 55-year-old Mr. Palmer, who has two grown children, and Sally Wain, who is considerably younger and has children in elementary school. Sally's husband, Larry, is a long-haul trucker who is frequently on the road. To keep herself occupied, she works as a Stanley Products woman, delivering orders. One day she arrives at the Palmers' to deliver a package, but finds Mr. Palmer there alone. They proceed to have a conversation, tell a few dirty jokes, and have sex. A few weeks later, he visits her house. Soon they are having a full-fledged affair. During one of their assignations at Sally's house, however, they are surprised by Larry's early return. Discovered, Palmer expects to get killed. Instead it is Larry who breaks down. He then slowly and painfully kills himself.

The details of this plot line don't begin to account for the true nature of "The Fling," however, for this tryst is a story within another story. The real protagonist here is Les Palmer, the adulterous man's son and the narrator of the tale. He speaks directly to the reader, telling us that he is going to "relate a story my father told me last year when I stopped over briefly in Sacramento" (*FS*, 62). Les does indeed repeat for us his father's version of the story summarized above. Although going to Sacramento to visit his father had been Les's idea—he stopped to have a few drinks with him in the airport lounge on his way from meetings in Los Angeles to his home in Chicago—it is clear that he still blames his father for his parents' divorce. He is particularly sensitive to the pain his mother has suffered as a result of the situation. When Mr. Palmer tells Les that the divorce is the least significant fact of the story, that "'there are things, things far more important than . . . your mother's leaving me'" (*FS*, 74), Les leaps to his mother's defense. Up to this point in time he has only heard of the infidelity from his mother's perspective, which he finds to be justified (as, indeed, does the philandering husband himself).

The death of Larry Wain is the "more important thing" to which Les's father is referring. He tells his son that "'It keeps coming back to me, I mean, and I can't get it out of my head that he should be dead for something I caused'" (*FS*, 76). Mrs. Palmer had never told her son about the death of the man cuckolded by her husband, if she even knew of it, and so the revelation comes as a great shock to Les. It is enough of a jolt to wake him out of his complacency, at least temporarily. While his father's narration continues, Les begins to come to realizations about his own life. Up until this point he has been listening to his father's explanation without "feeling anything one way or the other" (*FS*, 75), but now he realizes that he is supposed to reach out to his father, who hasn't been able to find anyone else to whom he could unburden himself. Yet Les is unable to offer such support. He "is not humane enough to respond to his father's pain" (Beattie, 180), and thus he discovers a great truth about himself: He doesn't have any feelings whatsoever. He tells us that "I felt a shaky, irrational fear begin to work through me, and the pain behind my eyes grew stronger. He kept staring at me until I began to squirm, until we both realized I had nothing to give him, nothing to give to anyone for that matter. I was all smooth surface with nothing inside except emptiness. I was shocked. I blinked my eyes once or twice. My fingers trembled as I lighted a cigarette, but I took care not to let him notice" (*FS*, 76). Les admits to having had an epiphany here, a real-ization of his own emptiness, but it doesn't seem as though he is going to make any conscious effort to change as a result of having seen the naked truth about himself. He still gets back on the plane and flies to Chicago.

There is yet another level to the story. In a final ironic twist, Carver gives the reader insight into Les's character, insight that Les himself has not yet reached. At the beginning of the story, Les nonchalantly lets the reader know that, although he is a married man with two kids, he and his wife Mary have "been living apart for nearly six months" (*FS*, 62). He doesn't see the significance of this fact, and he never mentions it to his father. He doesn't relate it to the situation between his parents, although it would seem logical that hearing about another marital break-up would cause him to consider his own. While his father is telling him the story of his fling, furthermore, Les's attention is constantly being drawn toward an attractive redhead in the airport bar. Mr. Palmer's statements about the Stanley Products woman are interspersed with Les's comments about the redhead. Later in the story, a band begins to play and the woman does a wild dance. The whole scene is somewhat surreal, but when Mr. Palmer says that he hasn't noticed anything we are led to wonder whether he is really that self-absorbed or whether Les is fantasizing about a fling of his own. In many ways, Les is replicating his father's behavior; despite the fact that he claims to be angry about the pain his father has caused his mother, he seems totally unconcerned about the pain Mary and the kids might be feeling because of his own departure. Mr. Palmer emphasizes this discrepancy by asking straight away about Mary and the kids after greeting his son. He even gives Les a sack with some candy and toys in it to take home to the children. As the story comes to a close, though, Les notes that "Half way to Chicago, I remem-bered I'd left his sack of gifts in the lounge" (*FS*, 78). His father has unwittingly provided him with the means to get back together with his wife—perhaps unconsciously hoping that Les would not follow the path that had led to such great pain in his own life—but Les's apathy makes such a reunion an impossibility. In fact, Les sounds very defensive in the final line of the story: "But, tell me, what could he expect from someone like me?" (*FS*, 78). He both realizes the problematic nature of his behav-ior and knows that he isn't going to change. If the story is "a prolonged rationalization by the narrator for his failure to respond sufficiently to the naked neediness of his father" (Saltzman, 92), as one critic maintains, then it has been an unsuccessful attempt; telling the story "has not explained his father to him nor excused him for his inaction" (Saltzman, 93). Like so many characters in Carver Country, Les is stuck in a rut from which neither a fling nor an epiphany is likely to free him. Claire Kane's nightmare, that something monumental will occur but will not cause any changes, is all too real in the life of Les Palmer.

"Pastoral"

"Pastoral," as its title indicates, is another of Carver's rustic stories, and it is perhaps the most Hemingwayesque piece of all of his works.[5] While the story turns on marital strife, for example, that element is rarely mentioned; instead, "following Hemingway's practice, Carver shapes the story as an 'iceberg,' its marital conflict seven-eighths submerged."[6] More obviously, the story's detailed descriptions of preparing to fish are reminiscent of "Big Two-Hearted River,"[7] while its notion of the return to nature as a return to order and wholesomeness recalls the fishing scenes in *The Sun Also Rises*. Predictably for Carver Country, however, the trip doesn't turn out as the fisher planned. Rather than experiencing a return to order, Harold's sense of the universe is almost entirely shattered.

As the story opens with Harold's arrival at the Castlerock campgrounds, we sense that he has been having some problems in his relationship with his wife, Frances. He has mixed feelings about having come on the fishing trip alone, even though she has urged him to go despite not wanting to accompany him. He remembers the time three years ago they stayed at the lodge together and how he caught a number of fish, yet this pleasant reminiscence only goads him today. Harold hopes that the fishing trip will signify a return of these positive feelings; he is looking forward to relaxation and rejuvenation. When he heads out to begin fishing the following morning, he is described in terms reminiscent of the chivalric tradition: He holds his rod "under his arm like it was a lance" and recalls how he used to "imagine himself in the lists coming down on his opponent" (*FS*, 86). After some time spent fishing, despite not having caught anything, he "beg[ins] to feel some of the old excitement coming back" (*FS*, 87). His growing sense of peace is rudely interrupted by the appearance of a wounded doe. Harold has expressed antihunter sentiments earlier in the story, and this encounter only provides further evidence for his view that hunters are "'dirty bastards'" (*FS*, 88). When the boys who are chasing the deer show up, Harold takes the opportunity to try to enlighten them about proper behavior in the natural environment. The leader's response, however, is to shoot a blank at him—"the barrel

pointed somewhere at his stomach, or lower down maybe" (*FS*, 89)—
after which the other boys pelt him with rocks. The leader threatens him
a bit more, telling him how lucky he is that they aren't going to do to
him what they did to the doe, and then they move off. To them this scenario is a joke, but to Harold, who really thought he had been shot, it is
quite serious; as Ewing Campbell aptly points out, "in the unexpected
confrontation between the imaginary good old days and the vulgar reality of the present, he stands like a stag brought to bay by the hounds"
(Campbell, 5).

After recovering his composure, Harold returns to the lodge, "feeling
unheroic, homeless, and alone" (Stull 1988, 466). He has, significantly,
lost his fishing rod, "the weapon of knighthood and the emblem of male
virility" (Campbell, 7). Harold now knows that the trip to the lodge has
been a mistake; the return to the pastoral no longer suffices to heal the
wounds from which he is suffering. Carver emphasizes this insight when
he writes in the story's final lines that "somehow [Harold] had missed it
and it was gone. Something heroic. He didn't know what he was going
to do. He couldn't very well go home. Slow, thick flakes sifted down
through the freezing air, sticking on his coat collar, melting cold and wet
against his face. He stared at the wordless, distorted things around him"
(*FS*, 91). The story thus ends on a note of sheer despair, the snowiness of
the scene and the bleakness of the outlook reminiscent of Jack London's
"To Build a Fire." "Pastoral" again demonstrates that, for Carver, as for
Hemingway, naturalism always seems to intrude into the pastoral idyll,
showing the uselessness "of nostalgia and self-deception as therapy for
malaise" (Campbell, 6). Any hope for reintegration and regeneration is
futile.

"Furious Seasons"

The next story, "Mine," is the volume's shortest and weakest; quite the
opposite is true of the subsequent text, the title story, which is one of the
volume's most fully developed and most effective pieces, as well as being
a fitting capstone to the collection by recalling many of its central
images and themes. Once again, for example, Carver uses an outdoor
scene, in this case a hunting trip, as the setting in which the protagonist
realizes that his life has fallen apart. As in "Pastoral," Lew Farrell, the
protagonist of "Furious Seasons," turns to nature in hopes of achieving
salvation, only to have those hopes dashed. From the very outset of the
story it is clear that nature is not always a comfort: "Rain threatens," the

story begins (*FS*, 94). Furthermore, Lew is looking at "the glossy pages [of a magazine] open now to a halftone, two page picture of a disaster scene, an earthquake, somewhere in the Near East" (*FS*, 95). He comes to associate the rain in his own part of the world with this distant earthquake, since both are examples of Nature's fury unleashing itself. When he looks out the rain-fogged window, "he could not see the other apartments and for a moment it was as if they'd been destroyed, like the houses in the picture he'd been looking at a few hours ago" (*FS*, 97). At the very end of the story, the moment at which Lew Farrell's world does indeed undergo an upheaval similar to an earthquake, the imagery returns to the threatening rain: "The gutter water rushed over his feet, swirled frothing into a great whirlpool at the drain on the corner and rushed down to the center of the earth" (*FS*, 110). Carver makes masterful use of weather imagery here and throughout "Furious Seasons," as the title indicates, to enhance his characteristic tension and menace. The note of utter despair that the whirlpool image so perfectly captures is reminiscent of the final notes sounded by "Pastoral" and "Mine," the preceding two stories.

In several other ways, however, "Furious Seasons" is a radical departure from the rest of the collection that bears its name. It is indeed rather an oddity in the whole of Carver's canon. In terms of its content, first of all, the story partakes of the Gothic tradition much more than do any of Carver's other texts. While "Mine" is reminiscent of Edgar Allan Poe's brief tales, "Furious Seasons" reminds us of Poe's use of the macabre. The story depicts, as do many others in the collection, a marriage on the rocks. While the wife is away, the husband is contemplating an extramarital affair. The twist here, however, is that the potential mistress also happens to be the husband's own sister. Lew recalls how he was once in his sister's room when she came in from the shower and dropped her towel. From this incident, he has concocted an elaborate incestual fantasy. Shortly before the story begins, Lew's sister, Iris, has come to stay with him and his wife, Lorraine, for a few months. The situation becomes a kind of inverse (and perverse) *A Streetcar Named Desire.* Lorraine, who thinks she is speaking metaphorically, ironically says, "'You're all mine, Lew. I hate to think of sharing you even for a little while with anybody. Even your own sister'" (*FS*, 103). With Lorraine gone, Lew wants to resist the pull of Iris's sexuality, but he is having a great deal of difficulty doing so, particularly when she emerges from the shower and sits down in front of the mirror to comb her hair. Shortly thereafter, Iris tells Lew that she is pregnant. His world is rocked. We don't know whether Lew could possibly be the father, but he seems to think that he is. He asks her what she is going to do, and appears to go calmly about his business. What we discover at the very end of the story, however, is that he has murdered her and placed her body under the blankets in the made-up bed she has been sleeping on. The violence is unexpected and quite shocking. It is at this point that Lew makes his pastoral remove; he goes goose hunting with his friend Frank. Lew shoots two geese, and at first this act seems to revive him. Soon, though, he begins to think of what he has done, and feels compelled to return home to face the sheriff. His conscience gets the better of him, as with several of Poe's characters, and he must submit to "the great whirlpool" that "rush[es] down to the center of the earth."

In addition to its Gothic content, the structure of the story is unusual for Carver "in its disruption of linear progression" (Saltzman, 96). He employs stream of consciousness devices, for example, slipping in and out of Lew's mind. Much of the story is presented in free association, as when the sound of the rain reminds Lew of the sound of the birds his sister captured when they were children. One passage, the one in which Iris comes out of the bathroom and tells Lew that she is pregnant, is repeated with minor variations three times, at the beginning (*FS* 95), in the middle (*FS*, 101–2), and at the end (*FS*, 108–9). In addition, Carver splits up narrative time in such a way that the true story is only gradually revealed, after which the reader can return to and understand previous portions of the text. An example is Carver's description of Lew's actions when Frank arrives to pick him up for the hunting trip: "He picked up his things and went out on the porch. Iris was there, stretched out under the twisted pile of heavy quilts" (*FS*, 100). It is only at the end of the story that we can understand the full impact of this scene, for at the time we are unaware that she is lying under quilts because he has put her corpse there.

Moreso in the manner of its telling than in the sordidness of its incestuous plot, "Furious Seasons" is reminiscent of the stories of William Faulkner, a writer whose aesthetic may seem diametrically opposed to Carver's. As Tess Gallagher has pointed out, this early story "represents perhaps the path not taken, since the borrowed devices—flashbacks and stream of consciousness—will seldom appear in his future work" (*NHP*, 12). Nor will such Faulknerian sentences as "For a minute, looking down over the porch to the black, ripply sidewalk, it was as though he were standing alone on a bridge someplace, and again the feeling came, as it had last night, that this had already happened, knowing then that it would happen again, just as he somehow knew now" (*FS*, 100–101). In a literary blindfold test, it is unlikely that many people would correctly identify Carver as the author of this passage. Although it is the only story in the volume that does not reappear in any of Carver's later collections, we should not let that distract us from the fact that "Furious Seasons" is an extremely effective work, and a fitting story with which to conclude the volume.

Conclusion

Furious Seasons is something of an odds-and-ends collection. Several of the stories included in it are actually older than those in *Will You Please Be Quiet, Please?*, and the earlier collection, ironically, does seem more mature than this one. That is not to deride these stories, however, for they do add substantially to Carver's canon. Ann Beattie, in one of the few reviews of the collection, asserted that the stories "are some of the most impressive of short fiction. The truth of them will make the reader restless and uneasy. There is a quality about them that defies paraphrase; the cumulative effect is overpowering" (Beattie, 182). Beattie perhaps overstates the case, but "So Much Water So Close to Home" is surely one of Carver's finest early achievements, and the stories "Furious Seasons" and "The Lie" are fascinating in their atypicality. Furthermore, the *Furious Seasons* stories will play an important role in the next chapter, as we turn our attention to *What We Talk about When We Talk about Love*, Carver's breakthrough volume.

Chapter Five

The Middle Years:
What We Talk about When We Talk about Love

Carver had stopped drinking by the time *Furious Seasons* was published, but he had not yet returned to writing. When he did, his stories were markedly different from what they had been. The obsessions were the same, but the stories were much darker, reflecting the hell of marital discord and alcoholism that Carver himself had experienced. Their style, moreover, was an exaggerated form of minimalism. Whereas he had once worried that a story like "Neighbors" might be "too thin, too elliptical and subtle" (*NHP*, 104), Carver was now writing stories that would make "Neighbors" appear positively lush. As one critic has pointed out, in these new texts "language is used so sparingly and the plots are so minimal that the stories at first seem to be mere patterns with no flesh and life in them. . . . Characters frequently have no names or only first names and are so briefly described that they appear to have no physical presence at all; certainly they have no distinct identity" (May, 78). Carver, looking back on the volume several years after its initial publication, told an interviewer that the texts in *What We Talk about When We Talk about Love* were "so pared down. Everything I thought I could live without I just got rid of, I cut out" (*Con*, 125). Urged on by his editor Gordon Lish, he began implementing Hemingway's "theory of omission. If you can take anything out, take it out, as doing so will make the work stronger. Pare, pare, and pare some more" (*Con*, 182). That phrase could in fact serve as a motto for *What We Talk about When We Talk about Love*, although critics have more often pointed to the following lines from "On Writing": "Get in, get out. Don't linger." (*F*, 22). The stories here are indeed shorter, on average, than those in *Will You Please Be Quiet, Please?* and *Furious Seasons*. They also have a more desolate outlook, which is amplified by their astringency of tone. Nowhere is Carver's minimalist aesthetic more clearly visible than in the five stories from *Furious Seasons* that reappear here in reduced versions, having been "subjected to rigorous cutting" (Campbell, 31).

Although Carver eventually reacted against this extremely pared-down style, the stories in *What We Talk about When We Talk about Love* continue to embody minimalism at its most distinctive. The collection has been nicknamed the "minimalist bible," and when readers and critics consider Carver a minimalist they generally have this volume in mind. Because it is the volume that established Carver as a major literary figure, it has remained the collection most often associated with him, even if it is, as we shall later see, his least representative.

"Why Don't You Dance?"

"Why Don't You Dance?," the leadoff story in Carver's third collection, focuses on the concerns that had so recently threatened to derail his own life, namely marital discord and alcoholism. As the story opens, an unnamed man has moved the entire furnishings of his house into his front yard. He has even "run an extension cord on out there [so that] everything was connected. Things worked, no different from how it was when they were inside" (*WWTA*, 4). The impetus behind this seemingly bizarre behavior is the recent departure of his wife, an event that has broken his spirit and left him with only the small comfort afforded by his drink. As the story continues, a young couple happens by the scene. Assuming it to be a yard sale, they stop to see if they can find some bargains. They proceed to lie on the bed and to try out the blender and the television set. The girl likes the bed, and she urges the boy to find out what the owners want for it, advising him to offer $10 less, since "'they must be desperate or something'" (*WWTA*, 6). When the man returns—he has been at the store buying more whiskey, as well as some beer and sandwiches—they do indeed dicker over the price of several items, and he ends up selling them the bed, the TV, and a desk. He clearly comes to see in this young couple an image of himself and his wife as a young couple, perhaps when they had first bought the furniture he is now selling. With a hint of nostalgia, he assures the girl that "'It's a good bed'" (*WWTA*, 6). He seems to enjoy watching the young couple and, after giving them a few drinks, he puts a record on the player and urges them to dance. The records are entirely unfamiliar to the youngsters, however. Once again the man is reminded of what he has lost, for these are songs that he and his wife had danced to. After the boy and girl dance, she comes over to dance with the man. While they embrace, he is taken back to his youth. For her part, she senses his sadness and wants to comfort him. She also seems to realize that, if she and her beau represent what he used to be, then he represents what they might become. Does his failed relationship presage a similar fate for them? "Will the young couple contract the same disease from the sofa he perched upon, his restless bed?" (Saltzman, 102). It seems so, for the story's conclusion emphasizes the repetitive patterns of relationship breakdowns.

In the story's final lines, the girl is telling everyone she knows about the incident. She feels that "there was more to it, and she was trying to get it talked out. After a time, she quit trying" (*WWTA*, 10). Here she may remind us of the waitress in "Fat," who was telling her story to Rita. In that case, though, Rita was the one who didn't understand; in this case it is the narrator herself who "has failed to discover the implications of what she has encountered" (Campbell, 44), and soon stops trying to gain insight into the situation. Carver's obsession with the importance and difficulty of communication resurfaces here. The girl, having stopped trying to talk her experience out, is most likely on her way to ending up as "desperate" (*WWTA*, 9) as the older man, even if she fails to comprehend what has been transferred to her along with the bed.

In its content and themes, then, "Why Don't You Dance?" is a fairly typical Carver story, judging by his first two collections. In its form, however, the story is quite a departure from most of the stories in the earlier volumes and provides a very good example of Carver's new minimalist style. Except for the lengthy description of the yard in the story's first section, the writing is short and clipped, as are the paragraphs; like Hemingway's works, adjectives are at a minimum. The characters by and large remain undeveloped and nameless. This absence of names may seem like a minor point, but it is quite indicative of the way in which the story leaves out much of what readers have come to consider necessary information about characters' pasts and about their feelings in the present. We don't really know what has happened to the man's wife, for example. She may have left him, but, for all we know, she may have died. We also don't know about the young couple: Are they married, or just setting up house together? These would seem to be important facts for an understanding of the dynamics of the triangular encounter, but Carver, employing the iceberg principle, leaves them unstated. Even when the narrator does step into one or another of the characters' minds, the reader fails to learn much about the character's feelings and motivations. At one point, for example, Carver writes that the man "looked at them as they sat at the table. In the lamplight, there was something about their faces. It was nice or it was nasty. There was no telling" (*WWTA*, 8–9). At the story's conclusion, as noted above, we are invited into the girl's mind only to discover that she doesn't understand the significance of the encounter, and has given up trying to comprehend it. The narration provides a kind of scrupulous objectivity, so that it is hard for the reader to get close to the situation. Nevertheless, the story does have a great deal of power. The reader senses the desperation that lies behind all three of the characters' lives and feels the same kind of indescribable menace that they do. In its starkness, this minimalist text provides a brief flash of insight into the characters' lives and forces the reader, like the girl, to work at trying to understand the message that is to be learned about the instability of relationships.

"Viewfinder"

Like the unnamed man in "Why Don't You Dance?," the unnamed first-person narrator of "Viewfinder" is in the process of coming to grips with the loss of his family. In this story, however, the protagonist seems to be moving in a more positive direction, facing the fact that he must become a survivor. He seems to understand the message that he is being given by the stranger who has entered his life, a man with hooks for hands who has come to his door hoping to sell a picture he has just taken with his Polaroid camera of the narrator's house. When the photographer comes into the house, he immediately senses the loss that the narrator has experienced; he says, "'You're alone, right?'" (*WWTA*, 12). Shaking his head, he remarks in a tone of commiseration, "'Hard, hard'" (*WWTA*, 13). He even seems to sense the facts of the situation when he remarks, "'So they just up and left you, right?'" (*WWTA*, 13). The man is able to understand the narrator's position so clearly, he says, because he has been in a similar situation himself. "'Hey, I had kids once. Just like you,'" he notes, motioning with his hooks; "'They're what gave me this'" (*WWTA*, 13). He doesn't explain to the narrator how his children caused the loss of his hands, but what is apparent is that he has not let either the loss of his hands or of his family bring him down. He continues to work and to earn a living, and he seems to be satisfied with his life.

Watching the man with no hands, the narrator comes to reassess his own life. He now realizes that his situation is not as tragic as he had felt it to be. After all, he still has the use of his hands, and he should be able to get along at least as well as the man with the hooks. Later in the story, the narrator asks the man to take more pictures of him and his house. The narrator climbs up on the roof, where he discovers some rocks on the chimney grate. When the man with the hooks is ready to take his picture, he picks up one of the rocks and, he tells us, "I laid back my arm and I hollered, 'Now!' I threw that son of a bitch as far as I could throw it" (*WWTA*, 15). As one critic explains this scene, "Carver seems to suggest that the narrator's throwing the rock frees him, at least temporarily, from the status of impotent object."[1] This action is thus symbolic of his discarding the ties to the past that have been constraining him. The narrator has listened to the photographer's statement that "'They're not coming back'" (*WWTA*, 14), and he realizes that he must find some way of moving on despite this loss, just as the photographer has learned to cope with the loss of his hands. Once he has entirely accepted his family's departure, which will be accomplished when he removes all of the rocks, he can begin to reassert himself and find a way of surviving in his new circumstances. As the story ends, he is preparing to throw another rock.

In several significant ways, then, "Viewfinder" is again reminiscent of "Fat." The oddity of the man with no hands, like the oddity of the extremely obese customer, forces the narrator to reevaluate his own life. This reexamination, moreover, results in a new sense of self. Although the title of the story explicitly refers to the camera—the narrator says that the man "would stand on the sidewalk in front of your house, locate your house in the viewfinder, push down the lever with one of his hooks, and out would pop your picture" (*WWTA*, 12)—it can also refer to the photographer himself, who has found a new view for the narrator. When the story opened, the narrator had been watching the man from inside his house, but he is now outside; rather than merely watching, he is actively participating in the photographs. "The narrator is no longer pinned by the camera's viewfinder, no longer a motionless loner trapped inside an edifice of alienation" (Lehman, 49). Through communication and communion with the other man, the narrator becomes able to begin putting his own life back in order. He is still in the early stages of this resurrection process as the story ends, but he does seem to be moving forward in a way that none of the characters in "Why Don't You Dance?" are. In Carver's world, this moment represents a victory, however limited.

"Mr. Coffee and Mr. Fixit"

In "Mr. Coffee and Mr. Fixit," on the other hand, there is nothing approaching even this level of success. Instead, the story presents us with a first-person account of a series of failed or failing relationships and seems to hold out little hope for any kind of redemption or salvation. The bulk of the story concerns events that transpired in the narrator's life three years before his present narration of them, events that do seem to give credit to his opening statement "I've seen some things" (*WWTA*, 17). He has seen his mother kissing a man other than her husband, for example. He had gone to her house "to stay a few nights" (*WWTA*, 17)—an indication of the problems he was experiencing in his own home—and had interrupted her and the man kissing on the sofa. He notes, furthermore, that he had been out of work at the time his "mother was putting out," and that his wife, Myrna, "was putting out too," having an affair with "an unemployed aerospace engineer she'd met at AA" (*WWTA*, 17). Ross, the man with whom Myrna was having her fling, had his own history of marital problems. He had been shot by his first wife, and he had been jailed by his second; at the same time he was sleeping with Myrna, moreover, he was also having an affair with "a twenty-two-year-old named Beverly" (*WWTA*, 19). Despite the fact that Ross was sleeping with his wife, the narrator doesn't seem to have any animosity toward the man. On the contrary, he notes that "we had things in common, Ross and me, which was more than just the same woman" (*WWTA*, 19). Like the homeowner and the photographer in "Viewfinder," the narrator and Ross prove to be "brothers—perhaps even twins—under the skin" (Runyon, 93). They are both unemployed, for one thing, and they are both alcoholics, as is Myrna. The narrator explains that "Ross and Myrna met when Myrna was trying to stay sober. She was going to meetings, I'd say, three or four times a week. I had been in and out myself. But when Myrna met Ross, I was out and drinking a fifth a day" (*WWTA*, 19). Even the narrator's relationship with his daughter, Melody, had been adversely affected by the chaotic situation. From all indications, then, the characters' personal lives had indeed been "crazy" (*WWTA*, 17) three years ago, as the narrator notes in retrospect. None of them seemed able to arrive at any kind of stability. "I don't know what we were thinking of in those days," he says (*WWTA*, 18).

The question we must ask ourselves, however, is whether things are really any different in the present. Although the narrator does try to assure us at the story's outset that "things are better now" (*WWTA*, 17), his story gives us little reason to accept that assessment. When he expresses his sympathetic attitude toward Ross, for example, stating that "I used to make fun of him when I had the chance. But I don't make fun of him anymore" (*WWTA*, 19), he uses the present tense, indicating an ongoing concern and sense of shared suffering. The same is true when he says "God bless and keep you, Mr. Fixit" (*WWTA*, 20), a nickname he bestowed on Ross when the latter had been trying unsuccessfully to make money during his layoff by fixing small appliances. The final lines of the story, in their ambiguity, also seem to indicate a lack of change in the narrator's life. What seems to be clear is a lack of intimacy and communication between the narrator and his wife, an apparently permanent and ongoing situation. The narrator may want to reunite with Myrna, despite all that has happened in the past, but she seems unwilling. The story thus ends without any hope for the narrator, who is unable to get his life into any kind of order. In its extreme attenuation and ambiguity, however, "Mr. Coffee and Mr. Fixit" is one of the least successful stories in the collection. The reader is given no access point from which to become engaged in these characters' lives. Since the reader doesn't know why the narrator is relating these things he has seen, the overall story has little impact. Perhaps this is a further indication of the story's obsession with the problem of communication, the way we manage to ignore one another. In any event, the story's message misses its mark.

"Gazebo"

Structurally, "Gazebo" shares much with "Mr. Coffee and Mr. Fixit." Once again we have a first-person narrator telling us the story of his troubled relationship, a bad situation that was exacerbated by the alcoholism of both parties. The story also features a disrupted chronology; we are constantly being moved from the narrative present, which consists of the telling of the events of an afternoon in the recent past, to a historical past that explains the germination of those events. Stylistically, however, the two texts are very different. While "Gazebo" would fit into most definitions of minimalism, it is not nearly as pared down as "Mr. Coffee and Mr. Fixit." Because the story is more fully developed, because we are given a more detailed picture of the situation and characters, we can arrive at a much deeper understanding of the story. In terms of its effectiveness, then, "Gazebo" is far superior to the previous story; indeed, it is one of the finest stories in the collection, and one of the few that Carver later chose for inclusion in *Where I'm Calling From.*

The protagonists here are another of Carver's "characteristic couples [who] lurch from disaster to disaster" (Jansen, 396). As the story opens, Duane is recalling that all-important afternoon when he and Holly finally acknowledged and talked over the strain in their marriage. From the opening sentences, the fact that their relationship has reached a breaking point becomes perfectly clear:

That morning she pours Teacher's over my belly and licks it off. That afternoon she tries to jump out the window.

I go, "Holly, this can't continue. This has got to stop." (*WWTA*, 21).

Duane's continual use of "I go/she goes" throughout the narration, besides being accurate to conversational norms of the 1980s, indicates that, for him at least, these actions are ongoing. Duane is continuing to replay them in his mind, and he feels that the ultimate outcome of the discussion is still in doubt. In this opening section we also discover that Duane and Holly run a motel and that they have closed up and gone into one of the rooms to have their talk. The overriding imagery, however, as is typical of Carver, shows the distinct lack of communication in their lives. The motel phone rings constantly, for example, but they do not answer it. More significantly, after she tells him that "'My heart is broken,'" the only response he can muster is "'Holly,' I go" (*WWTA*, 22).

The next section takes us back to the past, as Duane explains the factors that led up to this predicament. He and Holly had taken the motel jobs, as handyman and bookkeeper, with high hopes. For about a year the plan seemed to be working well. At that point, however, Duane, for no particular reason, began to have an affair with the hotel's maid, Juanita. His infidelity "has disturbed the trajectory of [their] hopes" (Campbell, 41), as well as causing an increase in their drinking. Duane says that "we both were hitting it pretty hard. Booze takes a lot of time and effort if you're going to do a good job with it" (*WWTA*, 26). Once the reader understands these facts, Holly's statements, such as "'Something's died in me. . . . You've killed something, just like you'd took an axe to it'" (*WWTA*, 23–24), become perfectly understandable and seem entirely appropriate. We also begin to understand Duane's take on the matter: He feels that Holly is completely right. He wants to comfort her, to hug her when she begins to cry, but he knows that "it's no good" (*WWTA*, 24). When Holly asks him whether he and Juanita made love in the room in which they are now having their talk, he tells us that "I don't have anything to say. I feel all out of words inside" (*WWTA*, 26). He would like to communicate, but for a variety of reasons he cannot. As he later says of that afternoon's conversation, "There was this funny thing of anything could happen now that we realized everything had" (*WWTA*, 27). Duane and Holly had clearly reached the nadir, and their only choices were to surrender or to begin the climb back up. They came to realize, Duane notes, that "we'd reached the end of something, and the thing was to find out where new to start" (*WWTA*, 27). As this statement makes clear, Duane would have liked the relationship to continue. He knew that he had been wrong, and that nothing he could say or do would change the facts, but he hoped that he and Holly could find some way to begin again.

This question of renewal is posed throughout the story by the way in which the downfall of Duane and Holly's relationship is paralleled in a series of images from nature, including that of the gazebo. Holly, thinking back to the time "'When we were just kids before we married'" (*WWTA*, 27), recalls having visited a farmhouse on the outskirts of Yakima. The old couple who lived there had showed them a gazebo where "men used to come around and play music . . . and the people would sit and listen" (*WWTA*, 28). Holly remembers the peacefulness of this pastoral scene with heartbreak and longing, as though she is lamenting the passing of those simpler, more innocent times. She emphasizes this point when she tells Duane that "'I thought we'd be like that too when we got old enough. Dignified. And in a place'" (*WWTA*, 28). When they first began to work at the motel, they seemed to be able to perpetuate such a feeling.[2] Following his affair, however, everything changed. Duane tells us that things at the motel "were going downhill fast. We just didn't have the heart for it anymore. I stopped cleaning the pool. It filled up with green gick so that the guests wouldn't use it anymore" (*WWTA*, 27). The destruction of the natural environment clearly parallels the destruction of Duane and Holly's relationship; as he tellingly notes, "we had fouled our lives" (*WWTA*, 27). Nevertheless, he feels that the relationship, like the pool, can still be reclaimed. He argues with Holly that "'these things, we'll look back on them too. We'll go, "Remember the motel with all the crud in the pool?"'" (*WWTA*, 28). Here he is clearly projecting a future for himself that also includes Holly.

We thus learn a good deal more about the narrative present in "Gazebo" than we did in "Mr. Coffee and Mr. Fixit," for we know what this narrator's personal feelings are. Carver does not tell us what effect his desires have had on the real world, however. The ending is again open:

> "Duane," Holly goes.
>   In this, too, she was right. (*WWTA*, 29)

Many critics take this ending as an indication that "the tide of desolation overcomes them" (Saltzman, 107), as is the norm in Carver Country. Arthur Saltzman, for example, asserts that "Holly needs only utter his name for him to take it as a sign that it—everything, now—is too late" (Saltzman, 108). Ewing Campbell similarly believes that "Gazebo" is "a story that concludes in tumult, the lives of the main characters devastated" (Campbell, 41). But I would argue to the contrary. The tension in the story comes from the fact that the issue has not yet been decided, as evidenced by the narrator's use of present tense. It is possible that, while Duane is talking, he is still "pray[ing] for a sign from Holly" (*WWTA*, 29). Although he has already accepted his guilt and knows that he must accept whatever decision Holly reaches, he doesn't yet know what she is going to say. He seems to be holding out hope that they can remain a couple. I would thus agree with Randolph Paul Runyon's claim that "Gazebo" shows "a wife and an unfaithful husband who work through their problem (*his* problem) and look forward to a new beginning" (Runyon, 100). Runyon also points out, interestingly, that Duane's crucial statement "the thing was to find out where new to start" was not present in the original version of the story in the *Missouri Review*, but was added for publication in this collection. Although the textual change is an indication of Carver's increased optimism, the story still leaves the reader very much on the cusp, not knowing whether Duane and Holly's relationship is over or merely on the verge of a rebirth. This kind of ambiguous ending is a Carver trademark, as we have seen, but here it seems to hold out a hint of promise rather than the sheer menace provided by so many of the other abrupt conclusions.

"I Could See the Smallest Things"

One of the minor masterpieces in the collection, "I Could See the Smallest Things" again sounds the two familiar Carver chords that form its dominant motif: the breaking down of relationships and the role alcohol plays in these breakdowns. In this case, drinking has ruined the friendship between two men, neighbors Sam and Cliff. Carver writes that "Sam and Cliff used to be friends. Then one night they got to drinking. They had words. The next thing, Sam had built a fence and then Cliff built one too" (*WWTA*, 33). These are events in the past, however, and the central relationship in the present is that of Cliff and his wife Nancy, the first-person narrator of the tale.

As the story opens, Nancy is awakened by the sound of the strong wind. Cliff is so deeply asleep that nothing will rouse him, but she decides to go out to see if any damage has been done by the wind. While closing the opened gate, she bumps into her neighbor, Sam, who invites her to come over to his house to "'see something'" (*WWTA*, 33). Nancy's dissatisfaction with Cliff has already been made apparent—she finds his

breathing "awful to listen to" (*WWTA*, 32), for instance—and her conversation with Sam seems rife with sexual tension; as she reminds us on
many occasions, she is walking around in her robe. The "something"
that Sam wants to show her, however, and therefore the reason he is up
in the middle of the night, is a bag full of slugs that he has been killing
and collecting. Their encounter thus ends innocuously, with Sam
expressing greetings to Cliff and wishing that they might try to become
friends again. Nancy returns home, but she cannot go back to sleep. Her
encounter with Sam causes her to look more closely at her relationship
with Cliff, and she again expresses dissatisfaction:

> I gave Cliff a little shake. He cleared his throat. He swallowed.
> Something caught and dribbled in his chest.
>   I don't know. It made me think of those things that Sam Lawton
> was dumping powder on. (*WWTA*, 36)

Having perceived this new image of Cliff as slug, Nancy seems ready to
break with him entirely. Nevertheless, she cannot bring herself to take
decisive action. As the story concludes, she notes that "I thought for a
minute of the world outside my house, and then I didn't have any more
thoughts except the thought that I had to hurry up and sleep" (*WWTA*,
36). She senses that the abyss is at hand, as is so often the case in Carver
Country, but she decides to pretend it doesn't exist. "She seeks to obliter-
ate her insight" (Stull "BH" 1985, 6), to become like a slug herself. Her
only thought is the oblivion of thoughtlessness.
    Like that of "The Student's Wife," Nancy's insomnia has led to
"an experience of seeing, of vision,"[3] as the title "I Could See the Smallest
Things" indicates. In this story, however, the protagonist refuses to
acknowledge the truth of her epiphany. Nancy fails to heed the message
that her identification of her husband with a slug should be giving her.
She might be able to see the smallest things about their relationship, but
she remains powerless to do anything about them. The end of the story
indicates that Nancy will stay with Cliff, despite her realization that all of
the love and enthusiasm has gone out of their marriage. In this way, then,
"I Could See the Smallest Things" supports Carver's claim in "Fires" that
insights "don't help any. They just make things harder" (*F*, 33).

"Sacks"

"Sacks," a revised version of "The Fling," is the first of the five *Furious
Seasons* stories to appear in this later collection in a significantly altered,

minimalized way. Examining the two of them together provides us with a very clear understanding of Carver's minimalistic aesthetic at this point in his career. In terms of style, it is easy to see the paring of needless words that Carver (spurred on by Lish) was now engaged in. A sentence such as "Just now, lights are coming on here and there in some of the buildings, and smoke from the tall stacks at the edge of town is rising in a slow thick climb into the darkening sky" (*FS*, 62), for example, becomes "I can see lights coming on in some of the buildings, smoke from the tall stacks rising in a thick climb" (*WWTA*, 37). This elimination of descriptive phrases occurs throughout the revised story. So does the breaking apart of compound sentences. "I straightened things around the couch and turned over the cushions, folded all the newspapers and even washed the two cups we'd used, and cleaned out the coffee pot" (*FS*, 69), for example, becomes "I fixed up the sofa and turned over the cushions. I folded all the newspapers and even washed the cups we'd used. I cleaned out the coffee pot" (*WWTA*, 43). In the inner part of the story, furthermore, the father's narration of his fling of two years ago, Carver shifts to the present tense, adding a heightened sense of immediacy and suspense to the telling. In the outer part of the story, Carver inserts a great deal of "he said"s and "I said"s to remind us of the frame. Both of these stylistic tics are typical of minimalism.

In terms of content, Carver's minimalistic aesthetic is also apparent here, for many of the most important sections of "The Fling" have been completely excised from "Sacks." As a result, Les's view of the situation, to cite one example, is made much harder to see. In the second paragraph of "The Fling," for instance, Les had explained that "the only thing that transpired between us in those few hours was that he caused me—*forced* might be the better word—to peer into my own abyss" (*FS*, 62). This inward peering does occur in "Sacks," but it is never so openly mentioned. Nor is Les's initial siding with his mother played up as much. The elimination of passages such as "it was all I could do to keep from telling him then what I thought of his dirty little affair, and what it had done to my mother" (*FS*, 71), makes it much more difficult for the reader to grasp the family dynamics. Much of the father's narration has been condensed as well; his long, involved story of how the affair was continued until he "'began to think I loved her'" (*FS*, 73) becomes "'so that's the way it went'" (*WWTA*, 43).

These deletions become most readily apparent in the story's ending. The explanation of the suicide of Larry, the cuckolded husband, has been entirely eliminated. All the reader of "Sacks" knows is that "'The man went all to pieces, is what. He got down on the floor and cried'"

(*WWTA*, 45). The father never explains the feelings of guilt that have been haunting him, and thus Les is not shocked out of his complacency and into the kind of epiphany that is apparent in "The Fling." He never senses that he is supposed to be reaching out to his father, and so he does not discover that he is void of feelings. In the story's first version, then, Les is made aware of the reality of his own situation, even if he fails to act on the knowledge; in the second version he never even realizes that he has been offered the opportunity for change. While the end of "Sacks" thus downplays the significance of the encounter between father and son, it compensates by emphasizing the importance of Les's relationship with his wife. We don't learn much about his marital relations early in the story, since the line "Of course, he didn't know we'd been living apart for nearly six months" (*FS*, 63) has been eliminated, but the story now ends by reminding us of this very important aspect of the frame story. Rather than venting his anger at his father when he realizes that he has left the sack of gifts behind, Les now verbally attacks his wife. "Just as well," he says. "Mary didn't need candy, Almond Roca or anything else. That was last year. She needs it now even less" (*WWTA*, 45). Such forced recalling of the reader to the present of the story's narration, with its implication of the end of Les's marriage, emphasizes how Les's narrative is similar to the monologues in "Mr. Coffee and Mr. Fixit" and "Gazebo."

Even in its minimalized form, "Sacks" is one of the fullest stories in *What We Talk about When We Talk about Love*, and it does have a great deal of impact. At least one critic has claimed, in fact, that the story "was improved by the omission of unnecessary elements" (Campbell, 34). I would disagree with such an assertion, however. The reader of "Sacks" does not have nearly as complete an understanding of what is important in the story as does the reader of "The Fling." There is such a "lack of context" (Vander Weele, 112) here that the reader who encounters this story alone could very well finish it in a state of bewilderment. In my opinion, Carver whittled "Sacks" down a bit too far, although looking at the differences between the two texts does provide an excellent example of the changes in Carver's style from his early to his middle period.

"The Bath"

"The Bath" has become one of Carver's best-known and most written-about stories. This distinction has been earned largely as a result of what the story anticipates rather than what it presents, however, since a later version of the story, *Cathedral*'s "A Small, Good Thing," is one of Carver's greatest achievements. Even in its own right, though, "The Bath" is a very effective story. It also conforms to the minimalism of this collection in its neutral, deadpan narration, its lack of description or detail (the main characters are most often referred to as "the man," "the woman," "the boy," and "the doctor," for example), and the suspension and menace of its ending. Stylistically, Carver lets us in on the story's method when he notes that the conversation between the woman and the baker contained "no pleasantries, just this small exchange, the barest information, nothing that was not necessary" (*WWTA*, 48). Although he employs minimalist techniques to do so, Carver is again exploring the problems of interpersonal communication, as in so many of his earlier stories.

The reason for the initial meeting of the woman and the baker seems innocent enough: She has gone to order a cake for her son Scotty's birthday. On the day of his birthday, though, Scotty is hit by a car and winds up in the emergency room. After several hours of waiting at the hospital, the boy's father goes home to take a bath, which symbolizes his need to be refreshed in order to face the ordeal of his son's medical problems. He muses that "it had been a good life till now. There had been work, fatherhood, family. The man had been lucky and happy. But fear made him want a bath" (*WWTA*, 49). His fear is exacerbated when, upon entering the house, he receives what he takes to be a crank phone call, in which someone says something about "'a cake that wasn't picked up'" (*WWTA*, 49). His wife had not told him about ordering the cake, having more important things to think of, and so the husband hangs up. Here, as in "Sixty Acres" and "Are You a Doctor?," the telephone functions as a "conduit for voices from the outside" (Clark, 242), and thus becomes a disruptive force. The baker calls back a bit later, forcing the husband to get out of the tub and making any kind of relief from thinking about his son's condition impossible. When the husband returns to the hospital the doctor arrives, but this only leads to another communication problem, since the medical practitioner does not use the same language as these laypersons. The parents want to know whether their son is in a coma, for example, but the doctor only replies "'I don't want to call it that'" (*WWTA*, 52), refusing to give them any concrete sense of the situation. The father intuits that the news is not good, and he wants to comfort his wife, but again Carver shows the difficulty he has in doing so. "He wanted to say something else. But there was no saying what it should be. He took her hand and put it in his lap. This made him feel better. It made him feel he was saying something" (*WWTA*, 53). This

kind of silent communication is the best that the couple can do, and
Carver indicates that it is perhaps the best anyone can do, even if the
message does not last for long.

Soon the mother decides to go home for a bath. She, too, feels the
need for "'something clean'" (*WWTA*, 55). As with her husband's
hoped-for bit of repose, however, her mood is shattered as she arrives
home by a ringing phone. The bath is obviously "a powerful healing
symbol," yet the telephone calls "deny Ann Weiss and her husband the
ritual healing that they most need" (Lehman, 52). She rushes to pick up
the receiver and anxiously asks the voice at the other end of the line
whether it is "'about Scotty'"; the voice replies, in the story's abrupt final
paragraph, "'It is about Scotty. . . . It has to do with Scotty, yes'"
(*WWTA*, 56). Just as the wife had not told her husband about ordering
the cake, so has the husband not told his wife about the phone call. She
therefore has no reason to suspect who is on the other end of the line,
and she assumes it's someone from the hospital. For her, then, the story
ends "inconclusively but ominously" (Cochrane, 85), because she doesn't
actually receive the bad news she expects to hear. She is left hanging
onto the telephone line for words of life or death. We know that the
voice on the other end is only the baker, though, and therefore no such
important communication is going to take place.

Nevertheless, the readers, to a certain degree, are left hanging along
with the wife. We also want to know what is going to happen to the boy,
and so we experience the same sense of anxiety and fear, a feeling that no
bath, even a completed one, is going to be able to eradicate. Here
Carver's minimalistic method achieves maximum impact on the reader.
As Ewing Campbell asserts, "in the empty space following the last full
stop, the reader involuntarily experiences the powerful emotions that
Ann would feel. The result is a story that exemplifies the Carveresque as
well as any story Carver ever wrote" (Campbell, 51). More precisely,
"The Bath" exemplifies the Carveresque mode of *What We Talk about
When We Talk about Love*, the minimalist style that made him famous. In
its rewritten version as "A Small, Good Thing," the style is very different,
as we shall see when we examine that later story in the chapter on
Cathedral.

"After the Denim"

The next story in the collection, "Tell the Women We're Going," is the
story that Altman used to close *Short Cuts*, but ultimately it is not one of
the more significant stories in the collection, presenting several of

Carver's standard themes in a rather typical, if somewhat horrific manner. "After the Denim" is a much more interesting piece, expressing aspects of Carver Country that are seldom touched on. The protagonists, James and Edith Packer, are unusual among Carver's characters for several reasons. As a couple, for example, they are fiercely devoted to each other (Towers, 37) and much happier than most of the pairs featured in the collection. More significantly, they are older than many of the characters in Carver's fiction. In fact, the story focuses on issues of aging, for during a night of bingo playing James Packer comes to realize that his life has passed him by, and that his world is far from being as solid as it might appear.

The story begins with the Packers being late to the bingo hall. When James discovers a van parked in his usual space he already feels the night taking a turn for the worse. "'I don't think I feel lucky now,'" he tells Edith. "'It's not lucky if you have to start out walking half a mile just to play'" (*WWTA*, 68). When they arrive in the hall, James receives a further shock and, as he sees it, indignity: the seats he and Edith normally occupy have been taken by a young, hippie-ish couple. He is incensed by what he sees as the younger couple's usurpation of his and Edith's bingo-playing space (as well as, he later finds out, his parking space). Edith tells him to calm down, and that "'they're not hurting anybody. They're just young, that's all'" (*WWTA*, 70). But James sees it as a personal affront; he might not be able to articulate his hurt, yet the reader comes to see that he feels the couple *is* hurting him precisely by being young, and by forcing him to acknowledge that he no longer is.[4]

James's animosity toward the young couple is increased throughout the evening, particularly when he witnesses the man playing a card he hasn't paid for. James wants to confront the man, but Edith again talks him out of it. During her trip to the restroom, though, he warns the young man that he is aware of his duplicity. James feels that he has asserted his manhood, but he is also "trembling" (*WWTA*, 73). His situation deteriorates further when Edith returns from the bathroom and informs him that she has begun "'spotting again'" (*WWTA*, 74), an indication that she has been beset by vaginal bleeding. James declares that "'this is the worst bingo night in history'" (*WWTA*, 74). The final indignity occurs when the denim-clad girl wins the night's big jackpot of $98. As the Packers are leaving the hall, James tells Edith to "'let those people get ahead of us'" because he "'can't stand to look at them'" (*WWTA*, 75).

For James, Edith's spotting, which seems to be getting worse as they arrive home, is equated with the "'lousy luck'" that characterized the

whole evening (*WWTA*, 76). He finds himself unable to sleep, and he
asks himself questions about his wife's illness, reflecting "bitterly upon
the unfairness of life" (Towers, 37): "Why not someone else? Why not
those people tonight? Why not all those people who sail through life as
free as birds? Why not them instead of Edith?" (*WWTA*, 77). He discovers that what bothered him the most about the young couple was
their "sauntering, arrogant gait" (*WWTA*, 77), indicative of their lack of
concern for the heartbreaks the future holds. "If only they knew," he
thinks. "If only someone would tell them. Just once! . . . If only they had
to sit with him in the waiting room! He'd tell them what to expect!
He'd set those floozies straight! He'd tell them what was waiting for you
after the denim and the earrings, after touching each other and cheating
at games" (*WWTA*, 77). James is concerned about his wife, but he is also
concerned about himself, for the evening has made him realize that he is,
in fact, after the denim, that is to say old. In a young man's world, he is
no longer a young man, nor is his wife a young woman.

At the end of the story, James is facing insomnia and he turns to his
needlepoint, something he took up to help cure his alcoholism. Carver
writes that he "stabbed at the eye [of the needle] with a length of blue
silk thread. Then he set to work—stitch after stitch—making believe he
was waving like the man on the keel" (*WWTA*, 78). The reference is to
an earlier description of a photograph that hangs on the wall of the
bingo parlor and shows "a boat that had turned over, a man standing on
the keel and waving" (*WWTA*, 69). James wants to think that he, too, is
in control, that he has escaped disaster, but he can only "make believe,"
for he now understands that in such a shipwreck he would be dragged
under. He also knows that needlepoint, his only defense against the void,
is not going to provide much protection. "After the Denim" may not be
one of Carver's better-known stories, but it is one of the most effective in
this collection, and a very good example of how Carver can be touching
without becoming sentimental.

"So Much Water So Close to Home"

The second of the *Furious Seasons* stories to appear in a revised form in
this volume, "So Much Water So Close to Home," despite its same title,
is very much changed. Surely this was one of the texts Carver had in
mind when he stated that his revisions often resulted in two entirely different stories (*Con*, 187); as with the change from "The Fling" to
"Sacks," this story has been severely minimalized. The second "So Much

Water" is half the length of the first, and long paragraphs and sentences are divided into many smaller ones. Carver has gone through the story and replaced long terms or phrases with shorter ones, cutting descriptive adjectives throughout the text. Once again, he has changed the internal narration—Claire's telling us what Stuart told her—to the present tense, and has added a healthy sprinkling of "I say"s and "he says"es. Finally, Carver has omitted entire passages of background material. In the minimalized version of "So Much Water," we learn much less about Claire, our narrator, than we did in the longer, *Furious Seasons* story. Carver eliminates many details of Claire's reactions to her husband's behavior, of her thoughts about their past relationship, and of the physical separation she imposes between him and her, making it harder for the reader to understand her motivation. The last line of the first version's opening paragraph—Claire's statement that "Something has come between us though he would like to believe otherwise" (*FS*, 41)—sets up, even sums up, much of the emotional conflict that is to be examined in the story, and so its deletion here leaves the reader less sure about the direction in which the story is headed.

Not only does the first version provide a fuller understanding of the main characters, but it also presents detailed pictures of some of the minor characters who are all but eliminated in the revision. Carver dramatically redraws his portrait of the murder victim, for example. It might seem like a minor detail, but there is a world of difference in the reader's perception when a character is called "Susan Miller" rather than "the body," as Carver calls the dead girl in this later version. The *Furious Seasons* version also contains a description of a television news report in which the girl's parents go into the funeral home to identify her body. Through this scene, Susan and her family come alive for the reader, who is able to identify with them as Claire does. When all we are told is that "the body has been identified, claimed" (*WWTA*, 84), however, we fail to reach this sort of understanding. Therefore we also fail to understand fully Claire's motivation in attending Susan's funeral. All of these omissions diminish our understanding of what is actually going on and, consequently, lessen our concern for the people involved.[5]

The most radical and significant alterations, however, occur in the story's ending. In the first version, Claire returns from the funeral and, when Stuart attempts to initiate physical contact with her, she rebuffs him, and even stomps on his foot. At the end of the story, still not understanding his actions or accepting his explanations, she says to him, "'For God's sake, Stuart, she was only a child'" (*FS*, 61). Her sense of continuing sympathy for Susan and her further separation from Stuart is perfectly in keeping with her previous actions and her decision not to give in to male domination, even if threatened with violence. As Ewing Campbell surmises, "In this version there can be no reconciliation between Stuart and Claire" (Campbell, 39). In the second version of the story, though, when Stuart attempts to initiate sexual activity, Claire allows herself to be symbolically raped. Her comment "I can't hear a thing with so much water going" (*WWTA*, 88)—although there is literally no water running in the story—clearly recalls the rape and murder of the other girl. She even goes so far as to take an active role in the violation: "'That's right,' I say, finishing the buttons myself. 'Before Dean comes. Hurry'" (*WWTA*, 88). Claire's reaction here comes quite unexpectedly. Perhaps she "sees sex as the means of a desperate and futile effort to hang on to life" (May, 79), but her reaction, like that of the wife in "I Could See the Smallest Things," demonstrates her willingness to return to the status quo, to "spin her own web of denial."[6] This closure thus indicates that her worst nightmare has come true, that the thing that should have dramatically changed her life won't have any lasting impact at all. As Ewing Campbell asserts, "her complicity with Stuart's sexual advances can be seen as yielding to his dominance and attempting to reconstruct on an unstable basis a world that has been reduced to chaos" (Campbell, 40). Her chances for success in such an endeavor are indeed limited.

What the reader of this version of "So Much Water So Close to Home" cannot understand is what causes Claire to change her mind about Stuart, why she wants to submit and allow herself, at least symbolically, to be killed. In this version of the story "there is no psychological movement in the paralysis of the couple" (Arias-Misson, 627), yet Claire's motivation for accepting, even welcoming, such a situation is left unclear. The violence that is done to Claire through Susan Miller, her "nightmare double" (Stull "RC" 1985, 240), seems to be accepted here, whereas it was openly rejected in the first version. There can be no doubt that in this rendition "So Much Water So Close to Home" is still quite an effective story, and that, being more despairing in both style and content, it better complements the rest of the stories in *What We Talk about When We Talk about Love*. Some readers have even expressed a preference for "the crisper version, whose ending is also more unsettling" (Stull 1984, 82). Once again, though, I would argue that Carver has gone a bit too far in his reductions. The fact that "the meaning must take shape in the mind of the reader" (Dickstein, 509) is indeed one of the strengths of

Carver's implosive style, but Carver has given us so few clues here that connections can barely be made. Of the *Furious Seasons* stories reprinted in this volume, "So Much Water So Close to Home" seems to have suffered more than the others in its truncation. Carver later came to share similar sentiments, and ultimately chose to stand by the first version, as we shall see in the next chapter.

"The Third Thing That Killed My Father Off"

In contrast to "So Much Water So Close to Home," of the five stories from *Furious Seasons* that reappear in altered forms in *What We Talk about When We Talk about Love* this story, a revision of "Dummy," probably benefits the most from its changes. The prose has been made much tighter with the elimination of descriptive passages. As with the other minimalized stories, the paragraph and sentence lengths have been reduced; long words have been exchanged for shorter ones. In terms of the minimalization of character and exposition, the changes are much less dramatic here than in the other transformations we have examined. Carver does eliminate some of the more obvious expository statements, and he does condense some of the background scenes, but he always leaves enough for the reader to fully understand what is going on. There are many times where, after eliminating a lengthy passage, Carver gets the same message across with one crystalline image, that is, by showing instead of telling. There are even a few places where Carver adds material to the text. The emotions that drive "Dummy" remain fully evident in "The Third Thing That Killed My Father Off," but they are indeed presented more sharply and effectively.

The second version of this story once again veers most dramatically from its original in the final paragraphs. The emphasis at the end of "Dummy" shifts away from the father and onto the son, our narrator. He notes that, "For myself, I knew I wouldn't forget the sight of that arm emerging out of the water. Like some kind of mysterious and terrible signal, it seemed to herald the misfortune that dogged our family in the coming years" (*FS*, 26). The emphasis at the end of "The Third Thing That Killed My Father Off," though, as should be expected given the new title, remains on the narrator's father and his reaction to the arm. The story now concludes:

> Just like Dummy, he wasn't the same man anymore. That arm coming
> up and going back down in the water, it was like so long to good times

and hello to bad. Because it was nothing but that all the years after
Dummy drowned himself in that dark water.

    Is that what happens when a friend dies? Bad luck for the people
he left behind?

    But as I said, Pearl Harbor and having to move back to his dad's
place didn't do dad one bit of good, either. (*WWTA*, 103)

Although a markedly different ending, this one is equally effective. The
listing of the other two factors that contributed to the death of the narrator's father recalls the new version's opening paragraph, and thus it
brings the story full circle. There is an equal sense of conclusion here,
even if it is an entirely different one. The son's role has clearly been
downplayed in the second version, but that is the only part of the story
that has been so slighted. All of the key points of the original story have
been retained, and usually presented in a more pointed form. For these
reasons, "The Third Thing That Killed My Father Off" is the superior
story of the two.

"The Calm"

The next story, "A Serious Talk," is not one of the strongest pieces in the
collection, although it does reinforce Carver's major theme of the problems caused by an inability to communicate; the story also upholds the
tone of the volume through hints of violence and a sense of menace.
There is a marked change in tone in the ensuing tale, "The Calm," as the
title indicates. This story presents an unnamed first-person narrator who
tells us about a crucial event in his past. In this case, the setting for the
revelatory moment was a barbershop. The narrator was getting his hair
cut, and there were some other men waiting, including Charles, a bank
guard, and Albert, an older man. When the barber asked Charles
whether he got a deer while hunting, Charles replied "'I did and I
didn't'" (*WWTA*, 116), explaining that, through the incompetence of his
hungover son, they had only wounded a deer and, despite trailing it, had
lost it when night fell. Charles's narrative, which details senseless and
horrific cruelty, thus aligns him with the barbaric doe-chasers who
harassed Mr. Harold in "Pastoral." Taking great offense at the barbarity
of the story, Albert told Charles, "'You ought to be out there right now
looking for that deer instead of in here getting a haircut'" (*WWTA*,
119). Anger rose between the two men, and the barber, representative of
order, had to work hard to prevent a fistfight from breaking out. Both

men subsequently left. The violence of the deer hunt was thus reenacted in the violence of the barber shop, and the narrator later learned that the presence of death suffused both encounters: After Albert left the barber explained that the man was "'about dead from emphysema" (*WWTA*, 120), the same kind of slow, lingering death that faced the wounded deer. This fact fully accounts for Albert's empathizing with the dying animal and cursing the malicious hunter.

Up to this point, then, the story's title seems ironic, for there is nothing calm about it. The entire focus of the story changes in the last paragraphs, however, as the narrator explains why he is telling us this story, why the haircut has proven to be one of the decisive moments in his life. "That was in Crescent City, California, up near the Oregon border," he says. "I left soon after. But today I was thinking of that place, of Crescent City, and of how I was trying out a new life there with my wife, and how, in the barber's chair that morning, I had made up my mind to go. I was thinking today about the calm I felt when I closed my eyes and let the barber's fingers move through my hair, the sweetness of those fingers, the hair already starting to grow" (*WWTA*, 121). It was through hearing the story of the hunt and witnessing the near-violence of the shouting match that the narrator came to see the problems in his own relationship and resolved to leave, perhaps before committing an act of violence himself. Looking back on these events, he sees that his decision to leave his wife and his achievement of a sense of calm occurred simultaneously, and there is no indication that he regrets the step he has taken. On the contrary, it seems that what he heard and saw made him "better able to bring order into his life" (Facknitz 1986, 290). More than anything, he recalls the sense of freedom, the feeling of casting off problems, that he experienced while the barber's fingers were running through his hair. The story itself does add a bit of calm to the disasters that permeate the rest of the volume, offering a truly rare moment of respite in an otherwise bleak landscape.

"Everything Stuck to Him"

The next story in the collection, "Popular Mechanics," is a revised version of "Mine" from *Furious Seasons*. Having been reprinted in several anthologies, it has gained a certain amount of acclaim, but I still find it to be one of the weakest efforts in Carver's repertoire. The following story, "Everything Stuck to Him," is a revised version of "Distance," and is the last of the five *Furious Seasons* stories to appear transfigured in the later collection. Carver has again minimalized the story somewhat. Like "The Third Thing That Killed My Father Off," however, the more concise version might be, for that reason, more effective. As in other revisions, Carver pares away needless words and phrases. He also makes some substantive deletions. Most significantly, a lengthy discussion of the mating habits of Canadian geese is omitted. In the earlier version, the young man explains that Canadian Geese "only marry once. They choose a mate early in life, and then the two of them stay together always" (FS, 30). His wife asks him if he's ever "killed one of those marriages" (FS, 30) by shooting one of the partners, and he admits that he has. He tells her that he always felt a little bit guilty about it, and shot the mate as well if he could, but he explains that "there are all kinds of contradictions in life. You can't think about all the contradictions" (FS, 31). Because we already know from the frame of the tale that the couple's marriage did not last forever, we look at this scene with a sense of irony and foreshadowing. Its omission in "Everything Stuck to Him" does reduce our appreciation of the situation somewhat, but not enough to make the story any less clear than it was before.

The most dramatic changes occur, once again, in the story's final line. What had been "They leaned on each other and laughed about it until tears came, while outside everything froze, for a while anyway" (FS, 36), is now "They had leaned on each other and laughed until the tears had come, while everything else—the cold, and where he'd go in it—was outside, for a while anyway" (WWTA, 135). The additional information in the second version shifts our focus back to the narrator of the tale, who is again reminded that this idyllic scene was fragile and destined to be short-lived. He would indeed be heading into the cold before too much longer. The narrator is remembering a moment at which he achieved a sense of stability, but he is doing so only to lament its subsequent loss. The new title, "Everything Stuck to Him," which refers explicitly to the breakfast plate he knocks into his lap, is an ironic reversal of the more straightforward title "Distance," but it has almost the same meaning, for it emphasizes how everything—his wife and daughter especially—did *not* stick to him, but instead became marked by their distance.

"What We Talk about When We Talk about Love"

The title story is the collection's longest and undoubtedly its greatest achievement, as well as being a fitting climax to the volume. Although its plot is rather thin, several of the obsessions that have run through the collection—the difficulty of sustaining relationships, the effect of alcoholism as a contributing factor to that difficulty, the problem of communication—are given their most extensive treatment. As the four characters (the narrator, Nick; his wife, Laura; their friend Mel McGinnis, a cardiologist; and his wife, Terri) sit around the table drinking gin, Carver is able to turn the question of love in several different directions. For this reason, more than one critic has likened the story's situation to Plato's *Symposium*,[7] which does indeed seem to be the model for the dialogue. Nevertheless, "the relative articulateness of these characters by no means enables them to reach a satisfactory conclusion" (Saltzman, 118). The only resolution reached in this version of the symposium is that we really have no idea what we talk about when we talk about love.

As the story opens, Terri, Mel's second wife, states that Ed, "the man she lived with before she lived with Mel[,] loved her so much he tried to kill her" (*WWTA*, 138). Mel argues, however, that she cannot really call Ed's emotions love. Having been a divinity student before he became a doctor, Mel feels that true love must contain a spiritual dimension. He argues that "'the kind of love I'm talking about is [an absolute]. The kind of love I'm talking about, you don't try to kill people'" (*WWTA*, 139). Terri's continuing insistence that what Ed felt was love only serves to anger Mel, and we begin to see signs of strain in their own relationship. To show what real love is, Mel tells the story of an old couple he had treated in the hospital. While recovering from a terrible car accident, the husband became depressed because, due to his bandages, "'he couldn't turn his goddamn head and *see* his goddamned wife'" (*WWTA*, 151). This old couple symbolizes for Mel what the old couple in the gazebo meant for Holly (Saltzman, 119), a sign of stable and long-lasting love. During his narration, however, he and Terri begin to argue more openly. When Terri kids Mel about sounding drunk, he quietly responds, "'Just shut up for once in your life. . . . Will you do me a favor and do that for a minute?'" (*WWTA*, 146). Mel begins to explain about the old couple's injuries, how they had only lived because they were wearing their seat belts, and Terri interrupts to say that Mel's story is a public service message. Mel doesn't find her jest the least bit funny. He is concerned with the true meaning of love, and he presses the point about the length of this older couple's commitment because, as he points out, all four of this symposium's participants have been married more than once. As the story points out, "the greatest obstacle to any ideal love turns out to be the transitoriness of love" (Saltzman, 118). Mel notes that "'sometimes I have a hard time accounting for the fact that I must have loved my first wife too'" (*WWTA*, 144) and he reminds the other couple that they "'both loved other people before [they] met each other'" (*WWTA*, 145). He even goes on to say that, should any of them die, he feels it wouldn't be long before the widowed person would remarry. This doesn't sit well with Terri, naturally, and the tension mounts.

Counterpoised to the disintegrating relationship of Mel and Terri are Nick and Laura, still-glowing newlyweds who, "in addition to being in love, . . . like each other and enjoy one another's company" (*WWTA*, 141). When Laura is asked whether she would call Ed's feelings toward Terri love, for example, she says, "'who can judge anyone else's situation?,'" and Nick tells us that "I touched the back of Laura's hand. She gave me a quick smile. I picked up Laura's hand. It was warm, the nails polished, perfectly manicured. I encircled the broad wrist with my fingers, and I held her" (*WWTA*, 139). Such physical intimacy continues throughout the story, although Terri tells them that they're "'still on the honeymoon'" and must "'wait awhile'" (143) to see what married life is really like. She seems to be making fun of them, yet her "remarks contain a hint of regret; she would like very much, it seems, to receive gestures of affection like those between Nick and Laura" (Carlin, 91). They are still in the first throes of love, whereas her marriage to Mel seems to have become stale.

At the end of the story, the gin is all gone and the four people, who had been planning to go eat at a new restaurant, seem exhausted and reluctant to move. Terri says that she will "'put out some cheese and crackers'" (*WWTA*, 153), but she makes no move to do so. Suddenly the story's tension level increases dramatically. Nick states that "I could hear my heart beating. I could hear everyone's heart. I could hear the human noise we sat there making, not one of us moving, not even when the room went dark" (*WWTA*, 153–54). As with other Carver stories of menace, such as "The Bath," the final note here is one of suspension, of tension threatening to explode but not yet ignited. The conversation began in the light of afternoon, but the participants fall silent in the dark of night and the story ends "in anxious isolation, enervation, and stasis" (Stull "BH" 1985, 2). Although one critic has asserted that "these moments together, deeply imbued with shared sensibilities, make up for the antagonisms, the regrets, the flirtations, [and] the spilled gin" (Saltzman, 120), such comments seem to miss the mark. Carver's use of the word "noise" in the passage indicates that, rather than having achieved some kind of peace beyond words, the four talkers have reached a point where no communication is effective, where nothing can be heard. The seemingly imminent explosion may be the one between Mel and Terri, but Nick and Laura are necessarily dragged into it and implicated as well,[8] since the newly married couple cannot avoid seeing themselves as Mel and Terri in a few years. As with all of Carver's first-person narratives, furthermore, we must ask ourselves who Nick is telling the story to, and when. The implication here is that he is fondly remembering that evening as a time when he and Laura shared a closeness that perhaps no longer exists.

Ultimately, the answer to Mel's question "'What do any of us really know about love?'" appears to be "not very much." A humorous digression in the middle of the story underscores this point. Mel, whose definition of love is based on "the chivalric code" (Saltzman, 117), asserts that he would like to have been a knight, because armor made it harder to get hurt. The narrator tells him, however, that sometimes the knights would die because they got too hot in their suits or because they fell off their horses and didn't have the energy to stand up, whereupon they could be trampled by their own horses or killed by rivals. What follows is a subtle but telling bit of dialogue:

> "That's right," Mel said. "Some vassal would come along and spear the bastard in the name of love. Or whatever the fuck it was they fought over in those days."
> "Same things we fight over today," Terri said.
> Laura said, "Nothing's changed." (*WWTA*, 149–50)

When it comes to talking about love—and understanding what we mean when we do so—Carver indicates that we are still in the dark ages.

"One More Thing"

As the title of this final story indicates, it is something of an epilogue or postscript, reprising "the fundamental plight of distance" (Saltzman, 120) and the picture of love's potential violence that have been developed in almost all of the stories. Its opening line sums up the entire plot of the story: "L.D.'s wife, Maxine, told him to get out the night she came home from work and found L.D. drunk again and being abusive to Rae, their fifteen-year-old" (*WWTA*, 155). The situation deteriorates from this point, until one of the characters (perhaps adding fuel to the antiminimalist fire) accurately calls it "another tragedy in a long line of low-rent tragedies" (*WWTA*, 156).

The focus of the story is clearly on L.D. and his reactions to his wife's order. At first, he becomes violent. The narrator notes that "L.D. had no intention of going anywhere. He looked from Maxine to the jar of pickles that had been on the table since lunch. He picked up the jar and pitched it through the kitchen window" (*WWTA*, 157). When Maxine threatens to call the police, L.D. calms down and claims that he's more than happy to get out of that "'nuthouse'" (*WWTA*, 157). Reluctantly, he begins to pack, seeking to revenge himself on Maxine by taking everything he can manage to stuff into a single suitcase and a shaving bag, including "the soap dish and the glass from over the sink and the fingernail clippers and her eyelash curlers" (*WWTA*, 158). He lingers over the doorway, expecting Maxine to call him back, but she continues to assert that she never wants to see him again. She is clearly right to feel this way—L.D. is in many ways a worthless drunk who brings nothing to the family and takes much away from it—yet Carver also manages to align our sympathies with L.D. We see the fears and insecurities that have led him to this position, and we feel for him in his effort to maintain what little stability he knows, however doomed that effort may be.

While removing all of the familiar objects from the home, L.D. also takes the ashtray, an action that clearly recalls the protagonist of "A Serious Talk." As in that story, furthermore, the lack of communication between husband and wife has created the rift whose end result Carver presents. The ending of "One More Thing" reinforces this fact:

> He said, "I just want to say one more thing."
> But then he could not think what it could possibly be. (*WWTA*, 159)

Once again, the titular act of communication fails to be effected; the protagonist is left stranded and needing desperately to communicate, but being entirely unable to do so. He "is capable only of childish retorts and gestures of impotent rage" (Cochrane, 80). This inability to communicate is the problem that has plagued so many of the couples in this collection. Once again, then, Carver confirms the theme of the volume: that "it ought to make us feel ashamed when we talk like we know what we're talking about when we talk about love" (*WWTA*, 146). At the same time, however, the story demonstrates that Carver himself does indeed know what he is talking about, for "One More Thing" is another brilliant depiction of love gone wrong.

Conclusion

Perhaps the most quoted quip concerning *What We Talk about When We Talk about Love*, and for good reason, comes from Donald Newlove's review of the collection; he writes that the book includes "seventeen tales of Hopelessville, its marriages and alcoholic wreckage, told in a prose as sparingly clear as a fifth of iced Smirnoff" (Newlove, 77). Newlove here highlights the main features, both of matter and manner, that unify the collection and give it a great deal of cumulative impact. By the end of the volume, having seen so much despair and so few spots of promise, we are as fatigued and numbed as the characters themselves. In these stories, then, Carver brilliantly weds his minimalistic style to his dispiriting themes. About the end of "One More Thing," for example, Hamilton E. Cochrane notes that "this conclusion reflects the unfinished business that is L.D.'s life. L.D. can make no sense of it—can make no connections, draw no conclusions—and the fragmentary and inconclusive form of the story itself seems to reinforce this" (Cochrane, 80). This marriage of form and content marks the style that Carver would become best known for, and that would so influence younger writers.

Many critics, particularly ones who don't like him, continue to take their measure of Carver from *What We Talk about When We Talk about Love*, which is, indeed, the finest book that minimalism has to offer. Yet, as Jay McInerney has noted, "Carver's career as a story writer and prose stylist had several distinct phases; only his [third] collection, *What We Talk about When We Talk about Love*, can really be called minimalism—a conscious attempt to leave almost everything out."[9] Carver himself noted that it "had been in many ways a watershed book for me, but it was a book I didn't want to duplicate or write again" (*NHP*, 127), and, following *What We Talk about When We Talk about Love*, Carver's stories did indeed change again, becoming broader, fuller, and more generous. We have passed through the narrowest point of the hourglass of Carver's minimalism—as exemplified by the truncations of the *Furious Seasons* stories—and we are now ready to broaden the form again as we turn to *Fires* and, especially, *Cathedral*.

Chapter Six
Carver the Reviser: *Fires*

Although *What We Talk about When We Talk about Love* was the volume that catapulted Carver into the literary spotlight, he soon became dissatisfied with the extreme minimalism of that collection. "I knew I'd gone as far [in reducing] as I could or wanted to go," he told one interviewer, "cutting everything down to the marrow, not just to the bone.[1] Any further in that direction and I'd be at a dead end—writing and publishing stuff I wouldn't want to read myself, and that's the truth" (*Con*, 44). He expressed much the same sentiments to other interviewers as well, telling Larry McCaffery and Sinda Gregory that "some of the stories were becoming too attenuated" (*Con*, 101), and commenting to William L. Stull that "it got to where I wanted to pare everything down and maybe pare too much. Then I guess I must have reacted against that" (*Con*, 182). The first fruit of Carver's reaction, his decision to return to a fuller style, was the story "Cathedral," which would become the title story of his next major collection. *Fires: Essays, Poems, Stories* is another sign of his new aesthetic.

In his afterword to the volume, Carver explains that Noel Young of Capra Press had approached him about republishing *Furious Seasons*, which had gone out of print. Instead of simply reprinting the earlier collection, however, Carver decided to rework the stories and to include a few newer ones. "I like to mess around with my stories," he wrote in the afterword, later retitled "On Rewriting." "I'd rather tinker with a story after writing it, and then tinker some more, changing this, changing that, than have to write the story in the first place" (*NHP*, 108). Such revising is surely not unusual for writers; what was rather unusual, however, was Carver's unwillingness to stop revising a piece even after it had been published.[2] We have seen this tendency, of course, in analyzing the stories that appeared in different forms in *Furious Seasons* and *What We Talk about When We Talk about Love*. When he came to assemble the stories for inclusion in *Fires*, then, Carver wasn't sure which versions to use. Ultimately he chose texts that, although reworked again, have much more in common with the fuller original versions than with their minimalized forms. Carver stated that he preferred these versions of the stories because they were "more in accord with the way I am writing stories these days" (*NHP*, 109), that is, the stories in *Cathedral*. As we look at some of the stories in *Fires*, therefore, we can trace the changes in Carver's style that led to his most mature work. He may still be a minimalist here, but not in the exaggerated way he had been in the previous volume.

"Distance"

The first story in *Fires* is particularly instructive. "Distance" is actually making its third straight appearance in one of Carver's collections, having been published under this title in *Furious Seasons* and as "Everything Stuck to Him" in *What We Talk about When We Talk about Love*. This version varies significantly from both of the previous texts, however, incorporating aspects of each. One the one hand, many of the superfluous words and descriptive phrases that Carver had eliminated in the second version remain eliminated in the third. On the other hand, much of the content that had also been excised is now reinstated. Most obviously, several long passages that were completely deleted in the minimalization process have been, more or less, fully restored. The tale of the ever-faithful Canada geese, for example, has been put back in, providing the reader with a fuller sense of the story's meaning. The scene of reconciliation toward the end of the story, which was greatly reduced in "Everything Stuck to Him," has also been returned to its meatier form. The elimination of such passages in the minimalized version of the story made it more difficult for the reader to understand the dynamics of the situation, and here Carver seems to be acknowledging and rectifying that situation. Although he does opt for the final lines as they appeared in "Everything Stuck to Him," by and large, and in the most significant places, Carver chooses the original, fuller version of the story. Ultimately, beneath the surface, this "Distance" is more similar to the original "Distance" than it is to "Everything Stuck to Him."

By examining this text, then, we can see how Carver combined elements of both his early and middle periods, thus arriving at the beginning of his mature style. The result is the best of both worlds, and this version of "Distance" is probably the most effective, for it is able to combine the more fully developed content of the first version with the more sharply pared-down style of the second. In this instance, the more Carver tinkered with the story the better it got, as Carver would later acknowledge by selecting the *Fires* version of "Distance" for inclusion in *Where I'm Calling From.*

"The Cabin"

The next story in the collection, "The Lie," appears virtually the same as the text in *Furious Seasons*. There are a few minor changes, but none of any substance. The same holds true for most of "The Cabin," a rewritten version of "Pastoral" from *Furious Seasons*. Many of the changes here, like those in "The Lie," are substitutions or rearrangements of individual words or phrases. At the end of the story, however, there is a major change. Not only is the writing itself entirely different, but so is the overall impression. The first version, as I noted earlier, ends on a note of total and unremitting despair, reminiscent of Jack London's "To Build a Fire." Here, though, the story ends with a much more optimistic outlook, "an outcome truer to Carver's mature style" (Stull 1988, 466). Following the encounter with the barbaric hunters, Mr. Harrold (Carver has changed the spelling of his name) returns to the lodge, only to find all of its lights on. The occurrence is "mysterious and impenetrable to him" (*F*, 155). He thinks of fleeing, but he gathers up the strength to reenter his cabin, where he finds that someone has built a fire in his stove. Here "The Cabin" directly counters the "To Build a Fire" parallels that "Pastoral" had called to mind. The story ends with Mr. Harrold in front of the fire: "He let the warmth gradually come back into his body. He began to think of home, of getting back there before dark" (*F*, 156). This sense of an impending return to normalcy and order is unthinkable in the first version, and the widening of Carver's vision here is a prelude of things to come in *Cathedral*. It is true that Mr. Harrold has been similarly unmanned in both stories—as seen by his having lost his fishing rod, which he had likened to a medieval knight's lance earlier in the story and which is clearly phallic in nature—but his reaction to the situation contrasts sharply in the different versions; whereas in the earlier version he felt that all hope had been lost, in the later one he feels that hope has in fact been restored, which was his motivation in going to the woodland cabin in the first place.[3] The change of title is instructive as well. The first version emphasizes the menacing side of nature, since the pastoral ideal has been invalidated and the landscape is reminiscent of London's Yukon, while the second version emphasizes the refuge that is to be found indoors, in a cabin that is warmed by human contact. Here we can clearly see the transitional nature of *Fires*, for Carver is moving away from the bleakness of *What We Talk about When We Talk about Love* and toward *Cathedral*'s generosity of both language and spirit.

"Harry's Death"

"Harry's Death" is the first of the two new stories in this volume, and it is a most affecting work. It tells us virtually nothing about either Harry or his death, but it does reveal quite a bit about the narrator, a friend and coworker of the recently deceased Harry. The subtitle tells us that the time and place of the story are "Mazatlan, Mexico—three months later" (*F*, 157), and the narrator's opening statements pick up on the oddness of the location: "Everything has changed since Harry's death. Being down here, for instance. Who'd have thought it, only three short months ago, that I'd be down here in Mexico and poor Harry dead and buried? Harry! Dead and buried—but not forgotten" (*F*, 157). Through the first part of the story, the narrator genuinely seems to be grieving for Harry, who was probably murdered. He notes that "I couldn't go to work that day when I got the news. I was just too torn up" (*F*, 157). Instead he goes to the bar where he and Harry used to hang out. The other regulars have also gathered there, although "none of us had much to say to each other. What could we say?" (*F*, 159).

Later on, however, the reader begins to sense some ambivalence on the narrator's part. He opts not to view the body at the funeral home, for example, and ultimately doesn't attend the funeral. What he does do, though, is comfort the bereaved daughter, "Little" Judith; at first he merely helps her take care of the funeral details, but then he begins to date her in earnest. Several months later they go to Los Angeles to look at a boat that Harry had inherited and that he had signed over to Judith so that his ex-wife couldn't claim it. The narrator notes that "Little Judith and I just looked at it and then looked at each other. It's seldom anything turns out better than you expected it to be. Usually it's the other way around" (*F*, 163). It is only in light of the story's conclusion, however, that the irony of this passage, and of the story's opening paragraph, becomes apparent. In the penultimate paragraph, the narrator rather absentmindedly informs us that "even Little Judith is out of the picture now, gone in a way that is tragic, and still has me wondering. It was somewhere off the Baja coast that it happened: Little Judith, who couldn't swim a stroke, came up missing" (*F*, 163). The police are also wondering about the circumstances of her death. They question the narrator, but he is able to convince them that her demise was purely accidental. The reader is not so easily convinced, however, since the narrator's lack of grief for Judith seems in direct contrast to his great initial grief over Harry's death.

In the final paragraph, the reader comes to question the narrator's motivations even further, for he appears quite satisfied with his present position. Not only has he gotten the boat, which Judith presumably left to him—"for luckily we'd been married just before leaving San Francisco" (*F*, 163)—but he has gotten it without the further encumbrance of Little Judith herself. Once again, the narrator seems to have stumbled upon something better than he could have possibly imagined—unless, of course, killing off Harry and Judith so that he could get the boat had been his plan all along. As the story ends, he is preparing for an extended cruise. His final comment, "sometimes I think I was born to be a rover" (*F*, 163), shows the hardness of his exterior, his lack of concern for others, specifically Harry and Judith. What the narrator really admired about Harry, it turns out, was his sharpness, his ability to "work it around so that in any deal he came up smelling like a rose" (*F*, 158). At the end of the story, then, we see the narrator's contentment and sense of accomplishment at having out-Harryed Harry. In this way, he comes across as something of a monster, his calmness belying his evil nature. Carver's use of first-person narration is brilliantly executed here, and he adds another intriguing character to his canon of self-revealing narrators. It is unfortunate that "Harry's Death" is not more widely known, for it is a finely crafted tale indeed, reminding us of the debt Carver owes to Poe and O. Henry that is not noticed often enough in critics' readings of his tales.

"The Pheasant"

The other original story in the collection, "The Pheasant," is also deserving of a wider audience than it has received. In many ways, it is a typical Carver story, focusing on a couple at the moment they are breaking up. The dissolution of their relationship again results from too much alcohol and too little communication. In the opening scene—which takes place, like most of the story, in a car traveling between two cities in California—we discover that Shirley Lennart has decided to leave Gerald Weber, whom she has given up "as a bad investment" (*F*, 165). In the next paragraph we discover that the feeling is mutual, that he feels their trip "had been a mistake" (*F*, 165). The sense of foreboding becomes even darker after their car hits and kills a pheasant, especially since Gerald knows that he has struck the animal deliberately. From this point on, the story takes a more analytical turn. As Arthur A. Brown explains, Gerald "uses the pheasant's death to discover his own identity."[4] He wants to investigate his actions and asks Shirley a series of philosophical questions, which she largely refuses to answer. To his question "'How well do you know me?,'" for example, she responds, "'I don't have any idea what you mean'" (F, 167), thus emphasizing their communication problems.

The further they go on their car trip, moreover, the further their relationship falls apart. Shirley becomes "sick of this whole thing. It was too bad she'd agreed to go with him. . . . She didn't like people who were forever trying to find themselves, the brooding, introspective bit" (F, 168). As for Gerald, he feels the sudden illumination of an epiphany later in the story. Carver, using the exact language of the line from Chekhov that he had tacked to the wall over his typewriter, writes that "Something became clear to him them. Partly, he supposed later, it was a result of the look of bored indifference she turned on him, and partly it was a consequence of his own state of mind. But he suddenly understood that he no longer had any values. No frame of reference, was the phrase that ran through his mind" (F, 169). When they stop for something to eat at a roadside cafe, they inevitably go their separate ways. Gerald wants to part as friends, reminding Shirley that "'We had some good times, right?'" (F, 170), but she refuses him even that much consolation. Instead she says that he was nothing to her, curses him, and then slaps his face. Gerald walks off into the sunrise, but certainly not in the uplifting tradition of the Hollywood hero.

What is unique about "The Pheasant" in Carver's canon, however, is embodied in that name: Hollywood. The characters in this story, rather than being Carver's typical blue-collar workers of Oregon and Washington, are, at least peripherally, members of the Hollywood jet set. In their jadedness and dissipation they are remotely akin to the valueless characters of Bret Easton Ellis's *Less Than Zero*, one of the most commercially successful minimalist novels. As such, many of their concerns are atypical for the characters of Carver's oeuvre, although they are quite normal in and of themselves. Gerald and Shirley's trip, for example, is intended to take them from Hollywood to Carmel, where Shirley has a beach house. When Gerald first met Shirley, we also learn, he "was just out of graduate studies at UCLA, a drama major—wasn't the city filled with them though—and, except for university theater productions, an actor without a salaried role to his credit" (F, 168). He saw in Shirley a golden opportunity, for he had always "wanted the kind of life he imagined she could give him. She had money and she had connections" (F, 168). For the next several years, then, he had been essentially kept by the woman, who was 12 years his senior. As the story opens, however, it

is "two days before his thirtieth birthday, [and] he'd felt at loose ends"
(*F*, 165). He is no longer suited for the partying life-style; rather, he
wants to think and explore, and, as Shirley disdainfully puts it, to find
himself. She, on the other hand, wishes simply to continue losing herself,
avoiding reality in favor of Hollywood's images.

Carver brilliantly emphasizes this point by including a number of the-
atrical terms in the final confrontation at the roadside cafe. Gerald, for
example, "felt as if they were doing a scene and this was the fifth or sixth
take" (*F*, 170). At the end he says, "'I suppose I'll say goodbye then,
Shirley. If that isn't too melodramatic'" (*F*, 170). The scene *is* rather
melodramatic, however, what with the cursing and slapping. In the
story's surprise ending, furthermore, Carver provides an audience for the
couple. Their argument is taking place in the parking lot outside the
cafe, while inside the patrons and waitresses are looking on, "at first
shocked and then amused with the scene" (*F*, 170), as good theatergoers
should be. As the story concludes, Carver shifts away from Gerald and
Shirley altogether to focus on this audience. A truck driver, for example,
contends that Gerald "'should turn around and just knock hell out of
her'" (*F*, 171). Gerald had already "knocked hell" out of the pheasant,
however, and that gratuitous act seemed only to have triggered his more
introspective side. In some ways, then, he is like the pheasant, while in
other ways Shirley is; all three of them have been given their lumps. The
story's themes thus turn out to be typically Carveresque, although the
characters and settings here show the range of his abilities beyond the
narrow scope that critics generally proscribe for him.

"Where Is Everyone?"

The expansive trend evident throughout *Fires* is nowhere more apparent
than in this story, which is a revision of "Mr. Coffee and Mr. Fixit" from
What We Talk about When We Talk about Love. Not only are sentences
combined and paragraphs consolidated in this new version, but the story
as a whole is considerably longer than it was before, and includes a great
deal more information than appears in the first version. Rather than
being attenuated, the tale is now fleshed out. As Marc Chenetier
explains, the longer story "makes plain a number of details that remain
quite puzzling in the shortened text" (Chenetier, 179). In the present
version, for example, there is a lengthy discussion of how the narrator's
children are handling the fractured familial situation. He notes that
"they fattened on it. They liked being able to call the shots, having the

upper hand while we bungled along letting them work on our guilt" (*F*, 175–76). The reader also finds out that Mike, the couple's son, has been abusive to his philandering mother, Cynthia; he had locked her out of the house one night when she was with her lover, Ross, and then hit her upon her return. The narrator expresses the opinion that Mike should join the service, and his wife tells him that Ross has said the same thing. He is again struck by the similarity between himself and the man with whom his wife is having an affair.

When the narrator tells us of his attitude toward Ross, however, he lets slip an incredibly pertinent fact: He asserts that Ross is "basically a good man. 'One of us,' was how I put it, trying to be large about it. He wasn't a bad or an evil man, Ross. 'No one's evil,' I said once to Cynthia when we were discussing my own affair" (*F*, 180). This is the only reference to the narrator's infidelity, and it adds an entirely new dimension to the story. So does a scene of marital tenderness that is presented in this version. His wife reminds him that "'When I was pregnant with Mike you carried me to the bathroom when I was so sick and pregnant I couldn't get out of bed. You carried me. No one else will ever do that, no one else could ever love me in that way, that much. We have that, no matter what. We've loved each other like nobody else could or ever will love the other again'" (*F*, 177). This is rather small consolation for the narrator, but the inclusion of the scene does help to explain the motivations of the characters. By providing a contrast, it also emphasizes the sad state of their current situation.

"Where Is Everyone?" differs most from "Mr. Coffee and Mr. Fixit" in its conclusion. The earlier story ended with the following cryptic lines:

> "Honey," I said to Myrna that night she came home. "Let's hug awhile and then you fix us a real nice supper."
> Myrna said, "Wash your hands." (*WWTA*, 20)

In the new version that bit of dialogue is replaced by several pages of new text. The narrator calls his mother and arranges to spend the night at her home. It is his mother, rather than his wife, who now says "Wash your hands," having already fixed his dinner and prepared a bed for him. She sees her son in pain and she wants to protect him, although the part that her own extramarital affair has played in creating his pain is not clear to her. His mother even tells him that Cynthia has been having an affair, not knowing that he has been aware of this for some time. She urges him to get some help and wishes him a good night. He does fall asleep, but he tells us that later, in the middle of the night, he "woke up with a start, the pajamas damp with sweat. A snowy light filled the room. There was a roaring coming at me. The room clamored. I lay there. I didn't move" (*WWTA*, 183). This ending of insomnia and terror, recalling several *What We Talk about When We Talk about Love* stories, is much more effective than the trailing off of "Mr. Coffee and Mr. Fixit." While the final lines of the earlier version might indicate a rapprochement between the two parties, this one indicates that the narrator is entirely on his own and must find some way to fill the vacuum. It is, moreover, a believable ending, since what leads up to it has been much more fully explored. This fleshed-out text allows the reader to have a much better sense of the narrator's personality and attitudes, and the story therefore has much greater impact.

In his lengthy review of *Fires*, William L. Stull says of this story that "some readers will prefer the explicit version, some the implicit, knowing now what is implied" (Stull 1984, 82). Even such a statement speaks in favor of "Where Is Everyone?," however, for it suggests, in something of a catch-22, that the readers who prefer the implicit version will do so only after they know the facts that can only be learned from the explicit version. Furthermore, this is another case in which Carver's own preference is clear, since the "Where Is Everyone?" that appears in *Fires* is nearly identical to the story as it first appeared in the journal *TriQuarterly*.[5] The text had in fact been minimalized into "Mr. Coffee and Mr. Fixit" for inclusion in *What We Talk about When We Talk about Love*. Once again, then, Carver, at a later point in time, chose the earlier, fuller version of a story rather than the one that had been more recently pared down. The three versions of this text thus conform to the hourglass pattern and confirm Carver's change in direction.

"So Much Water So Close to Home"

This hourglass pattern of development can also be seen in the last story in *Fires*, "So Much Water So Close to Home." Like the first story, "Distance," it is making its third straight appearance in a Carver collection. As with "Distance," moreover, this third version is much closer to the first than to the second, meaning that it is "considerably more explicit in style and substance alike" (Stull 1984, 82). In fact, the third version of "So Much Water So Close to Home" is almost identical to the one that appeared in *Furious Seasons*. What few changes have been made involve such minor details as commas, italics, quotation marks, and contractions; there are also a few places where phrases have been omitted or altered. More significantly, all of the material that had been slashed from the minimalist version of the story—the encounters with Dean, the scene of Claire slapping Stuart, her reminiscences about the past, her analyses of the present situation, the television story about the identification of Susan Miller's body, among others—have been reinstated. This version is much fuller than the stripped-down style of the one in *What We Talk about When We Talk about Love*, and Carver's returning to it here in *Fires* underscores the way in which this stopgap collection is more similar to the earlier volume than the immediately preceding one. This version also points the way toward the future maturation of Carver's writing style.

Conclusion

Looking at *Furious Seasons*, *What We Talk about When We Talk about Love*, and *Fires* in relation to one another, we find, as Stull has noted, "a dialectic of expansion, contraction, and restoration" (Stull 1989, 208). Carver at first moves toward, but then sharply away from, minimalism. In examining the revisions from the first of these volumes to the second, "we see Carver ruthlessly paring [his] tales down, roughing up the narrative, removing descriptive details, metaphors, and all traces of wistful, coming-of-age lyricism; we watch him turn long rolling paragraphs into choppy, staccato bulletins, often just fragments of dialogue separated by silence and vacancy" (Dickstein, 508). In examining the revisions from the second of these volumes to the third, on the other hand, we see the process in reverse; we see him beginning "to add, not to subtract" (Dickstein, 509). During this period he "restored and expanded the work that he had pared down under the influence of editor Lish" (Stull 1989, 208). Nowhere is this change in Carver's aesthetic more easily seen than in the stories published in all three of the collections, a fact on which we have been focusing in this chapter. The most important results of Carver's change in attitude, though, were the new stories he was publishing and that he would collect in *Cathedral*, the masterpiece to which we shall now turn our attention.

Chapter Seven

The Masterpiece: *Cathedral*

The notion that Carver's writing underwent a shift between *What We Talk about When We Talk about Love* and *Cathedral* has become a critical commonplace in Carver studies. By 1984, Michael Gearhart points out, most "critics acknowledged an unmistakable loosening of Carver's stark 'minimalist' prose style, and noted the development of human potential in his characters" (Gearhart, 439). Marc Chenetier, for example, asserted that the more recent stories signaled "a movement away from threatening ambiguity, a working towards hope rather than horror, and the abandonment of features Carver may have come to consider akin to the narrative 'gimmicks' he has always denounced" (Chenetier, 170). Many other critics made comments along the same lines. Carver's shift can actually be seen prior to the publication of *Cathedral* in *Fires*,[1] as I have shown, but the point is well taken; Carver's later writing is indeed very different from that of his middle period. Carver certainly felt that way. He told more than one interviewer that "after I'd finished [*What We Talk about When We Talk about Love*] and it was accepted for publication, I didn't write anything else for about six or eight months. Then the first thing I wrote was 'Cathedral' and I knew that story was different from anything I'd ever written, and all of the stories after that seemed to be fuller somehow and much more generous and maybe more affirmative" (*Con*, 125).

Asked to account for this movement away from the style that had made him famous, Carver asserted that "I suppose it reflects a change in my life as much as it does in my way of writing" (*Con*, 44). Having gained his sobriety and established a new relationship with Tess Gallagher, in addition to having achieved a degree of financial stability, Carver felt more optimistic and hopeful about his own life. This naturally reflected itself in his writing, both "structurally and thematically" (Cochrane, 79). With regard to structure, Carver explained that "I'm simply putting flesh on more things, putting color in the cheeks, rather than trying to take all the color out. . . . I'm adding to the characters, and adding to the situation itself, making it larger, making the stories give more, making them more generous" (*Con*, 145). With regard to theme, the stories are no longer so bleak. Instead, they offer a ray of hope. As Kathleen Westfall Shute explains, Carver "has begun to afford his characters the gift he has always granted the reader: some light by which to navigate, the chance for insight, a greater range of freedom and personal choice and, indeed, by implication, the moral responsibility which such an unfettering demands" (Shute, 2). Carver told an interviewer that "the vision now, today, is, I suppose, more hopeful than it once was. But for the most part, things still don't work out for the characters in the stories. Things perish. Ideas and ideals and people's goals and visions—they perish. But sometimes, oftentimes, the people themselves don't perish. They have to pull up their socks and go on" (*Con,* 161). Stories that feature survivors are indeed something new for Carver, and "A Small, Good Thing," "Where I'm Calling From," "Fever," and "Cathedral," all of which portray survivors, are generally considered to be among the finest works of his career. Even the stories of failure are more effective here than they were in the earlier collections, for the potential—as well as the mistake that was made to cause the protagonist to miss out on that potential—is more fully explained and developed. Carver is at the height of his powers here, having arrived at his full maturity, and *Cathedral* as a whole is certainly the most impressive of his collections, "confirm[ing] his place among the short-story writers of the first rank" (Campbell, 49).

"Feathers"

The opening story in the collection is also one of the strongest,[2] even if it doesn't demonstrate Carver's new, more hopeful attitude. Although the protagonists "experience a special moment which almost affords them a glimpse of something elusive" (Grinnell, 72), ultimately "they capitulate to the pervading despair of previous volumes" (Saltzman, 125). "Feathers," like "What's in Alaska?" and "What We Talk about When We Talk about Love," tells of an encounter between two couples. In this case the narrator, Jack, and his wife, Fran, go to dinner at the home of Olla and Bud. The story focuses on Jack and Fran, but Bud and Olla serve as important foils; it is in contrast to their marriage that Jack and Fran's relationship stands out in bold relief. In many ways, Bud and Olla are grotesques. When Jack and Fran arrive at their house in the country, for example, they are greeted by Bud and Olla's pet peacock, Joey,[3] who frightens them and momentarily prevents them from leaving their car. One of the first things Fran notices upon entering the other couple's living room, moreover, is "an old plaster-of-Paris cast of the most crooked, jaggedy teeth in the world"[4] sitting prominently on top of the television "like a prized relic" (Saltzman, 127). Bud explains that it is a mold of Olla's teeth that was made when he first took her to the orthodontist to have them straightened. Olla tells them that she keeps the casting around "'to remind me how much I owe Bud'" (C, 13), since her first husband didn't care enough about her to have her twisted teeth fixed, but Bud promised her that he would and carried through on his promise. Bud is aware of how these items might affect a visitor—" 'That dirty bird and your old pair of teeth!,'" he exclaims, "'What're people going to think?'" (C, 18)—but he laughs off the potential embarrassment. Later in the story we are introduced to Bud and Olla's baby, Harold, whom Jack describes as "the ugliest baby I'd ever seen. It was so ugly I couldn't say anything. No words would come out of my mouth. I don't mean it was diseased or disfigured. Nothing like that. It was just ugly. . . . Even calling it ugly does it credit" (C, 20). Despite the grotesqueries of their living arrangement, however, Bud and Olla seem remarkably happy; they enjoy bantering with each other, and with the bird and child, and represent a completely well-adjusted family. As Jack later notes, "It *was* an ugly baby. But, for all I know, I guess it didn't matter that much to Bud and Olla. Or if it did, maybe they simply thought, So okay if it's ugly. It's our baby" (C, 24). Bud's family, although "unrefined to say the least" (Saltzman, 126), is a tightly bound unit, happy in themselves and largely unconcerned about what others might think.

From the outset of the story, on the other hand, Jack and Fran's relationship shows signs of great strain. Fran seems particularly resistant to any kind of commitment or change. She has never met Bud and Olla, for example, and isn't "too thrilled" about meeting them now (C, 4). Following a brief argument about whether they should take something to the dinner, Jack interprets her look to mean "Why do we need other people? . . . We have each other" (C, 5). What he goes on to tell us, however, indicates that their life together is pretty empty. He notes that most evenings "she'd brush her hair and we'd wish out loud for things we didn't have. . . . Some nights we went to a movie. Other nights we just stayed in and watched TV" (C, 5). Whereas Bud and Olla's wishes come true, Jack and Fran's "never amount to anything" (C, 6). During their trip to the other couple's house, furthermore, the tension between them continues to rise. As in so many of Carver's other stories, the problems in Jack and Fran's relationship both stem from and are indicated by a lack of communication. When they encounter the peacock, for example, all they can do is swear, since "there was nothing else to say" (*C*, 8). When Olla tells them about the plaster teeth, Jack notes that "I didn't know what to say to this. Neither did Fran. But I knew Fran would have plenty to say about it later" (*C*, 14). Shortly thereafter he reports that "Fran turned her eyes to me. She drew her lip under. But she didn't say anything" (*C*, 15). The reader frequently senses Jack's attempts to put Fran at ease, but she remains distant, bored, and uncommunicative.

Even so, the end of the story indicates that Fran has been affected by Bud and Olla's closeness. In particular, the encounter has changed her attitude toward having children of her own. Earlier Jack had noted that "one thing we didn't wish for was kids. The reason we didn't have kids was that we didn't want kids. Maybe sometime, we said to each other. But right then, we were waiting" (*C*, 5). During the course of the evening at Bud and Olla's, however, through some comments that were made and through their playing with Harold, both she and Jack come to change their minds. As they drive back home Fran sits close to Jack and puts her hand on his leg; when they are in bed later she says to him, "'Honey, fill me up with your seed!'" (*C*, 25). Indeed, they conceive a child that night. For Jack, the evening at Bud and Olla's stands out as a positive moment in their lives. He tells us that "that evening at Bud and Olla's was special. I knew it was special. That evening I felt good about almost everything in my life. I couldn't wait to be alone with Fran to talk to her about what I was feeling. I made a wish that evening. . . . What I wished for was that I'd never forget or otherwise let go of that evening. That's one wish of mine that came true. And it was bad luck for me that it did" (*C*, 25). The end of this statement indicates that, despite the positive feelings it engendered, the evening became a curse for Jack and Fran, largely because of her reaction to it. While at first she was brought closer to Jack, he notes that "later, after things had changed for us, and the kid had come along, all of that, Fran would look back on that evening at Bud's place as the beginning of the change" (*C*, 25), a change that has now become entirely negative from her point of view. As Arthur Saltzman points out, "the child they ultimately produce does not avail them, and the marriage tenses, then unravels" (Saltzman, 128).

Rather than moving their relationship in a positive direction, the evening proves to have been but a brief stay in its inevitable decline. Jack comes to see the visit as "the final incident commemorating the halcyon days of his marriage" (Saltzman, 125). Toward the end of the story he tells us that "Fran doesn't work at the creamery anymore, and she cut her hair a long time ago. She's gotten fat on me, too. We don't talk about it. What's to say? . . . She and I talk less and less as it is. Mostly it's just the TV" (*C*, 26). Despite the positive example provided by Bud and Olla's closeness, the end result for Jack and Fran has been a further disintegration of their already tenuous relationship. Ultimately, the difference between the two couples' children parallels the difference between their relationships; just as Harold's outwardly noticeable ugliness is opposed to the "conniving streak" (*C*, 26) of Jack and Fran's son, which is particularly sinister for being under the surface, so is Bud and Olla's grotesque but undeniable love countered by Jack and Fran's outward appearance of community, which masks an inward lack of emotional attachment and commitment. Although the tone of Jack's narration is far from self-pitying, the reader does come to feel sorry for him as he finds himself trapped in a predicament from which nothing can provide a permanent means of escape. Like the father at the end of "Distance"/"Everything Stuck to Him," Jack's memory of the pleasantness of the evening at Bud and Olla's only exacerbates and reinforces the sadness of his present situation.

"Chef's House"

Like "Feathers," "Chef's House" presents the possibility of redemption and recovery for the main characters, only to take it away again. The story focuses on Edna, our narrator, and Wes, her estranged husband. Their breakup after many years of marriage was precipitated, in large part, by Wes's alcoholism. As the story opens, though, Wes is on the wagon and living in a house owned by a friend of his, another recovering alcoholic called Chef. Wes phones Edna and asks her to come and live with him, arguing that they can "start over" (*C*, 27). Edna agrees, after he promises that he will "try and be the Wes [she] used to know. The old Wes. The Wes [she] married" (*C*, 27). She tells her current boyfriend, who is also a recovering alcoholic, that "I have to do it for Wes's sake. He's trying to stay sober. You remember what that's like" (*C*, 28). The summer does indeed begin idyllically. Wes and Edna drink coffee, pop, and fruit juices, they fish, and Wes attends "his Don't Drink meetings" (*C*, 28). Their lives and their relationship appear back on track, and Edna, who puts her wedding ring back on, "confides that she has begun to believe in their solidarity again" (Saltzman, 129). She finds herself "wishing the summer wouldn't end" (*C*, 28).

As we should expect, however, paradise regained can only last for a brief period. One day Chef comes to the house to tell them that his daughter's husband, a commercial fisherman, has been lost at sea, and that he must ask them to leave the house so that he can help his daughter out by letting her move in. Edna is willing to take the change in stride, believing that their newly reestablished harmony can be maintained. For Wes, though, the change marks a necessarily catastrophic turning point. Although Edna tries to prop up his spirits, she is unsuccessful. "We'll get another house," she tells him, but he replies "Not like this one. . . . It wouldn't be the same, anyway. This house has been a good house for us. This house has good memories to it" (*C*, 30). Edna's primary concern seems to be that the depression Wes is sinking into will lead him to return to drinking, and that is in fact the implication with which the story leaves the reader. Edna notes that "Wes had this look about him. I knew that look. He kept touching his lips with his tongue. He kept thumbing his shirt under his waistband" (*C*, 30). Almost immediately, they both begin to talk about the idyllic summer "like something that was over" (*C*, 31).

Wes's sense of resignation dominates the last part of the story. Although Edna knows that "we have to do something now and do it quick" (*C*, 32), the chances of that "something" happening are highly unlikely. The story's concluding lines demonstrate the characters' return to despair: "Wes got up and pulled the drapes and the ocean was gone just like that. I went in to start supper. We still had some fish in the icebox. There wasn't much else. We'll clean it up tonight, I thought, and that will be the end of it" (*C*, 33). Alan Wilde notes that "the resignation of these statements, as laconic and disconnectedly paratactic as what precedes them, conveys the fatuousness of having believed, however briefly, that things might have been different, even better" (Wilde, 111). As with the evening at Bud and Olla's in "Feathers," the positive movement in Wes and Edna's relationship proves to be merely a brief respite from what has been, and is now once again. In many ways, moreover, "Chef's House" recalls one of Carver's earliest stories, "Neighbors," in which access to the Stones' apartment proves temporarily invigorating for the Millers, who thereafter find themselves plunged into even deeper despair when they accidentally lock themselves out of that apartment. Chef's house had proven to be the same kind of rehabilitation center for Edna and Wes, but by the end of the story they, too, are locked out, and the future looks quite bleak.

"Preservation"

The central theme of this story—"how the will to live and prevail can leak towards entropy" (Lehman, 46)—can be seen as turning on the dual meanings of the title. At first, we may think of preservation as being a positive sign, a kind of salvation. On the other hand, preservation also refers to keeping things intact, preserving them so that they do not change; this definition implies stasis rather than aspiration. In Carver's story, not surprisingly, it is the latter meaning of the word that prevails. During the course of the text, one of the characters reads from a book that tells of "a man who had been discovered after spending two thousand years in a peat bog in the Netherlands" (C, 36). Carver turns this fact into the central metaphor for the story, which details the way in which Sandy's husband is becoming similarly petrified.

As the story opens, we find out that Sandy's husband has been "terminated" from his job (C, 35).[5] Carver's use of that word is deliberate, for the event does seem to have ended his life. Since that time, three months prior to the story's present, he has done little more than lay on the sofa, watch television, read the newspaper, and occasionally study about the bog people. His total isolation from the outer world is reflected in the fact that he is never referred to by name in the story. Sandy, who is the central consciousness and true protagonist of the story, has difficulty dealing with her husband's inactivity. She wants to break him of his lethargy, and the opportunity seems to present itself when the refrigerator stops working. Just as all of the food in the freezer has thawed, so does the need to buy a new refrigerator begin to draw the husband out of his frozen shell. He looks through the newspapers and finds an ad for a used appliance auction, but when Sandy actually suggests that they go, he replies, "'I've never been to an auction in my life. . . . I don't believe I want to go to one now'" (C, 43). This refusal to face a new experience indicates that he is so frozen it is going to be difficult to thaw him out. Fed up, Sandy announces that "'I'm going to this auction. . . . Whether you go or not. You might as well come along. But I don't care'" (C, 43). He assures her that he is going to come, but as the story ends he returns to the couch.

In a final image, the defrosted food provides a very fitting metaphorical explication of his plight. As the story ends, Sandy discovers water running off of the table on which the thawing foods have been placed and pooling on the floor. "She looked down at her husband's bare feet. She stared at his feet next to the pool of water. She knew she'd never again in her life see anything so unusual. But she didn't know what to make of it yet. . . . She put her plate on the table and watched until the feet left the kitchen and went back into the living room" (C, 46). Here we see the husband literally afraid to get his feet wet. The sofa has become a kind of island to him, and he retreats to its security, fearing that if he ventures out he will only be swamped. As Sandy heads off to the auction at the end of the story, we sense that she is leaving him behind. Whereas her husband's future seems empty, she remains active and will survive; even her name, Sandy, as Daniel W. Lehman has noted, "distinguish[es] her, at least temporarily, from the peat bog that is enclosing her husband" (Lehman, 45). His preservation, like that of the bog people, has prevented his salvation, his return to a viable existence, but Sandy is determined to avoid becoming equally petrified.

"A Small, Good Thing"

The next piece in the collection, "The Compartment," also focuses on a character who has cut himself off from other people, and hence from any kind of meaningful life. The story's ending is ambiguous, however, in sharp contrast to the succeeding story, "A Small, Good Thing," the ending of which is undoubtedly optimistic. Winner of the O. Henry Award for the best short story of 1983, this is the text that most alerted critics to the new, more expansive Carver. A retelling of "The Bath" from Carver's arch-minimalist *What We Talk about When We Talk about Love,* "A Small, Good Thing" is fully three times as long as the earlier version, and everything about the story is examined in greater depth and detail. Although there are only a few extended additions in the revised story, much new material does appear in small doses throughout the narrative. In essence, Carver's revising here, as in several of the *Fires* stories, takes the form of maximizing rather than minimizing. Such maximizing does occur on a stylistic level, and that is certainly significant,[6] but what really draws people to "A Small, Good Thing" is the expansion of emotion that the new story presents. As William L. Stull has pointed out, "the minimally developed characters of 'The Bath' take on flesh, blood, and consciousness" (Stull "BH" 1985, 8). The fact that they are all given names here (whereas in "The Bath" the father was not named) is itself indicative of "a critical turn in Carver's work" (Shute, 6). The more detailed characterization serves "to decrease the distances that separate Carver's characters from one another and Carver's narrator from the story he relates" (Saltzman, 144), and the story is thus made "more sympathetic and accessible" (Saltzman, 143) to the reader.

While "The Bath" ended on a note of terror and menace, "A Small, Good Thing" moves through the conflict to achieve resolution. The point at which the earlier story ended is only the midpoint of the revision, and therefore much of the ambiguity at the close of "The Bath" is removed. The reader gets a more fully developed picture of the impact of Scotty's accident. What we discover in this expansion is that Scotty dies, the victim of "a hidden occlusion[,] a one-in-a-million circumstance" (C, 80). The story then focuses "on the efforts of the couple to confront catastrophe, share their sorrow, and gather up the fragments of the life that remains to them" (Lonnquist, 145). Scotty's parents do come to realize that the baker is the one who has been making the harassing calls, and, enraged, they drive to the mall to confront him. Cursing at him, Anne explains the reasons for her anger, breaking down in tears for the first time since Scotty's death. The baker, who becomes a fully rounded character in this version of the story, feels abashed. He pulls up chairs and makes the grieving parents sit down, apologizing profusely for the pain he has inflicted, and blaming it on the fact that he has no family of his own. He puts forth his own "story of suffering and endurance" (Cochrane, 85), explaining that "'I'm just a baker. I don't claim to be anything else. Maybe once, maybe years ago, I was a different kind of being. I've forgotten, I don't know for sure. But I'm not any longer, if I ever was'" (C, 87). The baker then offers the Weisses some fresh rolls, telling them that "'Eating is a small, good thing in a time like this'" (C, 88). Eating is also a group activity, unlike the solitary action of taking a bath, and for the first time since Scotty's accident the Weisses do take the nourishment that is offered.

The story thus ends, following this "final scene of dramatic recognition, reversal, confrontation, and catharsis" (Stull "BH" 1985, 10), on a note of communion,[7] of shared understanding and grief: "They talked on into the early morning, the high pale cast of light in the windows, and they did not think of leaving" (C, 89). Through the unlikely agency of the baker, then, the Weisses are "fortified [and] receive strength to face a new day, strength they could not bestow on themselves" (Cochrane, 86). Such a conclusion, rather than stressing the problems of communication that we saw in the harassing telephone calls, emphasizes the need for honest communication. As Miriam Marty Clark notes, this story "embraces conversation where other stories exclude it; it admits rather than shuts out other voices" (Clark, 241). In the revised version, then, Carver has moved from a story of utter despair to "one of healing and forgiveness" (Gearhart, 440), of temporary grief mingled with a ray of lasting hope. He "highlight[s] the small fires of optimism and endurance that human beings persist in building and rebuilding, even after they've been extinguished numerous times" (Johnson, 791).

Generally speaking, critics (and, I believe, readers) prefer the latter, more expansive version of the story. William Abrahams, the editor of the O. Henry Awards annual, for example, in explaining why he selected "A Small, Good Thing" for the first prize, noted that in revising "The Bath," which he considered one of Carver's "lesser achievements," the author "has lengthened, deepened, enriched, enlivened; and in so doing, he has produced a story of extraordinary power. What was latent in the original version, here finds ever deepening expression. Out of the simple sketch (and the analogy to painting seems peculiarly justified), a full-scale portrait, in all its lights and shadows, has been brought to the page."[8] William L. Stull similarly asserts that "the revision *completes* the original by turning the sum of its fragmentary parts into a coherent whole that has a powerful dramatic structure, a beginning, middle, and end" (Stull "BH" 1985, 7). Carver himself told an interviewer that

> the story hadn't been told originally; it had been messed around with, condensed and compressed in "The Bath" to highlight the qualities of menace that I wanted to emphasize—you see this with the business about the baker, the phone call, with its menacing voice on the other line, the bath, and so on. But I still felt there was unfinished business, so in the midst of writing these other stories for *Cathedral* I went back to "The Bath" and tried to see what aspects of it needed to be enhanced, re-drawn, re-imagined. When I was done, I was amazed because it seemed so much better. I've had people tell me that they much prefer "The Bath," which is fine, but "A Small, Good Thing" seems to me to be a better story.[9] (*Con*, 102)

Emphasizing the way in which "A Small, Good Thing" expands on "The Bath," however, should not obscure the very considerable achievement that is "A Small, Good Thing" in itself. The story is one of the most effective in the entirety of Carver's canon; it is, rightfully, one of the most anthologized, as well as one of the most written-about of his stories. In depicting the shared nature of suffering at the end of the story, Carver reaches beyond the cold confines of individuals' compartments, to use an image from the previous story, and touches the reader's heart. Carver would go on to write stories as good as this one, but none better.

"Careful"

The next story in the collection, "Vitamins," does not match its predecessor in either the hopefulness of its theme or in the mastery of its execution. One of the most despairing works in the volume, it is much less effective than "Careful," a story that is equally despairing, but one that has a much greater impact on the reader. "Careful" can be seen as a culmination of the several Carver stories that combine his obsessions with the problems of marital communication and the lure of alcoholism. As the story opens, we meet Lloyd, who has recently moved away from his wife, Inez, and is now living in a cramped room, completely cut off from everything. Carver writes, for example, that "he did not have a telephone, which was fine with him. He didn't want a telephone" (*C*, 113). Having one, after all, might require him to break out of his solipsism and talk to somebody. An alcoholic, Lloyd has taken to breakfasting on champagne and doughnuts. He notes that "time was when he would have considered this a mildly crazy thing to do" (*C*, 112), but now it seems like a perfectly reasonable routine.

When Inez unexpectedly comes to visit, however, his routine is interrupted. Lloyd would clearly like to reunite with his wife,[10] but he has trouble reaching out to her. He knows that "the visit [is] an important one" (*C*, 113) and he wants to be on his best behavior. Unfortunately, on the morning of her visit he has awakened to find one of his ears completely plugged up with wax. When the opportunity for communication presents itself, he literally cannot hear it. Moreover, the uncomfortable feeling of being in an echo chamber, another image of his isolation, is driving him crazy. Along with his hearing, he has "lost his sense of balance, his equilibrium" (*C*, 113). So much for making a good impression on Inez. She informs him that the visit is serious, that they "'have things to talk about'" (*C*, 116), but such dialogue has been rendered impossible. The parallel between the plug in Lloyd's ear and his inability to communicate with his wife is so clear it is almost allegorical.

Inez does help Lloyd with his ear problem, again offering the opportunity for communication. She states, philosophically, "'Anyway, we need to try *something*. We'll try [a makeshift Q-tip] first. If it doesn't work, we'll try something else. That's life, isn't it?'" (*C*, 116). This is so clearly a comment on their relationship that even Lloyd asks, "'Does that have a hidden meaning or something?'" (*C*, 117). While Inez is looking for some sort of implement in the bathroom, Lloyd "began thinking of all the things he ought to say to her" (*C*, 118), again indicating his desperate need to reestablish dialogue. As is to be expected in a Carver story, however, the moment is not taken advantage of: "When she came back into the room he couldn't say anything. He didn't know where to start" (*C*, 118). Anxious about what her response might be, Lloyd refuses to take the risk that conversation would entail and instead returns to his state of isolation. Inez continues speaking to him, "but he couldn't make out the words. When she stopped talking he didn't ask her what it was she'd said. Whatever it was, he knew he didn't want her to say it again" (*C*, 118).

The plug of wax is eventually removed, but Inez informs him that since she has spent all of the time she had for talking with him on helping him with his ear, she has to leave. On her way out the door she stops and says one more thing, but "he didn't listen. He didn't want to" (*C*, 123). At her departure, then, they still have not talked. As the story ends, Lloyd finds himself sitting on the couch in his pajamas at three o'clock in the afternoon, drinking champagne from the bottle, and watching TV. His life has come to such a pass that even this situation does not strike him as being anything that far out of the ordinary. Despite Lloyd's wish that the future bring a reconciliation with Inez, all the future seems to offer is the numbness of the bottle, and the added terror that his ear will clog up again and he won't have anyone there to unclog it. Because he is unable to communicate with another person, Lloyd remains "the perfectly inscribed subject of a fiercely repressive ideology,"[11] namely alcoholism. His future looks bleak indeed.

"Where I'm Calling From"

"Careful" and "Where I'm Calling From" create something of a diptych: Just as the first story depicts the descent into alcoholism and isolation, the second depicts the reversal of that process, a return to sobriety and community. The simple fact that the story is set at a recovery and rehabilitation center for alcoholics indicates a movement forward. Here the protagonists are able to communicate, and in this case "commiseration instigates recuperation" (Saltzman, 147). "Where I'm Calling From" thus emerges as one of the new, more open stories of *Cathedral*. Ostensibly, it details the history of J.P.'s relationship with Roxy, whom he first meets when she comes to his friend's house to sweep the chimney. On her way out after having done her job, she offers J.P.'s friend a good-luck kiss. J.P. takes her up on the offer as well, and then asks her out on a date. Eventually they get married, and J.P. becomes a partner in the family chimney-sweeping business. For some inexplicable reason, though, he starts to increase his drinking. From that point on, his life is a downward spiral. Alcohol completely overtakes him and he and Roxy begin to fight, physically as well as verbally. When J.P. finds out that Roxy has begun to see another man he destroys her wedding ring with a pair of wire cutters. The next day he gets arrested for drunk driving, and he finds himself "at Frank Martin's to dry out and to figure how to get his life back on track" (C, 135). In the story's present (New Year's Day, significantly), Roxy is coming to visit J.P. for the first time since he has been at the facility. Their reunion seems to go off without a hitch, and the last we see of the couple is them walking off arm in arm. Earlier in the story J.P. had recounted a time when, as a child, he had fallen in a well, but had been rescued unharmed, and Roxy's visit now seems to be as strong a lifeline as his father's was then.[12] As the story ends, J.P. is clearly on his way back up to the light; he provides a striking contrast to Lloyd in "Careful," who has the curtains drawn and his pajamas on at three o'clock in the afternoon.

That is the ostensible plot of the story, but the work really involves the narrator, another alcoholic who hopes to recover at Frank Martin's. His prospects don't sound good, though, for he informs us that this is his second visit to the facility. The first time he arrived there he was still trying to work things out with his wife, and she was the one who brought him. This time, his girlfriend accompanied him; both of them were drunk on champagne. Apparently, the day before Christmas she had received bad news about a Pap smear and the two of them had gone on a bender. A few days later the narrator decided it was time for him to return to Frank Martin's, and that same afternoon J.P. had been brought in by his father- and brother-in-law. The present of the story is a few days later, when J.P and the narrator meet on the porch and J.P. tells his story. The narrator knows that J.P. needs to talk, but he also appreciates the opportunity to listen; he notes that "It's helping me relax. It's taking me away from my own situation" (C, 134). Every time J.P. wants to stop his story, moreover, the narrator urges him to keep talking. He claims a certain amount of indifference, stating that "I would have listened if he'd been going on about how one day he'd decided to start pitching horseshoes" (C, 132), yet the very act of listening demonstrates a degree of sympathy. Furthermore, the parallels between J.P.'s story and his own become increasingly significant to him. As Hamilton E. Cochrane points out, "listening to J.P., paradoxically, seems both to take the narrator away from his own pain and, at the same time, to offer a paradigm that brings him back to his own experience with new understanding" (Cochrane, 82).

As J.P.'s story progresses, the narrator recognizes that he, too, has let alcohol cut him off from the important people in his life. He becomes increasingly desirous of making contact with his own loved ones. The next day he calls his ex-wife, for example, but there is no answer. As with Lloyd's clogged ear, it seems that the narrator here has been silent for so long that when he does want to speak he cannot. He tries again later, and then he starts to call his girlfriend, but he states that "I'm dialing her number when I realize I really don't want to talk to her. . . . I hope she's okay. But if she has something wrong with her, I don't want to know about it" (*C*, 142). The narrator's indecisiveness about opening up continues through the latter half of the story, and his status remains in doubt almost until the end. It is not clear whether he will be able to achieve the kind of reconciliation that J.P. has effected or whether he will end up like Tiny, a patient who suffered a seizure a few days before he was due to go home and now, instead of spending New Year's with his wife, is shuffling around the facility as a hopelessly broken man. Fearing that his own "night is coming on" (*C*, 146), that he must make some kind of connection or die, the narrator makes his final decision. He tells us that "I'll try my wife first. If she answers, I'll wish her a Happy New Year. . . . She'll ask me where I'm calling from, and I'll have to tell her. I won't say anything about New Year's resolutions. There's no way to make a joke out of this. After I talk to her, I'll call my girlfriend. Maybe I'll call her first. . . . 'Hello, sugar,' I'll say when she answers. 'It's me'" (*C*, 146). What's significant here is not so much where he's calling from but that he's calling at all, that he's beginning to climb out of his well. The narrator's "It's me" might seem an inconclusive note on which to end the story, but "this simple declaration suggests hard-earned self-knowledge and self-acceptance, the foundation on which the structure of a new life may be erected" (Cochrane, 82–83). Although the narrator has yet to actually place the call, the implication is certainly that he is going to.[13] Unlike Lloyd, the narrator shows that "he is not afraid to use the telephone to make contact with others to open dialogues" (Donahue, 61). The story thus "concludes with a glimmer of hope, with the possibility at least of resurrection" (Cochrane, 82). There is a good chance, for the narrator as well as for J.P., that it will indeed be a Happy New Year.

As several critics have noted, the reason for the success of J.P. and the narrator is that they are able to tell their stories, to become "dialogic selves who find their meaning, value and identity through and by inter-action with other selves, other stories" (Haslam, 57). At first the narra-tor is reluctant to say anything about himself, encouraging J.P. to talk instead. Eventually, though, he opens up as well. After all, he is telling us the story of his stay at Frank Martin's. Elliott Malamet likens this emphasis on dialogue and narrative to the "psychoanalytic 'talking cure,'" in which "language and storytelling can be employed to relieve emotional distress" (Malamet, 61). More often, however, the story is analyzed in light of the similar philosophy used by Alcoholics Anonymous. Peter J. Donahue, for example, notes that "the recovering alcoholic, as language user, is the technician of his own liberation" (Donahue, 57). He points out that "the implicit understanding among the characters in 'Where I'm Calling From,' which Lloyd fails to grasp in 'Careful,' is that only by maintaining an open-ended narrative can the alcoholic free himself from the dependency and begin his recovery" (Donahue, 62). Along these same lines, the sign at the entrance to Duffy's, the treatment center at which Carver himself stayed on two different occasions and which is clearly the model for Frank Martin's, states "They shared their experience, strength & hope with each other."[14] This is exactly what J.P. and the narrator have done, and it accounts for the optimism with which the story concludes. The positive ending doubtless attracts many readers to this story, which is in every respect one of Carver's masterpieces, and an excellent choice for the title piece of his volume of selected stories published a few years later.

"The Train"

Among the many revisions in Carver's canon, "The Train" is unique, for it is a revision of—or more precisely a sequel to—a story he didn't originally write, namely John Cheever's "The Five-Forty-Eight." The opening lines of "The Train" do a good job of summarizing both the plot and the theme of Cheever's story: "The woman was called Miss Dent, and earlier that evening she'd held a gun on a man. She'd made him get down in the dirt and plead for his life. While the man's eyes welled with tears and fingers picked at leaves, she pointed the revolver at him and told him things about himself. She tried to make him see that he couldn't keep trampling on people's feelings" (C, 147). To elaborate somewhat, Miss Dent, after having spent some time in a mental hospital, started working as a secretary for Mr. Blake. He took sexual advantage of and then fired her. In the story's present, she stalks him and exacts her revenge, which consists of humiliating him as he has humiliated her. Cheever's title, "The Five-Forty-Eight," refers to the train that Blake takes home to Shady Hill and upon which Miss Dent confronts him with her pistol; the actual humiliation takes place in an empty freight house north of the train station. After she rubs his face in the dirt she heads off down the tracks and returns to the railway station. It is on this station's platform that Carver picks up the story line in "The Train." Carver's sequel to Cheever's story is in many ways reminiscent of the other story in *Cathedral* that takes place on a train, "The Compartment." Once again Carver stresses the isolation of every person, the compartmentalization of human feeling that prevents any one individual from truly knowing any other. Although Carver stresses it much more in his tale, the theme is already present in Cheever's story. Because it is narrated from Blake's point of view, "The Five-Forty-Eight" shows his entire lack of understanding for Miss Dent's position. His coldness is evident in his decision to terminate her job after having slept with her, for example. The whole incident has meant so little to him that, when he first sees Miss Dent on the train, he can't even remember her name. He certainly can't understand why she would be following him in a threatening manner. He does eventually come to feel remorse, but it has nothing to do with his sexual harassment of Miss Dent. He feels guilty not because he has done something wrong, but because he has been dumb enough to get caught. Toward the end of the story, Miss Dent explains to him that, despite her problems, "'Still and all I'm better than you. I still have good dreams sometimes. I dream about picnics and heaven and the brotherhood of man, and about castles in the moonlight and a river with willow trees all along the edge of it and foreign cities, and after all I know more about love than you.'"[15] The reader certainly agrees with this assessment, but Blake, impervious as ever, dismisses her as a psychopath and feels quite "safe" (Cheever, 294) when she heads off down the tracks. His decision not to confront the truth parallels Myers's decision not to get off of the train in "The Compartment." Both characters show themselves to be emotionally dead, having cut themselves off from all meaningful contact with other people.

This sense of isolation is further emphasized in "The Train," for we see Miss Dent both misunderstanding and being misunderstood by other people. While she is sitting in the station's waiting room, her pistol-packing handbag clutched in her lap, an older man and a middle-aged woman enter. They are dressed well, but neither is wearing a coat in the cool evening, and the man has no shoes. Miss Dent tries to figure out from where they have come, for "they gave off an air of agitation, of having just left somewhere in a great hurry and not yet being able to find a way to talk about it" (*C,* 148). She even eavesdrops on their conversation, but it proves to be rather cryptic and she finds herself unable to understand what has brought them to their present situation. Carver brilliantly puts the readers into the same position in which Miss Dent finds herself: We can't help hearing what the couple says and attempting to make sense out of it, but we are also unable to do so.[16] At the same time, the woman begins to make comments about Miss Dent, demonstrating an ignorance as to what has happened earlier in the younger woman's evening (namely, the events of Cheever's story). The first time she refers to Miss Dent, for example, it is as the "'woman with the handbag'" (C, 151), yet she has no idea what that handbag contains. Later, she confronts Miss Dent directly, asserting that she's "'a sly boots'" who would "'rather just sit with [her] prim little mouth while other people talk their heads off,'" although the woman senses that Miss Dent has a real story to tell, that she "'could say a lot if someone got [her] started'" (C, 153). Miss Dent thinks about spilling her story to them, and she knows that her tale would be shocking, especially since it would come from such an unlikely source. At that moment, however, the train arrives, and communication is once again cut off. The characters remain ignorant of each other's situations.

As the story ends, Carver adds yet another layer of misunderstanding. As he enters the train, the man holds the door for Miss Dent as well as his companion, an action that is entirely misinterpreted by the train's passengers. Carver tells us that "the passengers naturally assumed that the three people boarding were together; and they felt sure that whatever these people's business had been that night, it had not come to a happy conclusion" (C, 155). The passengers thus show no more awareness of the relationship between Miss Dent and the couple than either of those parties has shown the other. Carver thus repeats and duplicates the pattern of misunderstandings to show us how hard it actually is to put oneself into another person's shoes. As the train goes speeding off into the night, all of the characters remain as isolated and compartmentalized as Carver's Myers and Cheever's Blake had been. Carver's revision of Cheever's story thus provides a natural bridge between the two writers, allowing us to see both of their texts in a new light.[17]

"Fever"

Although not as widely known as some of the other stories in this collection, "Fever" is one of the most effective[18] and most important. Carver told an interviewer that it was the last story he wrote for *Cathedral* and that "it's affirmative, I think, positive in its outlook" (*Con*, 101). In the character of Carlyle, Carver creates perhaps his most resourceful and resilient protagonist. During the course of the story he faces several crises, but in every case he is able to overcome his problems, and the story does end with a great deal of optimism for the future.

As the story opens, Carlyle seems like a perfect candidate for the kind of catatonia that we have seen enveloping Sandy's husband in "Preservation" and Lloyd in "Careful." The narrator informs us in the opening sentence, for example, that "Carlyle was in a spot. He'd been in a spot all summer, since early June when his wife had left him" (*C*, 57). Immediately following his wife's departure—she ran off to California with one of Carlyle's colleagues—Carlyle had isolated himself. He had no interest "in seeing other women, and for a time he didn't think he ever would" (*C*, 162); his drinking had begun to pick up, and he found himself "sitting in front of the TV with an unopened book or magazine next to him on the sofa" (*C*, 163). Although he would like to be reunited with Eileen, his wife, Carlyle can't do anything to facilitate that result. He is obviously at a low point, and he seems likely to capitulate to total inertia.

What saves him, though, is the fact that Eileen has left him with their children, Keith and Sarah. He feels a sense of added responsibility because he wants to make sure his children do not suffer emotional trauma from the familial shake-up, and this forces him to keep a moderately level head. Carlyle is a teacher, and so his wife's decampment in the spring allows him the summer vacation to move through the recovery process. His immediate problem, though, is finding a baby-sitter for his kids so that he can return to work. At precisely this point, Eileen calls to inform him that she has spoken to some people and that a Mrs. Webster will be calling him about the job. She tells him that "'things are going to get better'" (*C*, 168), and she is proved right. From the moment that Mrs. Webster steps into the house, Carlyle's life is transformed; "chaos has been banished [and] order is restored" (Campbell, 66). The children like her immediately, and her take-charge attitude infects even Carlyle. On his way to work he tells her that "'I feel, I really feel a hundred percent better'" (*C*, 171). By the midpoint of the fall semester, then, things are definitely looking up. Six weeks go by and the family is thriving. Carlyle, slowly reconciling himself to the fact that Eileen is not coming back, feels that "his life was beginning again" (*C*, 176). He even begins a new relationship with one of the secretaries at his school.

As we have come to expect in Carver Country, however, such a paradisal state cannot endure long. The first sign of trouble is that Carlyle comes down with a fever. Although a fairly minor event, the fever's immediate effect on Carlyle's state of mind can be likened to Lloyd's reaction to having his ear plugged with wax. The second blow is a more significant one: Mrs. Webster announces that she must leave, for her unemployed husband has been offered a partnership in their son's mink ranch in Oregon. This news is similar in its impact to Chef's announcement that he has to take his house back in "Chef's House." Unlike Lloyd and Wes, however, Carlyle is able to overcome both of these obstacles. His fever clears and he has no reason to think it will return; he knows that Mrs. Webster is doing what she has to, and he wishes her and her husband good luck. Before she leaves, furthermore, he has a long talk with her, "a burst of cathartic confession" (Campbell, 67) about the history of his relationship with Eileen. By talking with Mrs. Webster, Carlyle is finally able to close the books on that relationship and put it behind him. Mrs. Webster tells him that "'Sometimes it's good to talk about it. Sometimes it has to be talked about'" (C, 185), lines reminiscent of both "A Small, Good Thing" and "Where I'm Calling From." As in those two stories, here we see "the possibility of rebirth through the powers of community and narrative" (Cochrane, 83). Mrs. Webster assures Carlyle that he's going to be all right, and he believes her implicitly; he "finds his anxieties mitigated by the basic inducements of human contact" (Saltzman, 149). When she leaves, then, he feels "something come to an end" (C, 186), namely his life with Eileen. Having put her out of his mind, he is now able to turn to the children and begin a new phase in their lives. This final image allows the story to "end on [a] note of resounding uplift" (Con, 96). At the conclusion of "Fever," Carlyle, unlike so many of Carver's other protagonists in the volume, has indeed been made stronger by his ordeal and so his life is beginning again. His abilities to love and to open himself up have remained intact, and these capacities will allow him not merely to survive, but to thrive.

"The Bridle"

Like "Where I'm Calling from," "The Bridle" is a story that reflects more on the narrator's situation and character than on the people about whom she is telling. Unlike that earlier story, however, this one ends on a much less optimistic note, because the narrator here remains tightly reined. Ostensibly, the story concerns the stunned Holits family, recently dispossessed from their farm in Minnesota and trying to make a new start in Arizona. Holits himself remains unemployed, although his wife, Betty, does get a job as a waitress. One night Holits, drunk, attempts to dive from the roof of a cabana into a pool, but misses. He is now quite literally stunned, and he seems to have permanently entered a vegetative state. Betty is called upon to take full responsibility for leading the family. She does just that by leaving Arizona and "going someplace else to try their luck" (*C*, 206), although the narrative indicates that there is little chance their situation will change.

The tragic story of the Holits family is related by Marge, a part-time hair stylist and the full-time manager of the apartment complex in Arizona where Holits makes his fateful dive. As the story opens, she is quite sympathetic to the family's situation. Her first description of them, as they pull their car into the complex, is that they "look whipped" (*C*, 187), and when she gets the details of their situation she instantly "feel[s] sorry for them" (*C*, 190). She notes further that "these people seemed like dependable people. Down on their luck, that's all. No disgrace can be attached to that" (*C*, 192). In many ways they are typical Carver characters, and so, we will see, is Marge. The two women grow particularly close when, after her family has been in Arizona for a few weeks, Betty comes to Marge for a haircut. Betty has already started waitressing by this time, and Marge comments that they are "both wearing uniforms" (*C*, 197), a sign of their similar situations. Marge is able to "picture [her]self in Betty's shoes" (*C*, 201), recalling several of the stories in Carver's first collection, most obviously "Put Yourself in My Shoes." While Betty is having her hair done, she explains to Marge that she used to have dreams, but now she knows that dreams "'are what you wake up from'" (*C*, 200). She goes on to state that Marge doesn't "'know what it's like'" (*C*, 200), but the hairdresser tries to show her how wrong she is. "'Yes, I do,' I say. I pull the stool right up next to her legs. I'm starting to tell her how it was before we moved here, and how it's still like that. But Harley picks right then to come out of the bedroom" (*C*, 201). The bond between the two women is forged here, although it cannot be fully expressed. Nevertheless, the reader clearly understands how much the two women have in common.

Harley's interruption of this potentially intimate conversation is entirely appropriate, for he is Marge's Holits, as Carver indicates through the similarity in their names. Although mobile, Harley is another of Carver's petrified men. He is the groundskeeper for the apartments, but he spends most of his time eating, watching TV, and sleeping. Following the Holits family's departure, Marge notes that Harley is "settling into his chair. He has his can of pop, and he's wearing his straw hat. He acts like nothing has happened or ever will happen" (*C*, 207). Marge's position at the end of the story, then, is reminiscent of Betty's statement that "'For a long time, we had us a life. It had its ups and downs. But we thought we were working toward something.' She shakes her head. 'But something happened'" (*C*, 199). The reader senses that Marge and Harley also had a life once, but that it has soured since their removal to Arizona. Their attempt at a new start seems to have ended as poorly as Holits and Betty's, although their destruction has followed a more gradual course.

The ultimate effect of the Holits family's stay in the apartment complex is to show Marge the dashed hopes of her own life. In fact, there is even less chance of a fresh start for Marge than there is for Betty, as Carver makes clear through the image of the bridle. One of the first things Marge noticed when Holits was moving in was that he had a bridle, a reminder of his love for horses (the love that, according to Betty, started the family downhill in the first place). When she goes to clean their apartment after they have left, however, she finds that the bridle is still there. Betty had been in charge of the move, and Marge hopes that her discarding of the symbol of Holits's obsession will free her for better luck in the future. At the same time, though, she understands that Betty has bequeathed the bridle to her. She is now fully conscious of the restrictive life she is leading with Harley at the apartment complex. In the story's final image, which is almost frightening in its intensity, Marge looks at the bit and thinks that it's "heavy and cold. If you had to wear this thing between your teeth, I guess you'd catch on in a hurry. When you felt it pull, you'd know it was time. You'd know you were going somewhere" (*C*, 208). The force of the passage lies in Marge's full awareness that she is already wearing a bridle. In her case, furthermore, since the rider (Harley) suffers from such inertia, she won't be going anywhere at all. Earlier in the story, when Holits had paid his rent in $50 bills, she had dreamed of the places where those bills might end up. She had even written her name on them in hopes that someone somewhere might mention her, asking "'Who's this Marge?'" (*C*, 192). Unlike the bills, however, she is stuck. Marge can only be envious of Betty, even if she has two boys and a brain-damaged husband to take care of. The concluding paragraph of "The Bridle" is one of Carver's clearest evocations of the limited lives that most of his characters lead; it is only very rarely that the horse can manage to free itself from the bridle, and Marge is not going to find herself in that situation.

"Cathedral"

On the other hand, the narrator of "Cathedral," the final story in the collection, is just such a transcending individual, one who is able to turn an unexpected event into a positive element in his life. Carver termed this story a breakthrough, "a larger, grander story than anything I had previously written" (*Con*, 101), and it is surely one of his greatest achievements. Here, as in "Fever," Carver presents a character drifting toward inertia who is drawn back into life through an encounter with another person, in this case a blind man named Robert who is an old friend of the narrator's wife. The experience of being around a blind person is entirely new for the narrator, and he is not sure how to respond. At first the narrator is very reluctant to accept Robert into his home, an indication of his "rather repellent insularity and lack of compassion" (Saltzman, 152). He explains in the opening paragraph that "I wasn't enthusiastic about his visit. He was no one I knew. And his being blind bothered me. My idea of blindness came from the movies. In the movies, the blind moved slowly and never laughed. Sometimes they were led by seeing-eye dogs. A blind man in my house was not something I looked forward to" (*C*, 209). He is also somewhat jealous of Robert, a man from his wife's past. She had worked as a reader for him in Seattle one summer, and she has told her husband that she once let him feel her face. She now lives on the East Coast, but she and Robert have continued to stay in touch by sending each other tapes. Furthermore, the poems she writes, at the steady rate of one per year, are aimed more at Robert than at her husband.

As the story progresses, though, the narrator comes to reconsider his stance. When the narrator's wife explains to him how Robert's wife has recently died of cancer, the narrator "felt sorry for the blind man for a little bit" (*C*, 213). He also expresses sympathy for the blind man's dead wife, Beulah, who "could never see herself as she was seen in the eyes of her loved one" (*C*, 213). As soon as Robert arrives at the narrator's house, moreover, he begins to dispel all of the narrator's assumptions about blind people. For one thing, as the narrator notes in amazement, "this blind man, feature this, he was wearing a full beard! A beard on a blind man! Too much, I say" (*C*, 214). Robert neither wears dark glasses nor uses a cane, but he does smoke, something the narrator had heard blind people couldn't do. As they eat, the narrator responds "with admiration" (*C*, 217) to Robert's self-sufficiency. Later he is pleased to hear that the blind man enjoys television. By the time they've had after-dinner drinks and smoked some marijuana—a first for Robert—they are feeling like old friends. The narrator has clearly warmed up to his alien visitor.

Later in the evening, after the narrator's wife has fallen asleep, the narrator and Robert watch a television show about cathedrals. The narrator asks Robert if he understands what a cathedral looks like and, when the blind man replies that he does not, the host tries to explain it. He knows that the concept is not getting across, so he follows Robert's suggestion and gets a pen and some heavy paper. With the blind man's hand riding on top of his own,[19] the narrator begins to draw an elaborate cathedral. Although he is "no artist" (*C*, 227), the narrator continues drawing and he senses that Robert is finally able to "see" a cathedral. At the end of the story, Robert tells him to close his eyes but keep drawing, which the narrator does; "a moment of human, almost sacred communion ensues, collapsing distinctions between time and space" (Lonnquist, 149). The narrator notes, positively, that "it was like nothing else in my life up to now" (*C*, 228). Even when Robert tells him to open his eyes and look at the drawing, the narrator doesn't want to, and the story ends with the following passage, one of the most optimistic of all of Carver's fiction: "My eyes were still closed. I was in my house. I knew that. But I didn't feel like I was inside anything. 'It's really something,' I said" (*C*, 209). The sense of release from all constraints is so evident here that we are again reminded of Carver's affinity to Joyce in his use of epiphanies. Several critics, furthermore, have addressed the sight imagery in the story, commenting on the way in which "the blind man shows the narrator how to see" (Brown, 136). Mark A. R. Facknitz, for example, explains that "Carver redeems the narrator by releasing him from the figurative blindness that results in a lack of insight into his own condition and which leads him to trivialize human feelings and needs. Indeed, so complete is his misperception that the blind man gives him a faculty of sight that he is not even aware that he lacks" (Facknitz 1986, 293).[20]

The story, and the collection, thus ends on a note of exhilaration, a marked contrast to many of the individual stories in the volume. Unlike Marge in the preceding story, for instance, the narrator here is completely unbridled. By "enter[ing] imaginatively into the inner reality of his guest" (Lonnquist, 148), by "mov[ing] beyond isolation and xenophobia" (Clark, 245), he is able to respond in a positive manner and to learn the most valuable lesson of the collection: the importance of communication. Like the baker and the Weisses in "A Small, Good Thing," like the narrator at the end of "Where I'm Calling From," and like Carlyle in "Fever," the narrator of "Cathedral" is reaching out to another human being rather than succumbing to the ease of a petrified life.

Conclusion

In these four stories, then, we can see Carver moving away from the unremittingly bleak landscape of *What We Talk about When We Talk about Love* and the rest of the *Cathedral* texts. He is now "pointing the way out

of this 'dis-ease'" (Brown, 136), "focus[ing] on the way people wrest salvation from adversity" (*Con*, 167). As Carver's thematic outlook has
brightened, moreover, he has afforded a greater expansiveness to the
texts themselves, which are both more open and more detailed than
those in the previous collection. Although I concentrated on Carver's
thematic shifts in the discussions of the stories and did not spend much
time analyzing his movement away from stylistic austerity, few of the
stories in *Cathedral* can be considered minimalistic. In nearly every case
Carver provides precisely the kind of background material that he would
have previously excised. Even in the stories that present failure, the reader can now understand the causes of that failure. Whereas Carver could
have rightfully been accused of coldness in some of the earlier pieces,
that is no longer the case in this collection. Carver pointed out on
numerous occasions that *Cathedral* is more generous than his earlier volumes had been. At this point in his career, then, as William L. Stull has
noted, "Carver's journeyman days were over, as was his long revisionary
interlude. With *Cathedral*, he declared his independence as a master"
(Stull 1989, 208). Unfortunately, *Cathedral* would prove to be his last
book of new stories. In fact, he would only publish a total of seven additional stories before his untimely death. While reading this volume with
hindsight therefore causes us to consider what might have been,
Cathedral—deservedly nominated for both the National Book Critics
Circle Award and the Pulitzer Prize—remains Carver's masterpiece. In
writing of Chekhov, Carver defined "masterpieces" as "stories that shrive
us as well as delight and move us, that lay bare our emotions in ways
only true art can accomplish" (*NHP*, 146). The stories of *Cathedral* certainly live up to that high standard.

Chapter Eight

The Last Stories:
Where I'm Calling From

The final book of fiction Carver published during his lifetime is subtitled "New and Selected Stories," although they actually appear in reverse order. As a kind of introduction to or summation of his career, *Where I'm Calling From* serves several functions. It provides a clear picture of Carver Country, for example, in addition to showing the range of his talent. The volume also details the evolution of his narrative techniques in the hourglass pattern that I have been stressing. Carver made the selections for the volume and so he was able to weed out what he called "some of the stories which I just don't like and would never write again" (*Con*, 238). By looking at the texts that were included, then, we can see which of his own stories he ultimately chose to stand by. What we discover is that, throughout the collection, Carver chose optimism and fullness rather than pessimism and minimalism. The new stories, moreover, show Carver's writing expanding in unexpected directions. He asserted that "these new stories are different from the earlier ones in degree and kind" (*Con*, 186), for they "deal not just with husband and wife domestic relationships but with family relationships: son and mother, or father and children; and they go into these relationships more extensively. . . . And they're all longer, more detailed and somehow more affirmative, I believe" (*Con*, 210). On the whole, then, *Where I'm Calling From* is a fitting capstone to Carver's career, emphasizing his strengths and, once again, making us lament that he was not afforded the opportunity to produce more stories.

Selected Stories

The stories Carver opted to include here provide a strong indication of his aesthetic position toward the end of his life, for he selected more from the early and late periods than from the extreme minimalism of the middle period. The volume begins with 12 of the 22 stories from *Will You Please Be Quiet, Please?*, the most often overlooked work in his canon.

The stories included, which do represent a good cross section of that first volume, are, in their new order: "Nobody Said Anything," "Bicycles, Muscles, Cigarets," "The Student's Wife," "They're Not Your Husband," "What Do You Do in San Francisco?," "Fat," "What's in Alaska?," "Neighbors," "Put Yourself in My Shoes," "Collectors," "Why, Honey?," and "Are These Actual Miles?" If that last title sounds unfamiliar, the story itself was originally called "What Is It?," and except for its name, it is reproduced verbatim. All of these stories, in fact, are reprinted in their original versions. Next, Carver presents 6 of the 12 stories that made their first collected appearance in *What We Talk about When We Talk about Love*: "Gazebo," "One More Thing," "Why Don't You Dance?," "A Serious Talk," "What We Talk about When We Talk about Love," and "The Calm." Each of these appears as it did in the earlier volume, and several of the stories are indeed examples of Carver's minimalism at its most effective.

At this point in assembling the selected stories, Carver was faced with the same dilemma that had troubled him when he was preparing *Fires*: what to do with that set of stories that had appeared in several different versions. For the most part, Carver once again opted for the larger, more developed texts rather than the minimalistic ones. While an additional five stories that can be found in *What We Talk about When We Talk about Love* do appear in the selected stories of *Where I'm Calling From*, only two of them appear as they did in that arch-minimalist collection. "Little Things" is a new name for Carver's variation on the story that was originally titled "Mine" and then "Popular Mechanics." The text here comes from the second, *What We Talk about When We Talk about Love* version of the story, although the changes between the two texts are rather minor. "The Third Thing That Killed My Father Off," despite reverting to its *Furious Seasons* title, also presents the text as it first appeared in *What We Talk about When We Talk about Love*. However, Carver chose the more expansive forms of the other three stories. "Distance" (also known as "Everything Stuck to Him") and "So Much Water So Close to Home" are reproduced in the versions from *Fires*, versions that are much closer to their original, fuller texts than to the later, minimalized ones. Most tellingly, rather than reprinting "The Bath," Carver waits until he turns to the stories from *Cathedral* and includes "A Small, Good Thing," the greatly expanded version of that tale. The selection of these stories in these versions clearly demonstrates Carver's ultimate preference for the fuller style, as does his inclusion of two-thirds of the more generous *Cathedral* stories: "Vitamins," "Careful," "Where I'm Calling From,"

"Chef's House," "Fever," "Feathers," and "Cathedral," in addition to "A Small, Good Thing." The only stories from *Cathedral* that did not make the cut, furthermore, are the ones that depict a lack of communication or positive movement forward. That Carver should choose *Where I'm Calling From* as the title for the volume is additional evidence of his ultimately positive vision.

"Boxes"

The first of the new stories is also evidence of Carver's more optimistic side. Although its title might remind us of "The Compartment," the protagonist of "Boxes" *is* able to break out of his emotional isolation and reconnect with a family member. In the process he comes to more firmly understand himself as well. The general plot of the story, which Carver discloses in a rather roundabout way, centers on a male narrator who has moved to Washington following the emotional trauma he suffered in California after his wife left him. He is now living with Jill, a woman who has experienced traumas of her own: "Her two children were kidnapped by her first husband and taken to Australia. Her second husband, who drank, left her with a broken eardrum before he drove their car through a bridge into the Elwha River."[1] As though these events aren't bad enough, the fledgling relationship between the narrator and Jill is severely strained when his mother moves to town. After a short time in Washington, however, his mother claims to hate the place and longs to return to California. She even begins to pack up for a return move, although she puts off the actual trip for six months. As the relationship between mother and son becomes the focal point of the story, the narrator proves himself capable of navigating emotional straits and emerging with both a greater love for his mother and a greater sense of himself, although his future with Jill remains unsettled.

As the story opens, the mother is two days away from departure and she calls up her son and his girlfriend to invite them over for dinner. Jill, who has been hearing the older woman say that she is leaving for several months now, "has run out of patience" (*WICF*, 410) and is reluctant to go. Nor can the reader—or even the narrator—blame her, since the mother is very hard to deal with. She is elderly and might be getting senile, for one thing. During the long Northwestern winter she had told the narrator that "if this weather didn't improve she was going to kill herself" (*WICF*, 413), and at one point he thinks that he might be forced to commit her to an institution (*WICF*, 421). More significantly, this is far from the first time his mother has moved from one place to another and then back again; in fact, her moves are so frequent that the title of the story actually refers to the way her life is constantly being lived between unpacking and repacking boxes of her possessions. The narrator gives us a clear picture of her character when he explains that "she started moving years ago, after my dad lost his job. When that happened, when he was laid off, they sold their home, as if this were what they should do, and went to where they thought things would be better. But things weren't any better there, either. They moved again. They kept on moving" (*WICF*, 414). In this way she is like Holits and his family in "The Bridle," who moved to Arizona only to leave it again and try their luck somewhere else. The implication in both cases, though, is that such luck is probably not going to be found. Jill knows that her boyfriend's mother will be just as unhappy back in California as she has been in Washington. She even tries to tell her this, to force her to see reality. The mother briefly does seem to understand her predicament, but then she returns to her plans with renewed optimism. She tells her son that this will be her final move, although we have every reason not to believe her statement.

While Jill's attitude toward her boyfriend's mother is rather straightforward, the narrator's own emotions are much more complex and confused. Despite her many faults, she is still his mother, and he feels that he must look out for her. He has also run out of patience, but he doesn't see what his other options are. Although he agrees with Jill's assessment that his mother is losing her mind, he doesn't know how he should respond to such a situation. After his mother had expressed thoughts of suicide to him, for example, he reports that "I didn't have any idea what I was going to say next. I had to say something. But I was filled with unworthy feelings, thoughts no son should admit to" (*WICF*, 413). The stress begins to get to him and, during their farewell dinner, he breaks down in tears when he thinks that he may never see her again. The two women come to his aid, but unsuccessfully; he notes that Jill "is on one side of my chair, and my mother is on the other side. They could tear me apart in no time at all" (*WICF*, 421). Even two days later, when his mother actually does leave, the narrator expresses the ambivalence of his situation: "And I *am* going to miss her. She's my mother, after all, and why shouldn't I miss her? But, God forgive me, I'm glad, too, that it's finally time and that she is leaving" (*WICF*, 422). He is unable to say anything to his mother, and after she drives off he is "sad for a while, and then the sadness goes away" (*WICF*, 423).

When the mother calls to say that she has made it back to California, the narrator is at last able to have a serious talk with her. At first he is unable to respond to her complaints about California, but then he recalls how his father, when he wasn't drunk, would sometimes affectionately call his wife "Dear." He remembers that "always, hearing it, I felt better, less afraid, more hopeful about the future" (*WICF*, 424), and he says to his mother "'Dear, try not to be afraid'" (*WICF*, 424). He goes on, he notes, to "tell my mother I love her and I'll write to her, yes" (*WICF*, 424), evincing a strong desire to remain in close contact. During the course of the story the narrator has established a sense of communication with his mother, and they seem to understand each other better at the end of the story than they did at the beginning, even though, or perhaps because, she is hundreds of miles away. Moreover, the narrator's position at the end of the story is dictated by his own realization that "I'm never going back to California" (*WICF*, 421). For him, the lesson he has learned is to stay put, that the life he and Jill have together, despite its problems, is probably better than anything he could find anywhere else. Because he is able to overcome the emotional boxes in his life, therefore, he is able to avoid the literal boxes of moving as well. Even so, the ending of "Boxes" is somewhat ambiguous, particularly in regard to the narrator's continuing relationship with Jill. He has found a way to communicate with his mother, but he must now find a different way to talk with his girlfriend. So far the best he seems to be able to offer is a kind of inarticulate expression of caring. The hope with which the story ends is thus "vague [and] modest" (Saltzman, 174), although certainly present.[2]

"Whoever Was Using This Bed"

The opening of this story, in which the narrator receives a wrong-number call at three-thirty in the morning, instantly calls to mind "Are You a Doctor?" and "The Bath." The woman on the other end of the line is drunk, but she is also persistent. Finally Jack, the narrator, has to unplug the phone. He wants to go back to sleep, but Iris, his wife, seems to be awake for good. The couple begins to smoke cigarettes and talk. Iris tells Jack that she has been feeling a strange throbbing in her head, like an incipient stroke. He responds by telling her that he has been having heart palpitations himself. Neither has previously told the other about their respective symptoms, however, for fear that the spouse would be unduly worried. The topic of death thus enters the conversation and Iris raises the issue of "pulling the plug," that is, euthanasia, which had been much in the news of late. Up until this point Jack had only considered the topic on a hypothetical level, but with the detailing of his own and of his wife's afflictions he realizes that the discussion is now much more serious, and more personal. Iris pleads with Jack to promise that, should the situation arise, he will pull her plug, but he doesn't "know how [he] feel[s] about it yet" (*WICF*, 439). Then she asks him, more pointedly, what he would like her to do for him in the same situation. Jack is so stunned that at first he doesn't know how to respond. Ultimately he decides that, while he will honor her desire, he would like to stay plugged in himself. Jack and Iris both feel relieved for having talked the situation over, but the narrator knows that the conversation will always remain in his mind. He points out that "I feel as if I've crossed some kind of invisible line. I feel as if I've come to a place I never thought I'd have to come to. And I don't know how I got here. It's a strange place. It's a place where a little harmless dreaming and then some sleepy, early-morning talk has led me into considerations of death and annihilation" (*WICF*, 442). Once again we are reminded of "The Bath," where the sudden disruption of their lives forces the Weisses to think about things they had never before considered.

At this point Jack plugs the phone back in and it rings again. The caller is the same woman from many hours ago, but this time she is apologetic and no longer drunk. Nevertheless, Jack and Iris again react with horror to the intrusion in their lives. Jack warns the woman not to call again or "'I'll wring your neck for you'" (*WICF*, 443), and Iris lashes out at "'The *gall* of that woman'" (*WICF*, 443). She then bends over and roughly unplugs the phone. The last line of the story is the narrator's observation that "the line goes dead, and I can't hear anything" (*WICF*, 443). The parallel between unplugging a phone and unplugging a life support system is quite clear. While Jack and Iris have explored at length the issue of pulling each other's plug, they literally unplug this other woman without any kind of consultation. Admittedly, most of us would react as they do, yet the impression seems to be that this woman was in need of help and they nonetheless cut her off. Perhaps this is a statement about the perils of euthanasia, of how an impartial person might be overly willing to pull the plug on someone who could still be helped. In any event, the ultimate effect of the experience on the narrator is to make him more keenly aware of his own mortality, and the way his very life might at any moment be unplugged by his weak heart. Like "The Bath," then, "Whoever Was Using This Bed" ends on a note of suspension and menace. Jack and Iris are visibly shaken by their ordeal, and the line going dead seems to signal something about their own lives as well.

"Intimacy"

"Intimacy" also recalls the stories of the *What We Talk about When We Talk about Love* collection in several ways. The title, for example, is ironic, for the story is actually about the lack of intimacy between the narrator, a writer, and his ex-wife. One day he goes to visit her, but is met with "a tirade of complaint" (Runyon, 188). Most of the talking that makes up the story, in fact, is done by the ex-wife. The narrator himself has nothing to say, while she has been waiting for an opportunity to vent her hostility. Although they have not seen each other for four years prior to this meeting, he has kept her apprised of himself and his activities by sending her clippings about his writings and appearances. As it turns out, though, one of her greatest reasons for resenting him is that she feels she has been exploited as material in his works. Wondering why he has come to see her now, she accuses him of being "on a fishing expedition. You're hunting for *material*. Am I getting warm? Am I right?" (*WICF*, 447). Although this was probably not his original intention, the fact that we are reading the story proves her to have made an accurate prediction.[3] The narrator's ex-wife also resents the fact that he has found a new lover and is, according to his press clippings, "'happy now'" (*WICF*, 449). She wishes the newspaper people would ask her opinion, because she has a lot she could tell them. "I was there," she says. "I served, buddy boy. Then you held me up for display and ridicule in your so-called work. For any Tom or Harry to pity or pass judgment on" (*WICF*, 449). As the story progresses and the ex-wife rattles through her list of grievances, she grows ever more heated.

Through this entire harangue the narrator remains largely quiescent. He does not know how to respond to her complaints, many of which he acknowledges to be valid. Toward the end of the story he bends down and takes the hem of her dress, assuming a position of supplication.[4] His ex-wife then calms down and says that she forgives him, although she does so primarily in hopes that he will leave before her new husband comes home. Her final comments—"Maybe it'll make a good story, she says. But I don't want to know about it if it does" (*WICF*, 453)—indicate her desire for a complete break with her ex-husband. All she wants is to put that marriage completely behind her and to move on with her life. But the narrator doesn't seem to know what he wants. As he leaves his ex-wife's house he notices the disarray of the neighborhood and notes, in the image with which the story ends, that "somebody ought to make an effort here. Somebody ought to get a rake and take care of this" (*WICF*, 453). He would like a return to order and stasis, it seems, but will not actively do anything to bring it about. He wants "somebody" to do it, but he won't do it himself. While the narrator might be marked as a success in the public sphere, it is the ex-wife who can be marked a success in this story. She is relying on herself and moving forward, however tentatively, while the narrator seems to be languishing in indecisiveness. Perhaps in telling the story he is able to impose the kind of order that he would like to obtain, but he still comes off looking badly. For him, the story provides the sort of realization of failure that was a pronounced characteristic of some of Carver's earlier works.

"Menudo"

"Menudo" is very similar to "Intimacy," for it shares some of the same imagery and arrives at an equally pessimistic conclusion. Hughes, the narrator, like the narrator in "Intimacy," would like his life to return to order and normalcy, but he senses the impossibility of this outcome. Although he does rake the leaves in his yard—a clear reference to the end of "Intimacy"—there is no indication that his actions will have any kind of positive effect. His life has been full of "compulsion and error" (*WICF*, 461), as he notes at one point, and it seems that the future will be no different. The title of the story, for example, refers to a kind of tripe stew that the narrator's friend Alfredo had cooked for him when he developed a nervous condition shortly after his breakup with his first wife. Alfredo had told him, like the baker had told the Weisses in "A Small, Good Thing," that "it would be good for what ailed" (*WICF*, 467), that it would calm him down, but Hughes had fallen asleep while the menudo was simmering, and when he woke up it had already been eaten by somebody else. This scene is emblematic of Hughes's whole life, which is a litany of having missed out. The possibility of redemption had been offered to him, but he had been unable to take advantage of it and had subsequently moved into further stages of degeneration. The title, then, like the ironic title of "Intimacy," points to what the narrator lacks in his life rather than to what he actually has.

The narrator's having slept through the proffered menudo is made even more ironic by the fact that, in the present of the story, he is suffer-

ing from severe insomnia. Although "exhausted" (*WICF*, 454), he cannot sleep. As the night wears on he looks back over his life and goads
himself with recriminations about his inability to make contact with
another person. He recalls, for example, how his mother, to whom he
had been sending biannual support checks, had wanted a new clock
radio, but he had told her that he couldn't give her any more than he
was already giving. He knows, though, that he could have given more,
and his uncaring actions haunt him because, shortly thereafter, his mother died. Similarly, he remembers how he failed to come to his first wife's
aid when she needed him. He and Molly had known each other from the
time they were very young and they had vowed to love each other forever, "but it hadn't worked out that way" (*WICF*, 459). Hughes had
begun to see another woman, Vicky, and when Molly found out about it
she experienced severe mental problems, even to the point of being committed to an institution. He notes that "I bailed out on her" (*WICF*,
460), that "I didn't even go visit her—not once! . . . I intended to write,
but I didn't" (*WICF*, 465). He can now say that he is sorry, but he
knows that doesn't change anything. Molly had later informed him that
their destinies, their karmas, were linked, but he doesn't even know
where she is anymore and can hardly remember what she looks like. In
the present of the story, furthermore, his relationship with Vicky is most
likely coming to an end because he has begun to see another woman,
Amanda Porter, one of their neighbors. Going through yet another dark
night of the soul, Hughes puzzles over whether "this is where my destiny
has brought me? To this street in this neighborhood, messing up the
lives of these women?" (*WICF*, 466). He would like to believe something
else, but he cannot honestly do so.

Hughes's life has been brought to a crisis point because both Vicky
and Amanda's husband, Oliver, have found out about the affair. Vicky
had had an affair a year earlier, and while that episode had been weath-
ered, Hughes senses that this affair will not be so easily put behind
them. He knows that some decision must be forthcoming, and agrees
with Amanda's statement that "'we have to decide something real
important, real soon'" (*WICF*, 456), but he has no idea how to resolve
the situation. His primary impulse is simply to escape, to bail out again,
although he knows that he cannot do so. He states that "I wish I could
sleep and wake up and find everything in my life different" (*WICF*, 461),
but insomnia, an ally of reality, has him firmly in its grip. By the end of
the story, Hughes finds himself in the position of envying another of his
neighbors, a Mr. Baxter, who, he tells us, "is a decent, ordinary guy—a

guy you wouldn't mistake for anyone special. But he *is* special. In my book, he is. For one thing he has a full night's sleep behind him, and he's just embraced his wife before leaving for work" (*WICF*, 471). These small, good things, despite being all that Hughes aspires to, remain entirely beyond his reach. He can rake his yard, and he can rake Mr. Baxter's yard, as he is doing when Baxter goes to work, and he can even rake Amanda's yard, but he knows that these actions will not restore order to his life. He states that "now I don't know what to believe in. I'm not complaining, simply stating a fact. I'm down to nothing. And I have to go on like this" (*WICF*, 460–61). Even when he takes action at the very end of the story, then, telling us that "I look both ways and then cross the street" (*WICF*, 471)—presumably to Amanda's house, where she, too, has been spending a sleepless night—there is little reason to expect that his movement will alter his destiny. He seems much more likely to be hit by a car, despite the precaution of having looked out for one, than to reestablish a harmonious life with either Vicky or Amanda. For him, the dream of normalcy remains just that, a fantasy, while his real life seems to be going nowhere fast. The answer to his question "Is this what it all comes down to then?" (*WICF*, 469) seems to be that, for him, unfortunately, it is.[5]

"Blackbird Pie"

The next story in the collection, "Elephant," also presents a protagonist who is being dragged closer and closer to despair, and as such is a typical Carver character in a fairly typical Carver story. The same cannot be said of "Blackbird Pie," one of Carver's most inventive tales. Here the narrator moves from emotional blindness, through "'mystery [and] speculation'" (*WICF*, 508), to a serene understanding of himself and his life. The element that makes the story most memorable among Carver's later works is the narrator himself, a man who appears to be both incredibly smart and incredibly stupid at the same time. At the outset of the story he informs us that he "used to win prizes at school because of [his] ability to remember names and dates, inventions, battles, treaties, alliances and the like. [He] always scored highest on factual tests" (*WICF*, 491–92). When it comes to real situations that affect himself and his life, however, he is at a total loss. He doesn't seem to comprehend anything that is going on around him, even though he is able to make the situation blatantly clear to the reader. In explaining the events leading up to the evening of his wife's departure, for example, he notes that she had asked him whether he was "'planning to be in [his] room this evening'" (*WICF*, 497). Surely he should be able to sense the tension in the room and the tone of her question, yet he blithely replies "'Of course'" (*WICF*, 497). Heading off to his study, moreover, he totally misapprehends her attitude. He states that "I thought she might proffer a word or two of encouragement for the work I was engaged in, but she didn't. Not a peep. It was as if she were waiting for me to leave the kitchen so she could enjoy her privacy" (*WICF*, 498). This is not the case at all; she is waiting for him to leave the room so that she can leave the house forever.

Her reasons for leaving, as the narrator makes evident to the reader despite failing to see them himself, center precisely around his "work," the writing of a historian's text. Later on during the "evening in question" (*WICF*, 497) he is hard at work when an envelope is slid under his door. He informs us, in the story's opening paragraph, that "what was inside purported to be a letter from my wife. I say 'purported' because even though the grievances could only have come from someone who'd spent twenty-three years observing me on an intimate, day-to-day basis, the charges were outrageous and completely out of keeping with my wife's character. Most important, however, the handwriting was not my wife's handwriting" (*WICF*, 491). Carver's opening gambit, and much of the detective-fiction jargon in the story, recalls Poe's "The Purloined Letter," although here we are dealing with the "proffered" letter. The narrator knows where the letter comes from—he and his wife are the only people for miles around, which is one of the reasons she is leaving—but he cannot adequately account for his wife's behavior. He states that "I think her *decline*, as a historian might put it, was accelerated by our move to the country. I think she slipped a cog after that. I'm speaking from hindsight, of course, which always tends to confirm the obvious" (*WICF*, 495). Once again, however, the narrator has seen the wrong obvious, for it is clear to the reader that his wife is not crazy. On the contrary, it is the narrator who shows himself to be emotionally blind. The fact that the letter's handwriting is not his wife's convinces him of her instability, but Carver makes it clear to the reader that the change in her script is a manifestation of the explosion of her bottled-up emotions. The husband is suspicious of the letter's authenticity because words in it are underlined for emphasis, something his wife had never done in the thousands of letters she had written to him, yet he has already told us that she had recently begun speaking "as if virtually every other word out of her mouth ought to be emphasized" (*WICF*, 504). Once again, despite his high academic achievements, he shows himself to be unable to penetrate the mysteries of emotions. He knows that he must do something—like a detective, he must confront the parties involved—but he finds himself entirely unable to act. His wife is leaving and there doesn't seem to be anything he can do about it. In noting that "the moment had come and gone, and could not be called back" (*WICF*, 500), he echoes precisely the point that his wife had made in her letter describing the dissolution of their relationship.

Toward the end of the story, however, Carver moves the narrator forward to a kind of Joycean epiphany. The emotional stupidity he displayed in the first part of the story gives way to an emotionally charged self-realization of the irrevocable changes that have been wrought in his life. The story concludes with him philosophically musing that

> It could be said, for instance, that to take a wife is to take a history. And if that's so, then I understand that I'm outside history now—like horses and fog. Or you could say that my history has left me. Or that I'm having to go on *without history*. Or that history will now have to do without me—unless my wife writes more letters, or tells a friend who keeps a diary, say. Then, years later, someone can look back on this time, interpret it according to the record, its scraps and tirades, its silences and innuendos. That's when it dawns on me that autobiography is the poor man's history. And that I am saying good-bye to history. Good-bye, my darling. (*WICF*, 510–11)

The narrator is in fact the one who has left the record, and it is indeed full of "scraps and tirades." Nevertheless, there is also a certain amount of calm resignation here. The narrator seems to be wishing his wife well in her new life, even though he himself has nothing to look forward to since, by leaving, she has taken away both herself and his work, the two forces that had been competing for his attention. Like the maid in the "Sing a Song of Six-Pence" nursery rhyme to which the story's title alludes, the narrator has a little blackbird (his wife) fly out of the pie and snip off his nose. A wiser man at the end of the story, however, the narrator seems to have gained a sense of equilibrium, an emotional balance. He realizes what is in store for him for the rest of his life, and he seems willing to face that situation head-on.

"Errand"

"Errand," one of the crowning jewels in Carver's oeuvre, is unlike any other story he wrote, with the possible exception of "The Train." Just as that story borrowed from a separate text, John Cheever's "The Five-Forty-Eight," so does "Errand" work from the facts presented in another text: the story of the death of Anton Chekhov. There is a certain amount of factual material to be established at the outset of the story, and Carver presents it straightforwardly. He explains that, in the middle of the night, during a heat wave at the spa at Badenweiler, Chekhov finally succumbed to the tuberculosis that had been slowly killing him. The only people with him were his wife, the actress Olga Knipper, and his doctor, Dr. Schwohrer. Immediately prior to Chekhov's death, however, Schwohrer had ordered champagne for the three of them to raise a last toast. During the remainder of "Errand," Carver focuses our attention on the unsuspecting hotel delivery boy who fills this drink order. In a way, Carver prepares us for this unlikely focus in his explanation of the departure of Dr. Schwohrer following Chekhov's death. He writes that the doctor "picked up his bag and left the room and, for that matter, history" (*WICF*, 521). Schwohrer has played a significant role in the story—it was his idea, after all, to order the champagne—but we know nothing of his life outside of his encounter with the dying Chekhov. What, then, can be the importance of a person who didn't even play a significant role in this encounter, namely, the delivery boy? Carver imagines this character's position, returning to his old theme of putting oneself in another's shoes, and comes to view the events from a completely different perspective.

Carver projects that the bellhop had probably "been resting (slumped in a chair, say, dozing a little), when off in the distance the phone had clamored in the early-morning hours—great God in Heaven!—and the next thing he knew he was being shaken awake by a superior and told to deliver a bottle of Moet to Room 211" (*WICF*, 519). Naturally the boy is confused, and after he drops off the champagne Schwohrer quickly hustles him out of the room. Later on that morning, however, before the first official has gone to see about the situation in Room 211, the delivery boy, now fully awake and looking much more professional, returns to collect the bottle and glasses, and to present Olga with some flowers. He is made uneasy by Olga's distracted behavior, though, and he doesn't quite know what to do with the flowers. He senses that something is odd in the room, but he doesn't quite understand what has happened; there is no outward disturbance except for the cork from the champagne bottle which rests by the woman's foot, yet he is sure that something has gone wrong. Olga then charges him with an errand: to find, quietly and unobtrusively, the city's best mortician and to bring him to Chekhov's room. Olga emphasizes that he is to proceed slowly and methodically so as not to raise alarm about the great man's death. The bellhop nods his head, although he clearly hasn't grasped the significance of what is taking place. Instead, Carver notes, "at that moment the young man was thinking of the cork still resting near the toe of his shoe. To retrieve it he would have to bend over, still gripping the vase. He would do this. He leaned over. Without looking down, he reached out and closed it into his hand" (*WICF*, 526). While some critics see this action as showing the boy's total misapprehension of the difference between the trivial and the serious, there's more to it than that. The language of the passage has a remarkably upbeat tone to it, and the zen-like action indicates that a kind of grace has settled on the delivery boy. Carver indicates that if the boy can accomplish his errand, he will in fact have become significant to the story. Although in actuality history was not kind to the young man, for his "name hasn't survived, and it's likely he perished in the Great War" (*WICF*, 523), through his role in "Errand" he has indeed become an important figure, for in paying homage to Chekhov, Carver is paying homage to this anonymous bellhop as well. Thus, as Graham Clarke has written, "Errand" is "centrally Carver, for the waiter, like the figures in Carver's American stories, has been made visible: photographed, so to speak, as a singular being within a life as distinctive as the other characters in the story" (Clarke, 119). As much as Carver admired Chekhov, he also acknowledges that this anonymous delivery boy's life was equally important.

Conclusion

Another Carver tradition that "Errand" continued was the winning of awards; the story received the first prize in the 1988 O. Henry Awards and was included in *The Best American Short Stories, 1988*. The latter distinction is particularly interesting, since Mark Helprin, the guest editor for that year's volume, made his choices without knowing the various texts' authors, and included Carver's story despite spending the majority of his introduction railing against minimalism. By the time Carver wrote his final stories, he had obviously moved beyond the limiting style of extreme minimalism. Ewing Campbell, for example, writes that "the expressionism of 'Blackbird Pie' and imagined history of 'Errand' . . . signal a striking departure from the old, for which very little in Carver's realistic fiction could have prepared us" (Campbell, 71). Mark A. R. Facknitz concurs, stating that these two texts "seem to mark a new and more sophisticated tendency in Carver's work" (Facknitz 1989–90, 68).

As a matter of fact, none of Carver's final seven stories would be fully at home in *What We Talk about When We Talk about Love*, the text that defined the minimalist movement and gave Carver's career a major boost. Although many readers still associate him with the stories in that volume, it is in fact his least representative work, since the stories he produced both before and after that collection are markedly different.

All in all, then, *Where I'm Calling From* is a fitting conclusion to Carver's story-writing career. The collection contains 37 tales that, in addition to providing their own intrinsic merits, had a profound effect on American literature in the 1980s and 1990s. Hayden Carruth might have overstated the case a bit when he called *Where I'm Calling From* "the only certifiable masterpiece produced in the United States during the past quarter-century" (Stull 1989, 212), but it is certainly one of the few great works of that era, particularly among short-story collections. It is a book that will continue to be read and taught for many years to come. Carver's stories, like the works of his mentors, Hemingway, Joyce, and Chekhov, have become a permanent part of our literary landscape.

Chapter Nine

Poetry

Raymond Carver's reputation certainly rests on his short stories, but he was also a poet of considerable skill who published poetry throughout his career. His first published volume, in fact, was a collection of poetry entitled *Near Klamath* (1968). In his early years he published two more volumes of poetry, *Winter Insomnia* (1970) and *At Night the Salmon Move* (1976). In gathering the material for *Fires*, Carver returned to these volumes and reprinted (with some alterations[1]) a number of these poems. *Fires* also includes several poems that Carver had written between 1976 and 1982, the years he was drying out. These new poems indicate a growth and maturity in his poetic work. After he was given the Mildred and Harold Strauss Living Award in 1983, Carver moved to Port Angeles, Washington, Tess Gallagher's hometown, in order to escape the bustle of Syracuse. He intended to write stories, but instead he found himself writing poems at a furious pace; shortly thereafter he published *Where Water Comes Together with Other Water* (1985), probably his strongest individual collection of poems. Another spate of activity followed his return from a trip to South America, resulting in *Ultramarine* (1986). This volume received much praise and earned Carver *Poetry* magazine's Levinson Prize. Carver's final works were also poems, which were collected in the posthumously issued *A New Path to the Waterfall* (1989). In all of these volumes, particularly the last three, Carver produced poems that are deserving of much more attention than they have received to date. Nevertheless, Carver's poetry remains of interest primarily for its similarities to and differences from his fiction. The following discussion, therefore, rather than analyzing individual works, will attempt to group some of Carver's poems under various thematic banners.

In some ways, Carver's poems are very much like his stories. For example, he told one of his first interviewers that "I believe plot line is very important. Whether I am writing a poem or writing prose I am still trying to tell a story" (*Con*, 9). Poetic concerns like stanzas and meter mean little to him (*Con*, 191), except to the extent that such features help to move the plot forward. Carver also noted on several occasions that, due to the emphasis on the unity of effect, "there's more similarity between writing a short story and writing a poem than there is between writing a short story and writing a novel" (*Con*, 13; see also *NHP*, 140). For Carver, then, the writing of poems and stories goes hand in hand, with each genre helping to strengthen the other. And while his poems are known to be like stories, several critics have also pointed out that his stories are like poems, particularly in the clarity and intensity of their images (*Con*, 9, 106).

There are even a few illuminating cases in which Carver's imagery and content are found in both a story and a poem (or poems). A bridle, for example, appears in the poems "Energy"[2] and "The House behind This One,"[3] while depictions of voyeurism can be found in "The Man Outside" (*NHP*, 78–79) and "Locking Yourself Out, Then Trying to Get Back in" (*WWCT*, 32–33). The imagery in the poem "Distress Sale" (*F*, 56–57) is quite similar to that found in the story "Why Don't You Dance?," for both works explore the life of a person who is forced to put his belongings in the front yard in order to sell them off for whatever he can get. Carver explains that, in this case, he "wrote the poem first and then wrote the story, I suppose, because I apparently felt a need to elaborate on the same theme" (*Con*, 179), to "deal with it in a larger, fuller way" (*Con*, 223). The same is true of other crossovers, such as the poems that share material with the late stories "Boxes" and "Elephant." A mother much like the mother in "Boxes" can be found in several poems from *Ultramarine*, including "The Mail," "What I Can Do," "Son," and, especially, "Mother" (*U*, 13–14, 63, 68, 128). A narrator beset with family members' requests for money, the situation in "Elephant," appears in "Money" (*WWCT*, 39), "The Mail," "Stupid," and "What I Can Do" (*U*, 13–14, 21–22, 63). Parallels can also be drawn, for example, between the story "Intimacy" and the poem "The Schooldesk" (*U*, 93–95), in which the narrator notes that his ex-wife complains about being featured in his writings.

Many of Carver's poems are also depictions of life in Carver Country. For most of the protagonists, as Carver writes in a poem called "Shiftless," "the people who were better than us were *comfortable*" while "the ones worse off were *sorry*" (*U*, 59). "Fear," for example, is a litany of things the narrator, a typical Carver figure, fears, including policemen, bankruptcy, and even "Fear of anxiety!" (*WWCT*, 12); similarly, "Anathema" and "Next Door" are listings of all the things that have gone wrong in the narrators' lives before they were finally "beaten" (*WWCT*, 29, 62).[4] "Ashtray" tells of a relationship that is at the point of breaking apart; the woman in the poem is still trying to hold on, but the man has already moved on to the next phase in his life, a relationship with one of her friends (*WWCT*, 14–15). Perhaps the clearest example of Carver Country in the poetry is the diptych "Our First House in Sacramento" and "Next Year." In the first poem, the couple has just moved into the house when they are accosted by a man with a baseball bat who thinks they are the former occupants; this is a bad omen, and things only get worse until the couple decides to pack up and leave in the middle of the night in hopes of finding greener pastures elsewhere. In the second poem, set a year later in Santa Barbara, the narrator recounts all of the things that have gone wrong since they moved from Sacramento. He begins each item on his list with the haunting refrain "that wasn't the worst" (*WWCT*, 25). Again the poem ends with the hope that "this time next year / things were going to be different" (*WWCT*, 26), but by this point nobody is convinced that such a turn of events will actually take place.

This pair of poems also shows the contributing role alcohol plays in such disintegration; indeed, alcoholism is addressed at least as much in Carver's poems as it is in his stories. When Carver selected poems from his earlier volumes to include in *Fires*, for example, he grouped them based on their situations or obsessions, and the first group consists of poems dealing specifically with alcohol. These range from "Drinking While Driving" (*F*, 53), a poem that emphasizes the aimlessness of the alcoholic, and "Luck," in which the narrator dreams of "a house where no one / was home, no one coming back, / and all I could drink" (*F*, 55), to "Rogue River Jet-Boat Trip, Gold Beach, Oregon, July 4, 1977," a poem written only a month after Carver stopped drinking, and in which he writes that "I no longer know anything except / I am not drinking—though I'm still weak / and sick from it" (*F*, 71). Alcohol also plays an important part in several poems written about other members of his family. In "Photograph of My Father in His Twenty-Second Year," for example, he notes that his father is holding a beer along with his string of fish and concludes the poem "Father, I love you, / yet how can I say thank you, I who can't hold my liquor either, / and don't even know the places to fish?" (*F*, 59). In the later poem "To My Daughter," interestingly, Carver urges Christine to stop drinking, asking her "Didn't your mother and I set you / example enough?" (*WWCT*, 27). Other late poems that comment on alcohol and alcoholism include "The Old Days," "Yesterday, Snow" (*WWCT*, 22, 121), "NyQuil" (*U*, 56), and "Miracle" (*ANP*, 26–30).

The underlying reason for these crossovers between Carver's stories and poems, of course, is that they all grow out of the same set of experiences. In the depiction of those experiences, however, there is something of a divergence between the poetry and the fiction. He told Kay Bonetti, for example, that "the poetry can be much more personal than the fiction" (*Con*, 59), and he explained to Kasia Boddy that "I think I become more intimate in the poems, more vulnerable in ways I don't allow myself to be in the stories" (*Con*, 198). The poems certainly gibe more than do the stories with what we know of the historical facts of Carver's life. "Our First House in Sacramento" and "Next Year" certainly detail factual events in Carver's years of struggle, as does "Bankruptcy" (*F*, 61). Carver presents scenes from his own youth and adolescence as well, such as hanging out with his friends on "Wenas Ridge" (*WWCT*, 35–36), or working, as in "Woolworth's, 1954" (*WWCT*, 3). He also describes his job as a delivery boy for a pharmacist in the later 1950s in "Egress" (*U*, 44–45), and as a janitor at Mercy Hospital in the mid-1960s, the setting for the moving poem "The Autopsy Room" (*U*, 15–16). There are also many poems that are directed to or feature real people in Carver's life, particularly family members. He writes about his father, for example, in "Photograph of My Father in His Twenty-Second Year" (*F*, 59), "Bobber" (*F*, 116), "My Dad's Wallet" (*WWCT*, 55–56), and "The Kitchen" (*ANP*, 37–38), among others. His daughter—whose life has turned out much like one of Carver's hapless characters in that she married an abusive biker named Shiloh and tried to support two children—comes up in "To My Daughter" and "My Daughter and Apple Pie" (*WWCT*, 27–28, 51), while his son appears in "Ask Him" (*WWCT*, 59–61) and, especially, "On an Old Photograph of My Son" (*ANP*, 86–88). Carver addresses his first wife, Maryann, by name in a number of poems and by implication in several others; these include, in the first category, "Interview" and "The Windows of the Summer Vacation Houses" (*WWCT*, 79, 89–91), and, in the second category, "The Sensitive Girl," "The Author of Her Misfortune" (*U*, 38–39, 51), and "Miracle" (*ANP*, 26–30). Poems addressed to his second wife, Tess Gallagher, include "For Tess" (*WWCT*, 130), "Shooting" (*U*, 117–18), and "Hummingbird" (*ANP*, 92). In all of these poems, and in many others, Carver's autobiography is clearly to the fore.

In addition to being more personal and intimate, Carver's poems also feature several themes that were not of major importance in the stories. A number of texts, for example, focus on the workings of memory. The poet tends to recall an event from his past and then wonders why he thought of it and whether it has any connection to what he is experiencing in the present moment. The opening lines of "Woolworth's, 1954," for example, are "Where this floated up from, or why, / I don't know" (*WWCT*, 3), "this" being the memories of his first job and of "those early days in Yakima" (*WWCT*, 5). The poem "Wenas Ridge," also about the poet's early days, begins "The seasons turning. Memory flaring" (*WWCT*, 35). In "Interview," Carver tells of how the questions he has been answering make him think of Maryann, "that memory entering like a spike" (*WWCT*, 79). "The Meadow" is a list of several "crazy memories" (*U*, 103) that assail the narrator on a particular afternoon. Most significantly, Carver has published a poem simply entitled "Memory"[5]; here the speaker is cutting stems from strawberries and remembering what he had seen and heard that day, knowing that when he later eats the fruit he will "be reminded again—in no particular / order—of Tess, the little girl, a dog, / roller skates, memory, death, etc." (*WWCT*, 92). All of these poems detail the strange workings of memory and the role memory plays in the products of the creative artist.

The word "death" at the end of "Memory" also indicates an obsession of Carver's that, while apparent in several stories ("After the Denim" and "Errand," for example), is much more clearly pronounced in the poetry. Several of his poems, particularly early ones, are considerations of the deaths of people he has known. Such texts include "The Mailman as Cancer Patient" (*F*, 113), "Woolworth's, 1954," "My Dad's Wallet," "Blood" (*WWCT*, 3–5, 55–56, 80), "Egress," "Powder Monkey," "Migration," and "An Account" (*U*, 44–45, 52–53, 82–84, 101–2). Moreover, there are several poems in which Carver thinks of his own eventual death. In "In the Year 2020," for example, he hopes that he will be the last survivor among all of his friends, "lucky enough, privileged enough, / to live on and bear witness" (*WWCT*, 49), a sentiment very similar to that expressed in his later essay "Friendship" (*NHP*, 218). "My Death" (*WWCT*, 106–7) expresses the wish to die slowly so that he will have the opportunity to say good-bye to his loved ones. Carver also projects his death in "For Tess" (*WWCT*, 130) and "The Cobweb" (*U*, 9). All of these poems, however, like the essay "Friendship" and the story "Errand," were written well before Carver was discovered to have cancer. His final book, *A New Path to the Waterfall*, contains several poems written with the knowledge that his death was going to be sooner rather than later; these pieces—"Another Mystery," "What the Doctor Said," "Gravy," and "Late Fragment" (*ANP*, 48–49, 113, 118, 122)—are among the most touching works in Carver's canon.

Poetry also gives Carver a chance to pay homage to his literary mentors more openly than he can in his stories (with the exceptions of "The

Train" and "Errand"). For example, one of his longest works, "You Don't Know What Love Is" (*F*, 75–79), is subtitled "An Evening with Charles Bukowski" and is presented as a monologue given by the writer, whom Carver later recalled as "a kind of hero to me then" (*Con*, 36). Another revealing early poem is "Poem for Hemingway and W. C. Williams" (*F*, 114), in which the two writers discuss whether to catch and eat a fish or just to admire it. Two later poems take place in European cemeteries, where Carver is visiting the graves of two writers who have influenced him, namely Charles Baudelaire ("Ask Him") and James Joyce ("In Switzerland") (*WWCT*, 59–61, 69–71). He has also published poems titled "Balzac" (*F*, 93), "Kafka's Watch" (*U*, 69), and "Artaud" (*ANP*, 58). Other writers who have sparked poems by Carver include Flaubert ("The Blue Stones" [*F*, 84–85]), John Gardner ("Work" [*WWCT*, 48]), Sherwood Anderson ("Harley's Swans" [*WWCT*, 83]), and, of course, Chekhov ("Winter Insomnia" [*F*, 103] and "The Ashtray" [*WWCT*, 14–15]). *A New Path to the Waterfall* even includes passages from Chekhov's stories, which are reprinted to look like verse, as well as poems by Czeslaw Milosz, Jaroslav Seifert, and Tomas Transtromer.

Of all these writers, the one who probably exerted the most influence on Carver as a poet, and whom Carver called "my greatest hero" (*Con*, 108), is William Carlos Williams. Williams's responsibilities as a doctor, and his penchant for writing poems when and where he could, even on his prescription pads between seeing patients, certainly parallels the young Carver's problem of finding time free from wage-earning in which to write. More important, though, are Williams's valorization of "things," his simple wonderment at the vagaries and varieties of life, and his belief in the poetic occasion. With regard to the first of these concepts—Williams's dictum that there are "no ideas but in things"—Carver notes in "On Writing" that "it's possible, in a poem or a short story, to write about commonplace things and to endow those things—a chair, a window curtain, a fork, a stone, a woman's earring—with intense, even startling power" (*F*, 24). Carver achieved this effect in many of his stories, of course, but he did so perhaps most clearly in poems such as "My Dad's Wallet" (*WWCT*, 55–56), "The Schooldesk," and "The Phone Booth" (*U*, 93–95, 122–23). He also noted in "On Writing" that, "at the risk of appearing foolish, a writer sometimes needs to be able to just stand and gape at this or that thing—a sunset or an old shoe—in absolute and simple amazement" (*F*, 23). Williams made a career out of doing just that, and Carver follows in his footsteps in many of his own poems. Finally, Carver spoke of his poems as being spurred by specific occurrences; he noted that, unlike his stories, "every poem I've written has been, for me, an occasion of the first order. So much so, I believe, that I can remember the emotional circumstances that were at work when I wrote the poem, my physical surroundings, even what the weather was like" (*NHP*, 116). Undoubtedly Carver's situational memory is so strong because the poems were produced more quickly than the stories, but perhaps also because the brief flash of vision or insight that results in a poem is more intense. The occasional nature of Carver's poetry—like Williams's "This Is Just to Say," for example—can be seen in the following poems (and in many cases, even in their titles): "Rogue River Jet-Boat Trip, Gold Beach, Oregon, July 4, 1977," "Trying to Sleep Late on a Saturday Morning in November" (*F*, 71, 122), "Where Water Comes Together with Other Water" (written on the poet's forty-fifth birthday), "Interview," "Late Afternoon, April 8, 1984" (*WWCT*, 17–18, 79, 124–25), "An Afternoon," and "Earwigs" (*U*, 6, 54–55). As Arthur Saltzman has noted, Carver's "is a poetry of instants that often as not leaves the speaker gaping" (Saltzman, 158).

Carver stated more than once that he was "not a 'born' poet" (*NHP*, 105; *Con*, 48) and asserted that, if forced to choose between the two genres, he could not abandon writing fiction. Nevertheless, his poetry adds significantly to his body of work, which is still slim, unfortunately. Carver's best poems, as William L. Stull has noted, "have the virtues of his stories: photographic precision of image, disquieting turns of phrase and event, compelling immediacy, and lasting resonance" (Stull "RC" 1985, 244). By looking at them in conjunction with the stories, furthermore, we can get a more fully developed sense of Carver's world, in which the will to survive and create is able to overcome the oppressive forces that try to crush it. While few would suggest that Carver is equally adept in both genres, his poetry is of more than passing interest, and deserves a greater amount of serious scholarly attention.

Chapter Ten

Summation

Throughout his writing career, whether in poetry or short fiction, Raymond Carver was concerned with communication. Not only was it a nearly constant theme or obsession within his works, but it was the impetus behind the act of writing itself, a point that Carver made on several occasions. He told one interviewer, for example, that "in my view art is a linking between people, the creator and the consumer. Art is not self-expression, it is communication, and I am interested in communication" (Con, 58). The extent to which Carver's efforts at communication were successful can best be judged by the large number of readers who have enjoyed his works, who have felt that he is speaking about, for, or to them. Carver's works detail a particular time and place, but, like most significant artistic endeavors, they also explore issues of universal interest and appeal. In his essay "On Writing" Carver noted that good writers "want to stay in touch with us, they want to carry news from their world to ours" (F, 24), and to that end Carver proved himself to be a very good writer indeed.

When future histories of the American literary landscape of the 1970s, 1980s, and 1990s are written, the name of Raymond Carver will no doubt figure prominently. Not only did he play a large part in the revival of realism that characterized the period, and not only did he help to reinvigorate the genre of the short story, making it once again critically accepted as well as profitable, but he was also a major influence among a number of younger writers whose works gained notoriety during this time. The controversy over minimalism has tended to obscure Carver's true achievements somewhat, but we can look forward to the day when his works will be appreciated on their own merits as among the finest products of postwar American literature. Carver once wrote that "a writer who has some special way of looking at things and who gives artistic expression to that way of looking: that writer may be around for a time" (F, 22). Given that definition, Raymond Carver will indeed be around for a long time, for his works will continue to communicate with readers well into the next century. His life and career were unfortunately short, but he certainly made his mark.

Notes and References

Preface

1. Tess Gallagher, "Carver Country," in Bob Adelman, *Carver Country: The World of Raymond Carver* (New York: Scribners, 1990), 9; hereafter cited in text.
2. I will not be discussing Carver's early uncollected fiction—the stories "The Hair," "The Aficionados," "Poseidon and Company," and "Bright Red Apples," and the fragment of a novel "From *The Augustine Notebooks*"—all of which can be found in the posthumous volume *No Heroics, Please: Uncollected Writings*, ed. William L. Stull (New York: Vintage, 1992); hereafter cited in text as *NHP*.
3. Carver almost always revised his stories between their initial journal or magazine publication and their inclusion in a volume of collected stories; I have chosen not to examine these changes systematically.

Chapter One

1. Eugene Goodheart, "Four Decades of Contemporary American Fiction," in Boris Ford, ed., *American Literature: Volume Nine of the New Pelican Guide to English Literature* (New York: Viking Penguin, 1988), 634; hereafter cited in text.
2. David Jauss, "Literature at the End of the Century: An Editorial Perspective," *The Literary Review* 33 (1990): 167; hereafter cited in text.
3. Bruce Weber, "Raymond Carver: A Chronicler of Blue-Collar Despair," in Marshall Bruce Gentry and William L. Stull, eds., *Conversations with Raymond Carver* (Jackson: University of Mississippi Press, 1990), 84; hereafter cited in text as *Con*.
4. Morris Dickstein, "The Pursuit for the Ordinary," *Partisan Review* 58 (1991): 507; hereafter cited in text.
5. William L. Stull, "Raymond Carver," in *Dictionary of Literary Biography Yearbook: 1988*, ed. J. M. Brook (Detroit: Gale, 1989), 199; hereafter cited in text as Stull 1989.
6. William L. Stull, "Beyond Hopelessville: Another Side of Raymond Carver," *Philological Quarterly* 64 (1985): 1; hereafter cited in text as Stull "BH" 1985.
7. Raymond Carver, *Fires: Essays, Poems, Stories* (New York: Vintage, 1987), 13; hereafter cited in text as *F*.
8. Stewart Kellerman, "For Raymond Carver, a Lifetime of Storytelling," *New York Times*, 31 May 1988, C17; hereafter cited in text.
9. David Gates, "Carver: To Make a Long Story Short," *Newsweek,* 6 June 1988, 70.

10. The afterword doesn't appear in the Vintage edition of *Fires* cited in end-note seven of Chapter One, but it is reprinted in *No Heroics Please*. This passage is *NHP*, 108.

11. Jay McInerney, "Raymond Carver: A Still, Small Voice," *New York Times Book Review*, 9 Feb. 1986, 25; hereafter cited in text.

12. Sam Halpert, ed., . . . *When We Talk about Raymond Carver* (Layton, Utah: Peregrine Smith, 1991), 95; hereafter cited in text.

13. Tess Gallagher, "Raymond Carver, 1938 to 1988," *Granta* 25 (1988): 166.

14. Robert Towers, "Low-Rent Tragedies," *New York Review of Books* 14 May 1981, 38.

15. Charles E. May, "Raymond Carver," in *Critical Survey of Short Fiction: Supplement*, ed. Frank N. Magill (Englewood Cliffs, N.J.: Salem, 1987), 76; here-after cited in text.

16. The essays "My Father's Life" and "John Gardner: The Writer as Teacher" did not appear in the original Capra Press edition of *Fires*, but they are included in the Vintage edition cited in endnote seven of Chapter One.

17. Since *Dostoevsky: The Screenplay* is so different from Carver's other writings, I will not be discussing it in this book. For more information, see Carver's own introduction to the text in *NHP*, 111–15.

18. Mark A. R. Facknitz, "'The Calm,' 'A Small, Good Thing,' and 'Cathedral': Raymond Carver and the Rediscovery of Human Worth," *Studies in Short Fiction* 23 (1987): 287.

19. Raymond Carver, *A New Path to the Waterfall* (New York: Atlantic Monthly, 1989), 118; hereafter cited in text as *ANP*.

Chapter Two

1. Bill Buford, "Editorial," *Granta* 8 (1983): 4; hereafter cited in text.

2. Kim A. Herzinger, "Introduction: On the New Fiction," *Mississippi Review* 40–41 (1985): 7; hereafter cited in text.

3. This in part accounts for Robert Altman's ability to move his filmed version of Carver Country to Los Angeles without too great a sense of disruption.

4. Raymond Carver, *What We Talk about When We Talk about Love* (New York: Vintage, 1982), 156; hereafter cited in text as *WWTA*.

5. Anatole Broyard, "Diffuse Regrets," *New York Times* 5 Sept. 1983, 27; here-after cited in text.

6. Alan Wilde, *Middle Grounds: Studies in Contemporary American Fiction* (Philadelphia: University of Pennsylvania P, 1987), 110; hereafter cited in text.

7. Hamilton E. Cochrane, "'Taking the Cure': Alcoholism and Recovery in the Fiction of Raymond Carver," *University of Dayton Review* 20 (1989): 79; hereafter cited in text.

8. Tobias Wolff, "Raymond Carver Had His Cake and Ate It Too," *Esquire*, September 1989, 244.

9. Erich Eichman, "Will Raymond Carver Please Be Quiet, Please?," *New Centurion* Nov. 1983, 87.

10. Graham Clarke, "Investing the Glimpse: Raymond Carver and the Syntax of Silence," in his *The New American Writing: Essays on American Literature since 1970* (London: Vision, 1990), 117; hereafter cited in text.

11. Michael Wood, "Stories Full of Edges and Silences," *New York Times Book Review* 26 April 1981, 1.

12. Marc Chenetier, "Living On/Off the 'Reserve': Performance, Interrogation, and Negativity in the Works of Raymond Carver," in his *Critical Angles: European Views of Contemporary American Literature* (Carbondale: Southern Illinois University Press, 1986); 168; hereafter cited in text.

13. Paul Skenazy, "Life in Limbo: Ray Carver's Fiction," *Enclitic* 11 (1988): 80; hereafter cited in text.

14. Alain Arias-Misson, "Absent Talkers," *Partisan Review* 49 (1982): 626; hereafter cited in text.

15. William L. Stull, "Raymond Carver," in *Dictionary of Literary Biography Yearbook 1984*, ed. Jean W. Ross (Detroit: Gale, 1985), 239; hereafter cited in text as Stull "RC" 1985.

16. Anatole Broyard, "Books of the Times," *New York Times*, 15 April 1981, C29.

17. Michael Gorra, "Laughter and Bloodshed," *Hudson Review* 37 (1984): 156; hereafter cited in text.

18. Ewing Campbell provides a good, succinct discussion of how this religious term was adapted to literature by James Joyce; he also notes that "Carver's use conforms with Joyce's." See Ewing Campbell, *Raymond Carver: A Study of the Short Fiction* (New York: Twayne, 1992), 52; hereafter cited in text.

19. Alan Davis, "The Holiness of the Ordinary," *Hudson Review* 45 (1993): 653; hereafter cited in text.

20. Ralph Sassone, "Running on Empty: Minimalism and its Malcontents," *Voice Literary Supplement*, January/February 1989, S39; hereafter cited in text.

21. Gordon Weaver, ed., *The American Short Story, 1945–1980: A Critical History* (Boston: Twayne, 1983), xiv.

22. Reamy Jansen, "Being Lonely—Dimensions of the Short Story," *Cross Currents* 39 (1989/1990): 391; hereafter cited in text.

23. Frederick R. Karl, *American Fictions: 1940–1980* (New York: Harper and Row, 1983), 384–416.

24. Christopher Lasch, *The Minimal Self: Psychic Survival in Troubled Times* (New York: Norton, 1984), 130–62.

25. John Barth, "A Few Words about Minimalism," *Weber Studies* 4 (1987): 5; hereafter cited in text. This essay also appeared in the *New York Times Book Review*, 28 December 1986, 1–2, 25.

26. Ann-Marie Karlsson, "The Hyperrealistic Short Story: A Postmodern Twilight Zone," in Dunta Zadworna-Fjellestad, ed., *Criticism in the Twilight Zone: Postmodern Perspectives on Literature and Politics* (Stockholm: Amqvist and Wiksell, 1990), 145; hereafter cited in text.

27. John W. Aldridge, *Talents and Technicians: Literary Chic and the New Assembly-Line Fiction* (New York: Scribners, 1992), 48–49; hereafter cited in text.

28. Linsey Abrams, "A Maximalist Novelist Looks at Some Minimalist Fiction," *Mississippi Review* 40/41 (1985): 27; hereafter cited in text.
29. Joe David Bellamy, "A Downpour of Literary Republicanism," *Mississippi Review* 40/41 (1985): 37; hereafter cited in text.
30. Randolph Paul Runyon, *Reading Raymond Carver* (Syracuse: Syracuse University Press, 1992), 4; hereafter cited in text.
31. Mark A. R. Facknitz, "Raymond Carver and the Menace of Minimalism," *CEA Critic* 52 (1989–90): 70; hereafter cited in text.
32. See Adam Meyer, "Now You See Him, Now You Don't, Now You Do Again: The Evolution of Raymond Carver's Minimalism," *Critique* 30 (1989): 239–51; hereafter cited in text. This essay is also reprinted in Campbell 1992, 143–58.

Chapter Three

1. Raymond Carver, *Will You Please Be Quiet, Please?* (New York: Vintage, 1992), 3; hereafter cited in text as *WYP*.
2. Kirk Nesset, "'This Word Love': Sexual Politics and Silence in Early Raymond Carver," *American Literature* 63 (1991): 298; hereafter cited in text.
3. Arthur M. Saltzman, *Understanding Raymond Carver* (Columbia: University of South Carolina Press, 1988), 24; hereafter cited in text. Randolph Paul Runyon also points to the sexual repercussions of the scene, which reduce Rudy (and his penis) to a tiny thing while the narrator, sexually empowered by the fat man's penis like fingers, "is able to turn the tables on her usually dominant husband" (Runyon, 12).
4. David Kaufmann, "Yuppie Postmodernism," *Arizona Quarterly* 47 (1991): 98; hereafter cited in text.
5. See Campbell, 15, and Runyon, 13–14, for example.
6. Boxer and Phillips make the strongest points of several critics who have discussed Carver's use of voyeurism in this story and in others in the collection. Ann Beattie, interestingly, notes that Carver's narrative stance also places the reader in the position of a voyeur, "watching it all through a keyhole." See her "Carver's *Furious Seasons*," *Canto* 2 (1978): 178; hereafter cited in text.
7. Greg Johnson, "Three Contemporary Masters: Brodkey, Carver, Dubus," *Georgia Review* 43 (1989): 789; hereafter cited in text.
8. For further parallels and convergences along these lines, see Runyon, 17.
9. The symbolic nature of the huge fish is clear—it is obviously "an emotionally charged signifier" (Campbell 1992, 11)—but what exactly it symbolizes is up for debate. Saltzman provides a Freudian reading, indicating that the fish is "a prodigious phallic symbol for a boy who prizes potency" (Saltzman, 27), while Runyon sees the fish as symbolizing a woman. Ewing Campbell, on the contrary, offers an interpretation based on religious iconography, with the fish/boy serving as a Christ-like sacrificial victim. Campbell's claims are weakened, however, by his belief that the presentation of the fish has succeeded in ending the

parents' argument and "reestablish[ing] familial equilibrium" (Campbell 1992, 11), when it seems more likely that the change will only be temporary, and after they have finished with the boy they will return to fighting with each other.

10. See James Plath, "When Push Comes to Pull: Raymond Carver and the 'Popular Mechanics' of Divorce," *Notes on Contemporary Literature* 20, no. 3 (1990), 3.

11. As Runyon interestingly points out, the story also concerns an undercurrent of a mysterious future in San Francisco. Robinson is reminded of Marston when he sees a picture in the paper of a man who has killed his wife in San Francisco, and though he asserts that it isn't Marston, the reader has been given no evidence to the contrary. As Runyon speculates, the answer to "What Do You Do in San Francisco?" may be "murder."

12. Runyon is quite right to compare their behavior with that of Bill and Arlene Miller in "Neighbors," who also took their house-sitting a bit too far, literally putting themselves in other persons' shoes (Runyon, 45).

13. About this very story, for example, Alan Wilde asserts that "what makes the tale so revealing is . . . the unpleasantness and cruelty of its hero, whose confidence of superiority to his wretched hosts at least hints at Carver's own treatment of his characters" (Wilde, 118).

14. Jay McInerney, interestingly, notes that the first time he heard Carver read "Put Yourself in My Shoes" aloud, rather than experiencing the menace he had felt while reading it, he was struck by the story's humor, and by the way the audience "felt impelled to laugh at some of the most awkward moments" (Halpert, 47–48).

15. Kirk Nesset offers some interesting insights about Leo's motivation in sending Toni "out to do it" (*WYP*, 208). In particular, Nesset asserts that Leo, having committed his own adultery previously, sends Toni to do the same as "an act of retribution he inflicts indirectly upon himself" (Nesset, 305).

16. For a very interesting examination of these scenes see Miriam Marty Clark, "Raymond Carver's Monologic Imagination," *Modern Fiction Studies* 37 (1991): 243–45; hereafter cited in text.

17. Ralph both wants to know and not to know here; as Boxer and Phillips point out, "in the midst of pressuring his wife, Marian, to tell the full tale of her infidelity, Ralph Wyman feels the temptation to withdraw from revelation, to 'leave it at that'" (Boxer, 87). He thus displays, perhaps more clearly than any other character in the collection, "the devastating and contradictory nature of love" (Nesset, 309).

18. Charles E. May asserts that "the story captures a moment when things fall apart, never to be the same again" (May, 77), but his is certainly a minority view. Boxer and Phillips see the end as pointing to "the possibility of brighter futures" (Boxer, 87); Saltzman notes that it "displays an availability to life" (Saltzman, 71); and Nesset states that it "strikes an affirmative note that, as we have seen, is rare in the volume" (Nesset, 310).

Chapter Four

1. Raymond Carver, *Furious Seasons* (Santa Barbara: Capra, 1977), 15; hereafter cited in text as *FS*.
2. Carver expressed his admiration for O'Connor in several interviews; for a more in-depth analysis of their relationship, see Barbara Lonnquist's "Narrative Displacement and Literary Faith: Raymond Carver's Inheritance from Flannery O'Connor," in *Since Flannery O'Connor: Essays on the Contemporary American Short Story*, eds. Loren Logsdon and Charles W. Mayer (Macomb: Western Illinois University Press, 1987), 142–50.
3. Marilynne Robinson, "Marriage and Other Astonishing Bonds," *New York Times Book Review*, 15 May 1988, 35; hereafter cited in text.
4. Clarke also makes an interesting parallel between this story and James Dickey's novel *Deliverance*, a comparison that is worthy of further investigation.
5. See Beattie, 180. This does not mean, however, that Hemingway was the only influence at work in the story; Campbell is quite right in pointing to Joycean parallels as well, particularly to "Araby" (Campbell 1992, 4, 7–8).
6. William L. Stull, "Raymond Carver Remembered: Three Early Stories," *Studies in Short Fiction* 25 (1988): 466; hereafter cited in text.
7. Probably the best discussion of the similarities and differences between "Pastoral" and "Big Two-Hearted River" is in Graham Clarke's "Raymond Carver and the Syntax of Silence," 107–11.

Chapter Five

1. Daniel W. Lehman, "Raymond Carver's Management of Symbol," *Journal of the Short Story in English* 17 (1991): 49; hereafter cited in text.
2. For an interesting comparison and contrast of the gazebo and the motel, see Campbell 1992, 42.
3. Ernest Fontana, "Insomnia in Raymond Carver's Fiction," *Studies in Short Fiction* 26 (1989): 448; hereafter cited in text.
4. It may be that "the couple in denim are a younger version of the Packers" (Runyon, 114), as with the young couple and the older man in "Why Don't You Dance?," but Carver doesn't explore the possibility here to the extent that he did there.
5. For a more detailed discussion of these changes, see Meyer, 242–45.
6. Kathleen Westfall Shute, "Finding the Words: The Struggle for Salvation in the Fiction of Raymond Carver," *Hollins Critic* 24, no. 5 (1987): 8; hereafter cited in text.
7. See Saltzman, 117, 119; Stull 1985, 241; and, especially, Warren Carlin, "Just Talking: Raymond Carver's Symposium," *Cross Currents* 38 (1988): 87–92; Carlin hereafter cited in text.
8. In this way the younger couple parallels Nick and Honey in Edward Albee's play *Who's Afraid of Virginia Woolf?*, a text with which this story has much in common.

9. Jay McInerney, "The Writers of Wrong: A Novelist Carves the Critics," *Esquire*, July 1989, 114.

Chapter Six

1. It is interesting to compare this comment to Carver's later statement that he is not a minimalist because he doesn't cut his stories "to the bone" but "leave[s] a few slivers of meat on them" (*Con*, 80).

2. Carver frequently cited Frank O'Connor as a writer who continually reworked his previously published material, and this was, indeed, one of the things Carver admired most about him.

3. Not all critics see the ending of "The Cabin" in such an optimistic light. Saltzman, for example, asserts that the protagonist's "going home does not represent his positive determination to rebuild a relationship; it signals only one more retreat" (Saltzman, 99). Graham Clarke feels similarly, noting that his return is "not to a welcoming habitat as to a frightening lie" (Clarke, 111). The ending is certainly open enough to admit various interpretations, but even if these critics are right it still seems to be a softening from the extremely harsh ending of "Pastoral."

4. Arthur A. Brown, "Raymond Carver and Postmodern Humanism," *Critique* 30 (1990): 128; hereafter cited in text.

5. Raymond Carver, "Where Is Everyone?," *TriQuarterly* 48 (1980): 203–13.

Chapter Seven

1. In fact, according to Tess Gallagher (via Kirk Nesset), the change "began in *What We Talk about*, but because of severe editing by Gordon Lish, it did not become visible until [*Fires* and] *Cathedral*" (Nesset, 310)

2. For some negative assessments of the story, however, see Lehman, 53–55; Eichman, 87–88; and Michael J. Bugeja, "Tarnish and Silver: An Analysis of Carver's *Cathedral*," *South Dakota Review* 24, no. 3 (1986), 77–78; Bugeja hereafter cited in text.

3. For analysis of the relationship between this peacock and those of Flannery O'Connor, see Lonnquist, 144, and Saltzman, 128.

4. Raymond Carver, *Cathedral* (New York: Vintage, 1984), 12; hereafter cited in text as *C*.

5. He also says that he has been "'canned'" (*C*, 35), an interesting image, as Daniel W. Lehman points out, for a story titled "Preservation" (Lehman, 45).

6. For a more detailed look at some of these changes, see Meyer, 240–42.

7. Several critics have remarked on the Christian symbolism at the end of the story. See, for example, Lonnquist, 146; Facknitz 1986, 292; Shute, 6; Campbell, 55; and, especially, Stull 1984, 11–13. For an argument against this interpretation, see Runyon, 149–51.

8. William Abrahams, Introduction to his *Prize Stories, 1983: The O. Henry Awards* (Garden City, N.Y.: Doubleday, 1983), xi

9. As Carver points out, there are some dissenters, some who prefer "The Bath," largely because they find the ending of "A Small, Good Thing" to be overly sentimental. Among critics, see Bugeja, 73–77; Josh Rubins, "Small Expectations," *New York Review of Books*, 24 November 1983, 41–42; and Dorothy Wickenden, "Old Darkness, New Light," *New Republic*, 21 Nov. 1983, 38–39. Although Campbell never actually says he prefers "The Bath," that seems to be the point of his lengthy discussion of the renewed acceptance of sentimentality as seen in the praise lavished on "A Small, Good Thing" (Campbell 1992, 48–56).

10. As Arthur Saltzman points out, though, there is little chance of their reconciliation. Inez arrives at Lloyd's apartment "with new clothes and new vitality; she is set to thrive" (Saltzman, 136), a direct contrast to Lloyd's own inertia.

11. Peter J. Donahue, "Alcoholism as Ideology in Raymond Carver's 'Careful' and 'Where I'm Calling From,'" *Extrapolation* 32 (1991): 61; hereafter cited in text.

12. This story of a chimney sweep who had once fallen into a well also appears in Tess Gallagher's story "Turpentine," a text with which Carver helped her as much as she helped him with "Where I'm Calling From." See Tess Gallagher, "Turpentine," in *"The Lover of Horses" and Other Stories* (New York: Harper and Row, 1987), 59–60. For an interesting discussion of the parallels between falling into a well and sweeping chimneys see Elliott Malamet, "Raymond Carver and the Fear of Narration," *Journal of the Short Story in English* 17 (1991): 68; hereafter cited in text.

13. Interesting analyses of this open ending are offered by Thomas J. Haslam in "'Where I'm Calling From': A Textual and Critical Study," *Studies in Short Fiction* 29 (1992): 64 (hereafter cited in text), and, particularly, Donahue, 61, 62, who notes that alcoholics are never recover*ed* but are always recover*ing*. We should also remember, though, to the extent that the story is autobiographical, that Carver twice visited Duffy's, a facility much like Frank Martin's, but was not successfully cured during either stay.

14. The sign can be seen in one of the photographs in Bob Adelman's *Carver Country: The World of Raymond Carver* (New York: Scribners, 1990), 96.

15. John Cheever, "The Train," in *The Stories of John Cheever* (New York: Ballantine, 1980), 280–94; hereafter cited in text.

16. As Runyon points out, this strategy also "puts Miss Dent in the same situation in which "The Train" puts the reader who does not know Cheever's story" (Runyon, 173).

17. On the whole, though, I would agree with Michael J. Bugeja's assessment that the story almost demands comparison with Cheever's "classic" and that, "in such a comparison, 'The Train' suffers" (Bugeja, 78).

18. For a less than positive assessment of the story, however, see Campbell 1992, 66–68.

19. As Barbara Lonnquist points out, "paradoxically, the movement from ver-

bal to tactile communication, a seeming reduction, is actually a movement upward, to a higher level of communication between the two" (Lonnquist, 149).
20. Along these same lines, several critics have discussed the similarities between "Cathedral" and D. H. Lawrence's story "The Blind Man." See, most notably, Monroe Engel, "Knowing More Than One Imagines; Imagining More Than One Knows," *Agni* 31–32 (1990): 165–76. Although I have not been able to obtain a copy of it, I have also seen references to the following article: Keith Cushman, "Blind, Intertextual Love: 'The Blind Man' and Raymond Carver's 'Cathedral,'" *Etudes Lawrenciennes* 3 (1988): 125–38.

Chapter Eight

1. Raymond Carver, *Where I'm Calling From* (New York: Vintage, 1989), 409–10; hereafter cited in text as *WICF*.
2. Some critics are not willing to grant the story even that limited amount of optimism; see Campbell, 77.
3. In Sam Halpert's interviews with some of Carver's friends, several of them mention how "Intimacy" is based on Carver's relationship with his first wife, Maryann, although Carver always denied the connection. Douglas Unger, for example, who taught with Carver at Syracuse and also happens to be married to Maryann's sister, notes that the story is "the writer asking forgiveness for having allowed their lives to be so used and abused in his stories and by the world,—then, of course, the ironic twist of making use of that very apology as fresh meat for another story" (Halpert, 69). We might also be reminded of Myers from "Put Yourself in My Shoes," who might not have stolen Morgan's records but is, in a sense, stealing his identity for the story that he is telling (see Brown, 131–32).
4. Ewing Campbell likens this scene to "the diseased men of Gennesaret seeking wholeness by touching the hem of Christ's garment" and "Jacob refusing to release the angel until he is blessed" (Campbell 1992, 73, 74).
5. Ernest Fontana presents a more optimistic interpretation of "Menudo," asserting that Hughes discovers "an unsuspected capacity for courage and resolution" (Fontana, 449), that "his insomnia represents an intensification of his will to live and choose the future" (Fontana, 450). To arrive at this position, however, he must read an awful lot into the text. Mark Facknitz is much more accurate when he states that "'Menudo' is not about salvation but about a soul who waits for it, wants it, and needs it, but misses his few slim chances. . . . Within the boundaries of the story, there is no hope for a bright new prospect" (Facknitz 1989–90, 69–70).

Chapter Nine

1. Since these revisions, while interesting from a technical point of view, are for the most part minor, I have chosen not to discuss them in the body of this chapter. I also will not be quoting from *Near Klamath*, *Winter Insomnia*, or *At Night*

the Salmon Move, bacause all of the poems in these volumes can be found, in one version or another, in *Fires, No Heroics, Please*, or, in a very few cases, *A New Path to the Waterfall*.

2. Raymond Carver, *Where Water Comes Together with Water* (New York: Vintage, 1986), 31; hereafter cited in text as *WWCT*.

3. Raymond Carver, *Ultramarine* (New York: Vintage, 1987), 34; hereafter cited in text as *U*.

4. Another litany poem along these lines is "The Car" (*U*, 19–20).

5. Actually, Carver has published two different poems titled "Memory," the second of which (*U*, 18) is not nearly as successful.

Selected Bibliography

Primary Works

Short Stories

Will You Please Be Quiet, Please? New York: McGraw-Hill, 1976. Reprint. New
    York: Vintage, 1992.
Furious Seasons and Other Stories. Santa Barbara, Calif.: Capra, 1977.
What We Talk about When We Talk about Love. New York: Knopf, 1981.
    Reprint. New York: Vintage, 1982.
Cathedral. New York: Knopf, 1983. Reprint. New York: Vintage, 1984.
Where I'm Calling From: New and Selected Stories. New York: Atlantic Monthly,
    1988. Reprint. New York: Vintage, 1989.
Short Cuts: Selected Stories. New York: Vintage, 1993.

Poems

Near Klamath. Sacramento, CA: English Club of Sacramento State College,
    1968.
Winter Insomnia. Santa Cruz, Calif.: Kayak, 1970.
At Night the Salmon Move. Santa Barbara, Calif.: Capra, 1976.
Where Water Comes Together with Other Water. New York: Random House, 1985.
    Reprint. New York: Vintage, 1986.
Ultramarine. New York: Random House, 1986. Reprint. New York: Vintage,
    1987.
A New Path to the Waterfall. New York: Atlantic Monthly, 1989.

Short Stories, Poems, Prose

Fires: Essays, Poems, Stories. Santa Barbara, Calif.: Capra, 1983. Reprint. New
    York: Vintage, 1989.
No Heroics, Please: Uncollected Writings. New York: Vintage, 1992.

Screenplay

Dostoevsky: The Screenplay. With Tess Gallagher. Santa Barbara, Calif.: Capra,
    1985.

Secondary Works

Interviews

Gentry, Marshall Bruce, and William L. Stull, eds. *Conversations with Raymond Carver*. Jackson: University Press of Mississippi, 1990. Containing all of the most significant interviews with Carver, this is an indispensable volume.

Books

Campbell, Ewing. *Raymond Carver: A Study of the Short Fiction*. New York: Twayne, 1992. Campbell provides a good overview of Carver's career and interesting readings of 27 of his stories. The book also includes the essays by Shute, Facknitz (1989–90), and Meyer listed below.

Halpert, Sam. . . . *When We Talk about Raymond Carver*. Layton, Utah: Gibbs Smith, 1991. Interviews with 10 of Carver's friends and associates, including his first wife. Valuable for biographical information.

Nesset, Kirk. *The Stories of Raymond Carver*. Athens, Ohio: Ohio University Press, 1994. An expanded version of the first dissertation on Carver, this provides a useful introduction to his works.

Runyon, Randolph Paul. *Reading Raymond Carver*. Syracuse, N.Y.: Syracuse University Press, 1992. Runyon argues that we need to examine Carver's stories in their sequences within the collections. He makes some good points, but his thesis seems flawed and the book as a whole is forced and overly cute.

Saltzman, Arthur M. *Understanding Raymond Carver*. Columbia: University of South Carolina Press, 1988. The first full-length study of Carver's work, Saltzman's text is solid and quite useful, despite its brevity and some occasional misreadings.

Stull, William L., and Maureen P. Carroll, eds. *Remembering Ray: A Composite Biography of Raymond Carver*. Santa Barbara, Calif.: Capra, 1993. Like Halpert's text, this is a collection of interviews with and essays by Carver's friends and associates, here turned into a kind of oral biography.

Parts of Books

Aldridge, John W. *Talents and Technicians: Literary Chic and the New Assembly-line Fiction*. New York: Scribners, 1992. Aldridge condemns a wide array of authors whom he feels enjoy inflated reputations. Carver comes under particularly fervent attack because of the undeniable influence he has had over so many of the other writers Aldridge doesn't like.

Chenetier, Marc. "Living On/Off the 'Reserve': Performance, Interrogation, and Negativity in the Works of Raymond Carver." In *Critical Angels: European Views of Contemporary American Literature*, edited by Marc Chenetier. Carbondale: Southern Illinois University Press, 1986. An important theoretical examination of Carver's rhetoric, his way of using omission, elision, and indeterminacy to indicate the importance of what is absent or remains unsaid.

Clarke, Graham. "Investing the Glimpse: Raymond Carver and the Syntax of Silence." In *The New American Writing: Essays on American literature since 1970*, edited by Graham Clarke. London: Vision, 1990. Something of an introduction to Carver for the British, Clarke provides a very good overview of some of Carver's major obsessions: silence, absence, death, communication, and the glimpse.

Karlsson, Ann-Marie. "The Hyperrealistic Short Story: A Postmodern Twilight Zone." In *Criticism in the Twilight Zone: Postmodern Perspectives on Literature and Politics*, edited by Danuta Zadworna-Fjellestad. Stockholm: Almqvist and Wiksell, 1990. Karlsson finds similarities among the dirty realists/minimalists in their subtle attack on traditional realism, their reticence, their small-town settings, their profusion of details, their emphasis on absences and silences, and their sense of narrative immediacy gained through the use of present tense.

Lonnquist, Barbara C. "Narrative Displacement and Literary Faith: Raymond Carver's Inheritance from Flannery O'Connor." In *Since Flannery O'Connor: Essays on the Contemporary American Short Story*, edited by Loren Logsdon and Charles W. Mayer. Macomb: Western Illinois University Press, 1987. Lonnquist makes a convincing argument for O'Connor's influence on Carver, particularly in the narrative structure of his stories and his use of epiphany.

May, Charles E. "Raymond Carver." In *Critical Survey of Short Fiction, Supplement*, edited by Frank N. Magill. Englewood Cliffs, N.J.: Salem, 1987. A good reference book overview of Carver's life and career. Solid discussion of the overall course of Carver's writings, his "shift" to openness, as well as interesting analyses of several stories from the major collections.

Stull, William L. "Raymond Carver." In *Dictionary of Literary Biography Yearbook: 1984*, edited by Jean W. Ross. Detroit: Gale, 1985. An excellent introduction to Carver's life and works by one of his most astute critics. Stull does a particularly good job describing Carver's early years, explaining how the biographical facts of his life impinged on his writings, and presenting an overview of Carver's critical reception.

————. "Raymond Carver." In *Dictionary of Literary Biography Yearbook: 1988*, edited by J. M. Brook. Detroit: Gale, 1989. An obituary updating the article listed above. Here Stull provides the fullest and most compelling commentary to date on the Carver/Chekhov connection.

Wilde, Alan. *Middle Grounds: Studies in Contemporary American Fiction*. Philadelphia: University of Pennsylvania Press, 1987. Wilde generally denigrates the work of the "Catatonic Realists." He uses Carver as a foil for the writers he is naming and acclaiming as midfictionists, including Grace Paley, Max Apple, and, especially, Donald Barthelme.

Articles

Barth, John. "A Few Words about Minimalism." *New York Times Book Review*, 28 December 1986, 1–2, 25. Here Barth, one of the preeminent maximalists, provides a cogent and useful investigation of minimalism. He does an excellent job of defining the term as it is applied to Carver and other writers of the era, and he explores several possible causes for the popularity of minimalism in the 1970s and 1980s.

Barthelme, Frederick. "On Being Wrong: Convicted Minimalist Spills Bean." *New York Times Book Review*, 3 April 1988, 1, 25–27. In this spirited defense of minimalist writers, Barthelme provides a good history of American literary trends in the 1960s, 1970s, and 1980s. He sees the minimalists as post-postmodernists who embody a direct turn away from a concentration on language and toward a concentration on people.

Bell, Madison. "Less Is Less: The Dwindling American Short Story." *Harper's*, April 1986, 64–69. A general attack on the minimalists in which Carver comes under particularly heavy assault. Bell finds Carver to be a dangerous influence on younger writers.

Boddy, Kasia. "Companion-Souls of the Short Story: Anton Chekhov and Raymond Carver." *Scottish Slavonic Review* 18 (1992): 105–13. Boddy compares the ways in which Chekhov and Carver dealt with their impending deaths, and then fruitfully explores "Errand" and two of Chekhov's tales.

Boxer, David, and Cassandra Phillips. "Will You Please Be Quiet, Please?: Voyeurism, Dissociation, and the Art of Raymond Carver." *Iowa Review* 10 (1979): 75–90. The first scholarly article on Carver, and still one of the best discussions of his first collection. The authors point to several "obsessions" that run through the volume, particularly voyeurism and dissociation.

Brown, Arthur A. "Raymond Carver and Postmodern Humanism." *Critique* 31 (1990): 125–36. Brown argues that Carver is a postmodern writer and explores the metafictional ramifications of "The Pheasant," "Put Yourself in My Shoes," and "Cathedral." He asserts that the roles of writer, narrator, and reader become intertwined in these self-reflexive texts.

Bugeja, Michael J. "Tarnish and Silver: An Analysis of Raymond Carver's *Cathedral*." *South Dakota Review* 24, no. 3 (1986): 73–87. Bugeja takes a rather mixed view of the volume. On the one hand, he praises the more expansive, more optimistic stories; on the other hand, he lambastes Carver for the weak endings of several stories.

Carlin, Warren. "Just Talking: Raymond Carver's Symposium." *Cross Currents* 38 (1988): 87–92. A clever—and credible—paralleling of "What We Talk about When We Talk about Love" and Plato's "Symposium." Carlin charts the way in which Carver's text is structured along the lines of a theological dialogue.

Clark, Miriam Marty. "Raymond Carver's Monologic Imagination." *Modern Fiction Studies* 37 (1991): 240–47. Clark describes Carver's work as going against Mikhail Bakhtin's influential stress on heteroglossia, play, and carnival. Carver's characters reject intrusions from other voices, and this solipsism leads to the stories' despairing endings. Clark also notes that in some of the later stories the characters do break out of this mode and move toward the dialogic.

Cochrane, Hamilton E. "'Taking the Cure': Alcoholism and Recovery in the Fiction of Raymond Carver." *University of Dayton Review* 20 (1989): 79–88. Cochrane focuses on the way in which Carver's stories of recovering alcoholics are grounded in the traditions established by Alcoholics Anonymous. Cochrane also demonstrates, convincingly, how the shift to expansiveness in Carver's later stories is a function of his regained sobriety. Provocative and highly recommended.

Dickstein, Morris. "The Pursuit for the Ordinary." *Partisan Review* 58 (1991): 506–13. A ruminative obituary in which Dickstein does a good job of tracing the hourglass outline of Carver's life and career toward and then away from minimalism, commenting briefly on a number of the revisions.

Donahue, Peter J. "Alcoholism as Ideology in Raymond Carver's 'Careful' and 'Where I'm Calling From.'" *Extrapolation* 32 (1991): 54–63. Donahue, like Cochrane, uses the methodologies of Alcoholics Anonymous in examining Carver's texts, stressing the importance of communication and open-endedness.

Engel, Monroe. "Knowing More Than One Imagines; Imagining More Than One Knows." *Agni* 31–32 (1990): 165–76. An interesting comparison of the structural similarities in "Cathedral" and D. H. Lawrence's "The Blind Man."

Facknitz, Mark A. R. "'The Calm,' 'A Small, Good Thing,' and 'Cathedral': Raymond Carver and the Rediscovery of Human Worth." *Studies in Short Fiction* 23 (1986): 287–96. One of the seminal articles in tracking Carver's shift to openness and generosity in the later stories. Facknitz demonstrates that the heroes in these three stories are able to succeed because they find a way to communicate.

———. "Missing the Train: Raymond Carver's Sequel to John Cheever's 'The Five-Forty-Eight.'" *Studies in Short Fiction* 22 (1985): 345–47. A brief but informative look at these two stories, emphasizing the more pessimistic tone of Carver's text.

———. "Raymond Carver and the Menace of Minimalism." *CEA Critic* 52 (1989–90): 62–73. Facknitz's point is that the true menace of minimalistic style is what it says about the conditions of modern life, which it approximates. Good discussion of the final seven stories. Reprinted in Campbell 1992, cited above.

Fontana, Ernest. "Insomnia in Raymond Carver's Fiction." *Studies in Short Fiction* 26 (1989): 447–51. Fontana examines the protagonists of "The Student's

Wife," "I Could See the Smallest Things," "Menudo," and "Whoever Was Using This Bed." He provides very optimistic readings of the last two stories, for he interprets the characters as moving out of insomnia and back into the world of relationships.

Gearhart, Michael Wm. "Breaking the Ties That Bind: Inarticulation in the Fiction of Raymond Carver." *Studies in Short Fiction* 26 (1989): 439–46. Gearhart examines "A Small, Good Thing" to see how the characters manage to escape the problems of inarticulation, and he concludes that it is through the use of nonverbal communication. His analysis of body language is quite persuasive.

German, Norman, and Jack Bedell. "Physical and Social Laws in Ray Carver's 'Popular Mechanics.'" *Critique* 29 (1988): 257–60. The authors place a lot of emphasis on the title, and make some good points about the laws of physics in the story's plot, but they don't take into account that Carver published the same story with two other titles.

Gilder, Joshua. "Less Is Less." *New Criterion*, February 1983, 78–82. Another attack on the minimalist aesthetic. Gilder feels that Carver trivializes his characters' lives and condescends to them, and that he writes an elementary prose.

Haslam, Thomas J. "'Where I'm Calling From': A Textual and Critical Study." *Studies in Short Fiction* 29 (1992): 57–65. A good look at Carver's revising practices. Haslam closely examines the versions of the story published in the *New Yorker* and in the collected stories, *Where I'm Calling From*.

Hathcock, Nelson. "'The Possibility of Resurrection': Re-Vision in Carver's 'Feathers' and 'Cathedral.'" *Studies in Short Fiction* 28 (1991): 31–39. A solid discussion of post-shift Carver that focuses on the characters' new-found ability to communicate. Hathcock convincingly describes "Feathers" as one of *Cathedral*'s more generous stories, and provides a solid analysis of "Cathedral" itself.

Henning, Barbara. "Minimalism and the American Dream: 'Shiloh' by Bobbie Ann Mason and 'Preservation' by Raymond Carver." *Modern Fiction Studies* 35 (1989): 689–98. Henning argues that these minimalist texts force the reader to make active use of metaphors to resolve the textual dilemmas.

Herzinger, Kim A. "Introduction: On the New Fiction." *Mississippi Review* 40–41 (1985): 7–22. In this introduction to the crucially important special issue on minimalist fiction, Herzinger explains how the collection of essays came together. She provides a very good definition of minimalist fiction and does an excellent job of explaining both the problem of terminology and the problem of inclusion, as well as of defending the style against its many attackers. The essays themselves are also valuable, although I have not included any of them in this bibliography.

Jansen, Reamy. "Being Lonely—Dimensions of the Short Story." *Cross Currents* 39 (1989–90): 391–401, 419. Jansen places Carver in the main line of the short story tradition that stresses loneliness and isolation. The author then demonstrates how Carver's post-"Cathedral" narrators break out of this isolation and move toward connectedness.

Jauss, David. "Literature at the End of the Century: An Editorial Perspective." *Literary Review* 33 (1990): 164–71. Jauss, editor of the journal *Crazyhorse*, provides an engaging account of the dominance of minimalism among America's *un*published literature, the rejected submissions to journals like his own.

Kaufmann, David. "Yuppie Postmodernism." *Arizona Quarterly* 47 (1991): 93–116. A fascinating account of the success of the trade paperback industry, particularly Vintage Contemporaries, which successfully marketed stories of unemployed, blue-collar alcoholics to yuppies. Carver is plumbed for examples of his paratactic writing style.

Lehman, Daniel W. "Raymond Carver's Management of Symbol." *Journal of the Short Story in English* 17 (1991): 43–58. Lehman argues, rather persuasively, against the prevailing notion of the stylistic shift in Carver's writing, since he finds Carver to have been supremely in control of his material's symbolic structures throughout his career.

Malamet, Elliott. "Raymond Carver and the Fear of Narration." *Journal of the Short Story in English* 17 (1991): 59–74. A very interesting reading of narratorial reticence in "Where I'm Calling From." The story stresses the restorative powers of the talking cure for J.P., but Malamet points out that the narrator himself remains unommunicative. As the story progresses, however, the narrator feels increasingly comfortable and finally does reach out.

McInerney, Jay. "Raymond Carver: A Still, Small Voice." *New York Times Book Review*, 9 February 1986, 1, 24–5. A touching reminiscence of Carver the teacher by his best-known student. McInerney speaks of Carver's respect for language, points to his effect on the younger generation, and claims that "his example reinvigorated realism as well as the short-story form."

Meyer, Adam. "Now You See Him, Now You Don't, Now You Do Again: The Evolution of Raymond Carver's Minimalism." *Critique* 30 (1989): 239–51. An earlier version of the present study, in which the hourglass pattern of Carver's career was first proposed. The author explains this metaphor by comparing early, middle, and late versions of several stories. Reprinted in Campbell 1992, cited above.

Nesset, Kirk. "'This World Love': Sexual Politics and Silence in Early Raymond Carver." *American Literature* 63 (1991): 292–313. In this chapter from the first dissertation on Carver, Nesset emphasizes the role love and sex play as the creators of both problems and the possible solutions to them in *Will You Please Be Quiet, Please?*

Plath, James. "When Push Comes to Pull: Raymond Carver and the 'Popular Mechanics' of Divorce." *Notes on Contemporary Literature* 20, no. 3 (1990): 2–4. Emphasizes the story's parallels to and divergences from the story of King Solomon, which Carver uses as an underpinning.

Sassone, Ralph. "Running on Empty: Minimalism and Its Malcontents." *Voice Literary Supplement*, January/February 1989, S39–40. A humorous and balanced account of, and possible explanation for, the antiminimalism backlash. Sassone points out that the term is slippery, and in many cases stands for whatever the critic doesn't like.

Skenazy, Paul. "Life in Limbo: Ray Carver's Fiction." *Enclitic* 11 (1988): 77–83. A brief, eulogistic overview of Carver's life and career, this article provides a good summary of the dominant milieu that Carver created in so many of his stories.

Stull, William L. "Beyond Hopelessville: Another Side of Raymond Carver." *Philological Quarterly* 64 (1985): 1–15. In this essay—one of the most important and influential pieces of Carver criticism—Stull argues that, if we take our stock of Carver from the arch-minimalist *What We Talk about When We Talk about Love*, we are not getting the whole picture, for Carver's writing, both before and after that volume, is more expansive and optimistic. Stull is among the first to chart Carver's movement from existential to humanistic realism by comparing "The Bath" and "A Small, Good Thing."

———. "Raymond Carver Remembered: Three Early Stories." *Studies in Short Fiction* 25 (1988): 461–77. A valuable rundown of Carver's early writing career, it includes analyses of the three reprinted stories, "The Aficionados," "Poseidon and Company," and "The Hair," all of which later appeared in the Stull-edited volume *No Heroics, Please*.

———."Visions and Revisions." *Chariton Review* 10 (1984): 80–86. Ostensibly a review of *Fires*, this article contains much more—namely, a thorough-going examination of the ways in which the texts in the collection have been revised from earlier versions. Stull gives generally higher remarks to the fuller versions.

Verley, Claudine. "Narration and Interiority in Raymond Carver's 'Where I'm Calling From.'" *Journal of the Short Story in English* 13 (1989): 91–102. Verley's structuralist examination of the story is sometimes hard to follow, but she does demonstrate that the protagonist's movement from being a controlling and manipulative narrator to being a more open and honest character parallels his difficult recovery and readjustment process.

Wolff, Tobias. "Raymond Carver Had His Cake and Ate It Too." *Esquire*, September 1989, 240–48. A touching tribute by one of Carver's oldest and closest friends. Wolff's discussion of Carver's postalcoholic personality is quite moving.

Index

The Author

Adam Meyer is currently an Assistant Professor of English at Fisk University. He was educated at Kenyon College (B.A.), the University of New Mexico (M.A.), and Vanderbilt University (Ph.D.). In addition to his previous work on Raymond Carver, Professor Meyer has published articles on William S. Burroughs and Franz Kafka, Grace Paley, and Mike Gold and Daniel Fuchs, and his essays on Lore Segal and Paule Marshall are forthcoming. His essay "The Need for Cross-Ethnic Studies: A Manifesto (with Antipasto)" received third prize in the annual awards from the journal *MELUS*. This piece is part of his current project, an examination of encounters between African-Americans and Jewish-Americans in contemporary African-American and Jewish-American literatures. Along with his wife and two children, Professor Meyer resides in Nashville, Tennessee.

The Editor

Frank Day is a professor of English and department head at Clemson University. He is the author of *Sir William Empson: An Annotated Bibliography* and *Arthur Koestler: A Guide to Research.* He was a Fulbright Lecturer in American literature in Romania (1980–81) and in Bangladesh (1986–87).